BISON
BOOKS

HANDCART EMIGRANTS

From a painting by Dan Weggeland. Courtesy of the Latter-day Saints Church Historian's Office.

HANDCARTS TO ZION

the story of a
Unique Western Migration
1856-1860

with contemporary journals, accounts,
reports; and rosters of members
of the ten Handcart Companies

by
LeRoy R. Hafen
and
Ann W. Hafen

Published by the
University of Nebraska Press
Lincoln and London
in association with
The Arthur H. Clark Company
Spokane, Washington

First Bison Book printing: 1992
Most recent printing indicated by the last digit below:
10   9   8   7

Library of Congress Cataloging-in-Publication Data
Hafen, Le Roy Reuben, 1893–
Handcarts to Zion: the story of a unique western migration, 1856–
1860: with contemporary journals, accounts, reports, and rosters of
members of the ten handcart companies / by LeRoy R. Hafen and
Ann W. Hafen.
p.   cm.
Includes index.
Originally published: Glendale, Calif.: A. H. Clark Co., 1960.
ISBN 0-8032-7255-3
1. Mormons—United States—History—19th century.   2. Migration,
Internal—United States—History—19th century.   I. Hafen, Ann W.
(Ann Woodbury), 1893–1970.   II. Title.
BX8611.H25   1992
289.3′78′09034—dc20
91-40163   CIP

Reprinted by arrangement with the Arthur H. Clark Company

⊗

To Mother
MARY ANN HAFEN
Who, as a child of six years,
trailed a Handcart to Utah in 1860

Contents

Illustrations

Foreword

The past hundred years has witnessed an interesting evolution of overland transportation – pack horse train, ox-drawn wagon, stagecoach, pony express, railroad train, motor car, airplane – each in turn. And interspersed with these more common conveyances have appeared unusual or freakish devices, ranging from the wheelbarrow to the camel caravan.

But at only one period, 1856-60, was the handcart employed for mass migration – the most remarkable travel experiment in the history of Western America.

Nearly three thousand men, women and children, pulling their worldly possessions in hand-made, two-wheeled carts, trudged some thirteen hundred miles to the Zion of their hopes. Across prairies and mountains, rivers and deserts, creaked their fragile vehicles, motored by muscle and fueled with blood.

There were the blind and deaf; little children and infants in arms; gray veterans of Waterloo; old ladies and pregnant women.

Babies were born on the journey; marriages were performed at the camps; old and young were buried along the trail. Overpowered by summer heat, former factory workers fainted beside their carts. Scores froze in the biting cold of Wyoming blizzards.

For some there was the joy of fulfillment as, dust-stained and travel-worn, they trailed down from the yellow-aspened Wasatch Mountains to walk proudly into Salt Lake City behind a brass band, pulling their carts between lines of welcoming brethren. For others, deep tragedy. Caught in the claws of an unseasonable winter, they struggled through mounting drifts with little clothing, less shelter, and no food, and came to a complete halt in the white desolation.

To save these thousand souls stalled in the snow, more than three hundred miles from any settlement, was staged the most heroic mass rescue the frontier ever witnessed.

Under the commanding leadership of Brigham Young, these stranded Saints were saved from certain death. And it was accomplished by Mormon colonists who, but nine years before, had squatted upon a desert with empty wagons and bare hands.

The womb of the Handcart has produced a numerous progeny. From less than three thousand emigrants, who pulled or trailed a cart one hundred years ago, have come a half million Americans. Cherishing a unique heritage, they are proud to claim descent from Handcart pioneers.

A special interest has drawn us to this topic. As a little girl of six, our mother, fresh from the green hills of Switzerland, trailed a handcart the long dry miles to the Great Salt Lake, in the last handcart caravan. Our master's thesis on the Handcart Migration, written forty years ago, has been rewritten and expanded into the present story.

Introduction

Mormonism, from the days of its founding in 1830, has been a missionary religion, vigorously proselyting the "honest in heart." Zion, as a gathering place for the faithful, was proclaimed almost from the beginning. And "gathering to Zion" became a powerful force in the rise and development of the Church of Jesus Christ of Latter-Day Saints (better known as the Mormon Church).

The idea reached its fullest vigor in the mid-nineteenth century, when the missionary efforts in England had succeeded so well that thousands of enthusiastic converts clamored for the privilege of going to the "Promised Land." The fervor reached such a pitch that obstacles and sacrifices were no longer deterrents; many were so eager to go that they offered to "walk from their homes to Liverpool, and from New York to the Great Salt Lake."

With thousands of the poor "panting to gather to Zion," and with inadequate means for wagon transportation, there was born the plan for travel by handcarts to Utah.

The startling story of that unique experiment is disclosed on the ensuing pages of this volume.

Handcarts to Zion

The Handcart

A crude and lifeless thing of wood –
Two wheels, two shafts, and a box.
Yet it rolled the road to a Zion home
With never a mule or ox.
Propelled by blood of the human heart
The wood became a walking cart.

Creeping thirteen-hundred miles
It squeaked and groaned and whined
Through dust, and rivers of mud and sweat,
Greased with a bacon rind.
At night, as silent as the graves
New-hidden under grassy waves.

Hand-fashioned, this rude family cart
Of Iowa hickory, oak.
No iron strength in the rustic art
Of axle, shaft, or spoke.
Creaking along while the pioneers plod,
Choraling anthems to their God.

But the lowly cart, with its miracle wheel
As timeless as the poor,
Was a circle of faith that eased the way
To an inland Salt-Sea shore.
A man and wife, its walking team,
Trundling a baby and a dream!

Ann W. Hafen

The Gathering

Within six months after the founding of the Mormon Church (April 6, 1830), the new Prophet, Joseph Smith, announced a Revelation: "And ye are called to bring to pass the gathering of mine elect; . . . they shall be gathered in unto one place upon the face of this land." Zion, the Gathering place, he announced, "shall be on the borders by the Lamanites" (Indians) ; in other words, upon the frontier.

"The glory of the Lord shall be there," he promised, "and it shall be called Zion. . . The righteous shall be gathered out from among all nations, and shall come to Zion, singing with songs of everlasting joy." [1]

As early as 1830, missionaries were sent out to the Indians of the West – quite a journey from New York. In the following spring, Joseph Smith himself traveled to the frontier. While there, at the outpost of Independence, he announced that Missouri was the place appointed for the gathering. "Wherefore, this is the land of promise, and the place for the city of Zion." [2]

During the earliest years of the Church, proselyting was carried on in the United States and Canada; but beginning in 1837, ardent missionaries went to England. Here the response to the new gospel was so ready that within eight months, two thousand converts were

---

[1] *The Doctrine and Covenants of the Church of Jesus Christ of Latter-Day Saints, Containing Revelations given to Joseph Smith, the Prophet* (Kirtland, Ohio, 1835, and numerous subsequent editions), Sec. 29, ver. 7, 8; Sec. 28, ver. 9; Sec. 45, ver. 67, 71.

[2] *Ibid.,* Sec. 57, ver. 2.

baptized.[3] Despite this success, the neophytes were not then urged to emigrate to America, for Zion was not yet ready to receive them.

Western Missouri, where the Saints had settled, was torn by bitter conflicts; and presently the Mormons were expelled from the state. They backtracked some three hundred miles to Illinois. Here they established themselves on the east bank of the Mississippi, and built their magic Nauvoo into the largest city of Illinois.

This place now became a "stake of Zion," and from it the call again was trumpeted for the gathering: "Send forth unto foreign lands; call upon all nations, . . . Go ye out from among the nations, even from Babylon, from the midst of wickedness, which is spiritual Babylon." [4]

By 1840 there were nearly seven thousand converts in Britain, and of these some five thousand migrated to the gathering place in Illinois.[5] Britain's unemployment and hard times produced ready ears for a gospel that promised both material and spiritual salvation.

The *Millennial Star,* Mormon organ in Liverpool, observed in February, 1842: "In the midst of the general distress which prevails in this country on account of want of employment, the high price of provision, the oppression, priestcraft and iniquity of the land, it is pleasing to the household of faith to contemplate a country reserved by the Almighty as a sure asylum for the poor and the oppressed – a country every way adapted to their wants and conditions."

---

[3] Gustive O. Larson, *Prelude to the Kingdom, Mormon Desert Conquest; a Chapter in American Cooperative Experience* (Francestown, New Hamp., 1947), 39. This is an excellent study of Mormon migration and of the Perpetual Emigration Fund, developed to aid the migration.

[4] *Doctrine and Covenants, op. cit.,* Sec. 133, ver. 8, 14.

[5] Larson, *op. cit.,* 96.

Nauvoo, the Mormon haven, soon proved to be an uncertain refuge. Seeking protection from mob violence, and reimbursement for property destruction in Missouri, the Prophet had journeyed to the nation's capital in 1839, asking redress. The response was President Martin Van Buren's pathetic admission, "Your cause is just, but I can do nothing for you." [6] For self-defense, the Nauvoo Legion was organized and trained under Joseph's direction.

With difficulties continuing, the Mormon leader came to the conclusion that the unsettled region of the far West would ultimately become the site of his people's Zion. In August, 1842, he prophesied that the "Saints would continue to suffer much affliction and would be driven to the Rocky Mountains. . . some of you will live to go and assist in making settlements and build cities and see the Saints become a mighty people in the midst of the Rocky Mountains." [7]

On a later occasion, the perturbed leader sketched with chalk on the floor of the Masonic Hall in Nauvoo, the general location of what he called the Great Salt Lake Basin.[8] In February, 1844, Joseph organized the Oregon and California Exploring Expedition to seek a possible refuge in the western country. Twenty-five men were to go equipped to make the survey.[9] Hoping to get cooperation from the government, he directed a petition to Congress, asking authorization to raise a

[6] *History of the Church of Jesus Christ of Latter-Day Saints, Period* 1: "History of Joseph Smith, the Prophet, by Himself," (Salt Lake City, 1949 edition), IV, pp. 39-40, 80.

[7] *Ibid.*, V, p. 85.

[8] Larson, *op. cit.*, 52, quoting from the entry of July 26, 1897, in the Latter-Day Saints Journal History, located in the Church Historian's Office, Salt Lake City. Hereafter this important collection of sources will be referred to as Journal History.

[9] *History of the Church*, VI, pp. 222-27.

company of one hundred thousand armed volunteers. The request was ignored.[10]

Before further action could be taken on a westward move, hostilities burst wide open in Nauvoo. Joseph Smith was imprisoned in Carthage jail, and was there murdered by a masked mob on June 22, 1844.

Brigham Young and the others who succeeded to leadership, conscious of a continuing insecurity in Illinois, investigated various possible havens in Texas, Oregon, California, and the Great Basin. The *Nauvoo Neighbor* published fifty or more descriptive articles pertaining to the West, and ran Fremont's Reports serially, concluding with an account of his experiences at the Great Salt Lake.[11]

By the fall of 1845 the Mormons announced that they would leave Nauvoo for the West the following spring. At the October Conference, held in the new Temple, Parley P. Pratt philosophically observed: "The Lord designs to lead us to a wider field of action, where there will be more room for the Saints to grow and increase, and where there will be no one to say we crowd them, and where we can enjoy the pure principles of liberty and equal rights." [12]

During the winter of 1845-46 the city of Nauvoo was transformed into a gigantic outfitting center. Homes were converted into workshops. Twelve thousand wagons were made ready for the exodus. Persistent friction, however, caused the Mormons to depart even earlier than they had planned. The contemplated spring exodus became a February escape into the merciless arms of an Iowa winter.

---

[10] *Ibid.*, pp. 274-77; *Congressional Globe*, May 25, 1844 (28 Cong., 1 sess., vol. 13, p. 624).

[11] A. L. Neff, *History of Utah, 1847 to 1869* (Salt Lake City, 1940), 35-37.

[12] *History of the Church*, VII, p. 464.

Again the gathering from foreign lands had to be suspended, while the beleagured children of modern Israel sought out a new Zion in an unclaimed area of the far West.

In 1847 the new leader, Brigham Young, piloted the vanguard of homeless Saints across the plains and into the Rocky Mountains. Looking out over a generally barren valley with the Great Salt Lake shimmering in the distance, he rose from his sick bed in the wagon and announced: "This is the place."

Adopting a system of irrigated agriculture, the Mormons began to transform a desert land. It was no small project for twenty thousand people, many of them destitute through the forced sale of their homes, to trek fifteen hundred miles across plains and mountains, and with bare hands in a barren land, create a new home.[13]

The resilience of the Mormons under these disheartening circumstances was something remarkable. A city was laid out with the site of Zion's temple in the center block. Adobe houses rose beside the camped wagons. Irrigation ditches led water from mountain creeks to thirsty acres. Community fields were encircled by a common fence, to guard them from foraging cattle.

To build their new empire – a Kingdom of God on earth – the Mormons soon realized that they would need more workers and an increased population. Once again the word went forth, counseling the Saints abroad to gather to the new Zion. Their coming would help fulfill the ancient prophecy of Isaiah, about the Lord's house being established in the tops of the mountains, and that all nations would flow unto it.[14]

---

[13] The removal of the entire membership from the Illinois-Iowa region to the Great Basin required several years.

[14] *Book of Isaiah*, Ch. 2, ver. 2.

"To all Saints in England, Scotland, Ireland, Wales, and the adjacent islands and countries," ran the General Epistle, issued by the Church leaders on December 23, 1847, "we say emigrate as speedily as possible to this vicinity . . . bringing with you all kinds of choice seeds, of grain, vegetables, fruit, shrubbery, trees and vines, everything that will please the eye, gladden the heart, or cheer the soul of man, that grows upon the face of the whole earth; also the best stock of beast, bird, and fowl of every kind; also the best tools of every description, and machinery for spinning, or weaving, and dressing cotton, wool, flax, and silk, etc. . . So far as it can be consistently done, bring models and drafts, and let the machinery be built where it is used, which will save great expense in transportation, particularly in heavy machinery, and tools and implements generally." [15]

The missionaries abroad were instructed: "Tell them to flee to Zion. . . Should any ask 'where is Zion' tell them in America, and if any ask 'what is Zion' tell them the pure in heart. . . The Kingdom of God which we are establishing is not of this world, but the Kingdom of the Great God." [16]

Exultantly, Orson Spencer, Mormon leader in Britain, proclaimed on February 1, 1848: "The channel of Saint's Emigration to the land of Zion is now opened. The long wished for time of gathering has come. Good tidings from Mt. Zion! The resting place of Israel for the last day has been discovered." [17]

In the Second Epistle – October 12, 1849 – the Mormon leaders appealed: "We want men; brethren, come

---

[15] *Millennial Star* (Liverpool, England), x (1848) 81-88.
[16] *Ibid.*, 83.
[17] *Ibid.*, IX (1847) 41.

from the States, from the nations, come! and help us build and grow, until we can say enough, the valleys of Ephraim are full." [18]

Despite the desires of the Saints to follow the counsel of their leaders, and migrate to the Salt Lake Valley, many were too poor to purchase transportation. With the purpose of aiding the hopelessly poor Saints, Brigham Young proposed the creation of a revolving fund to be used for transporting the faithful to Zion. Those assisted were to repay the loan after arriving in Utah, where public work would be provided.

At the General Conference of the Church in October, 1849, the plan was approved. Five thousand dollars was contributed by the Saints to launch the movement.

"The few thousands we send out by our agent at this time," explained the Fund's Letter of Instructions, "is like a grain of mustard seed in the earth; we send it forth into the world and among the Saints, a good soil, and we expect it will grow and flourish, and spread abroad in a few years so that it will cover England, cast its shadow in Europe and in the process of time compass the whole earth." [19]

In 1850 the Perpetual Emigration Fund Company was incorporated, and Brigham Young was elected president.[20] This organization was to play an exceedingly important role in the gathering and transporting of the Saints to Zion. At first it was utilized in assisting those on the Missouri frontier to migrate to Utah;

---

[18] "Second General Epistle," of Oct. 12, 1849, in J. A. Little, *From Kirtland to Salt Lake City* (Salt Lake City, 1890), 207-208.

[19] Quoted in Larson, *op. cit.,* 109-110.

[20] The incorporation Act by the extra-legal "State of Deseret" was accepted and legalized by the Utah legislature on October 4, 1851. It was further amended by the legislature on January 12, 1856.– *Compiled Laws of Utah* (1876), Secs. 556-68.

later it was devoted to helping the foreign Saints gather to Zion. Functioning for nearly forty years, it was to assist in the removal of fifty thousand individuals over land and sea to Utah.[21] And, as we shall see in this study, it was to be the major force in the handcart migration.

Another agency, that was immeasurably helpful in gathering Saints to Zion, was the *Millennial Star,* first foreign publication of the Mormon Church. It served as a bulletin board for conveying church messages to the Saints in Europe. Founded in 1849, it is still being published.

Not until 1852 was the Perpetual Emigration Fund used to assist Saints in Europe to come to Utah. The 251 persons helped that year were shown special honor as the "poor company." [22] Upon their approach to Salt Lake City President Young, accompanied by other Church leaders, many Saints, and a brass band, went east of the city to welcome them. The emigrants "danced for joy, and their hearts were made glad by a distribution of melons and cakes," the *Deseret News* reported. Then the procession marched into the city.

"As the escort and the train passed the Temple Block, they were saluted with nine rounds of artillery, which made the everlasting hills shake their sides with joy; while thousands of men, women, and children gathered from various parts of the city to unite in the glorious and joyful welcome." [23]

The operations of the Fund in Europe having proved successful, except for a financial deficit, plans were

---

[21] A. L. Neff, *op. cit.,* 580.

[22] The cost of emigrating this group took the 1410 pounds sterling then in the Perpetual Emigration Fund in Europe and required an advance of 1000 pounds from other Church sources.

[23] *Deseret News,* Aug. 21, Sept. 18, 1852.

pushed for the next year's operations. Church leaders fanned the fire of hope.

"Let all who can procure a loaf of bread and one garment on their backs, be assured there is water plenty and pure by the way, and doubt no longer, but come next year to the place of gathering, even in flocks, as doves fly to their windows before the storm." [24]

Enthusiasm for emigration mounted in Britain. A "ten pound" plan was announced for through transportation, and with the aid of the P.E. Fund, 2,312 Mormons journeyed to Utah in 1853. Saints in England contributed twelve hundred pounds to the P.E.F. in 1854, and of the 3,167 Mormons who emigrated from Britain that year, 1,075 traveled by aid of the Fund.[25]

Heber C. Kimball, Counsellor to President Young, made an appeal at the General Conference of the Church in Utah, on October 6, 1854, for enlargement of the P.E. Fund: "Look at the poor in Old England. . . In the last letter that came from my son William, he wrote that 'I feel to weep and mourn and lament when I behold the poverty of the people; they are starving to death, and there are scores and hundreds of my brethren in the poor houses of the country.' . . . That is the case with our brethren there, and while you are here in the midst of luxuries; while you are enjoying these blessings of the Lord, can you see your own brethren afflicted? It is not only so in England, but in Ireland, in Scotland, in Denmark, in Sweden, and in all the nations of the earth. . . Let us go to work now and enlarge this Fund. . ." [26]

[24] *Millennial Star*, XIV (1852) 325.

[25] The summaries of emigration, 1852-1854 are taken largely from Prof. Larson's study, previously cited.

[26] *Deseret News*, Oct. 19, 1854, reprinted in *Millennial Star*, XVII (1855) 162.

While contributions were solicited in Utah and abroad to enlarge the P.E. Fund, the Gospel of the Gathering was pressed with continuing fervor. An editorial in the *Millennial Star* of April 21, 1855, warned:

"The clouds of war have continued to gather thicker and darker over the horizon of the nations. . . Famine has stared multitudes in the face during the past winter. . . The present is full of calamity and evil. At this moment thousands are anxiously inquiring in their hearts, 'Is there no way of escape from these evils?' . . . There is beyond the sea a haven of peace, and a refuge from the impending storms. . . The Spirit whispers: 'Get ye up out of these lands for the judgments of the Almighty are being poured out upon the nations, for they are ripening in transgression.' " [27]

In the same paper, on September 22, 1855, the Mission President argued at length the necessity of saving every penny and bending every effort toward the goal of emigration, and urged:

"The Lord never yet gave a commandment to His people, but what, if they would go to with full purpose of heart and try to obey it, they could do so. The commandment to gather out to the land of America is just as binding on the Saints, so far as it is possible for them to accomplish it, as it was in the first place to be baptized for the remission of sins. . . Every impulse of the heart of the Saint, every hope of the future says, Gather up to the land of America." [28]

The Saints in Britain responded enthusiastically.

[27] *Millennial Star,* XVII (1855) 248-49.
[28] *Ibid.,* 601-603.

The refrain was echoed in this song, composed by Richard Smyth of Dublin.

COME TO ZION

Israel, Israel, God is calling –
Calling thee from lands of woe;
Babylon the Great is falling;
God shall all her towers o'er throw.
Come to Zion,
'Ere his floods of anger flow. . .[29]

The wisdom of the Gathering, for the advancement of the Church, was evident. Having established themselves in a desert country and undertaken there the building of a commonwealth, the Mormons were in need of more settlers to develop the resources of the land. Also, experience had proved that the Church thrived best when concentrated, and thus under the influence and encouragement of its leaders.

During the early fifties, harvests in Utah had been abundant. The optimism resulting had encouraged the Mormons to proselyte actively and to urge heavy emigration to their new and expanding Zion. From 1849 to 1855 some 16,000 European emigrants had been transported to Utah; and the Perpetual Emigration Company had expended £125,000 during 1852-55 in emigrating the "poor Saints" from Europe to the Salt Lake Valley.[30] The emigration of 1855 had been especially heavy, with a total of 4,225. Of these, 1,161 had been transported by the Fund, at a cost of approximately $150,000.

Upon reaching Utah in the fall of 1855, these new

---

[29] The complete song is given in Appendix K.

[30] L. J. Arrington, *Great Basin Kingdom; an Economic History of the Latter-Day Saints, 1830-1900* (Cambridge, Harvard University Press, 1958), 99.

arrivals found Zion in distress. A grasshopper plague
had brought havoc to crops. Millions of the pests had
descended upon fields and eaten up every green thing.
All efforts to stay their destruction seemed futile. To
add to the distress, the summer had been hot and dry;
the irrigation water supply was diminished. As a result
of the grasshoppers and drouth, the harvest of 1855
was reduced by from one-third to two-thirds, depend-
ing upon the locality.[31]

With a diminished food supply, the large immigration of this year was not an asset, but instead an added
burden upon the strained economy. Rigid rationing of
food would be necessary through a severe winter.

The sharp decrease in food production, the unemployment and distress in 1855, caused marked falling-
off in tithing receipts (the Church's revenue), and reduced donations to the Perpetual Emigration Fund to
a dribble. Faced with these conditions, some Mormons
advised curtailing foreign immigration for 1856. But
the leaders, in the General Epistle of October 29, 1855,
announced that the emigration should not be reduced,
because "the cry of our poor brethren in foreign lands
for deliverance is great, the hand of the oppressor is
heavy upon them, and they have no other prospect on
earth through which they can hope for assistance." [32]
Despite heroic efforts heretofore to assist emigration,
the Mormons had been able to bring to Utah only one
out of twenty of those who wanted to come. In view of
this situation and the economic conditions prevailing,
a cheaper mode of transportation was urgently needed.
Under these circumstances was born a unique plan for
overland migration – by handcart.

[31] *Ibid.,* 150.
[32] Thirteenth General Epistle, in *Millennial Star,* XVIII (1856), 51-52.

The New Plan

Walking across the plains and mountains of western America was no novelty in the days before the coming of the railroad. Bullwhackers regularly tramped beside their yoked cattle on the Santa Fe Trail; and the covered wagon emigrants, who first rutted the Oregon Trail, often trudged beside their monotonous rolling wagons. Gold seekers to California, and to other eldorados, sometimes carried their worldly goods flung over their shoulders. The Mormons who pioneered the route to the Salt Lake Valley and those who trekked after them, walked much of the way beside the ox-drawn trains.

But never had *handcarts* been employed as means of transport for an entire emigrant company. Now, this humble vehicle was to be adopted and put to the test.

"I have been thinking how we should operate another year," wrote Brigham Young to the President of the European Mission in September, 1855. "We cannot afford to purchase wagons and teams as in times past. I am consequently thrown back upon my old plan [1]– to make hand-carts, and let the emigration foot

---

[1] The "General Epistle" of October, 1851 in *Millennial Star,* XIV (1852) 23, contained the following: "Some of the children of the world have crossed the mountains and plains from Missouri to California with a pack on their back to worship their God – Gold! . . . Some of the Saints now in our midst came here with wagons or carts made of wood, without a particle of iron, hooping their wheels with hickory, or rawhide or ropes and had as good

it, and draw upon them [the carts] the necessary supplies, having a cow or two for every ten. They can come just as quick, if not quicker, and much cheaper – can start earlier and escape the prevailing sickness which annually lays so many of our brethren in the dust. A great majority of them walk now, even with the teams which are provided, and have a great deal more care and perplexity than they would have if they came without them."

Getting down to specifics, Brigham Young continues: "They will only need 90 days' rations from the time of their leaving the Missouri River, and as the settlements extend up the Platte, not that much. The carts can be made without a particle of iron, with wheels hooped, made strong and light, and one, or if the family be large, two of them will bring all that they will need upon the plains. . .

"I think we might as well begin another year as any time, and save this enormous expense of purchasing wagons and teams – indeed we will be obliged to pursue this course, or suspend operations, for aught that I can see at the present. . .

"I think the emigration had better come the northern route from New York, or Philadelphia, or Boston, direct to Iowa City, . . . Their passage through

---

and safe a journey as any in the camps, with their wrought iron wagons. And can you not do the same? Yes, start from the Missouri River with Cows, handcarts, wheel-barrows, with little flour and no unnecessaries and come to this place quicker, and with less fatigue, than by following the heavy trains with their cumbrous herds which they are often obliged to drive miles to feed."

The next spring a handcart plan was presented to the General Conference in Salt Lake City and 93 men volunteered to go east with teams and provisions to meet such walking immigrants.– *Millennial Star*, XIV, p. 325. But the scheme was not put into operation at that time.

to Iowa City will not cost more than 8 or 9 dollars, and they will only have to be supplied with money for provisions and a few cows, which should be of the very best quality. . . Of course you will perceive the necessity of dispensing with all wooden chests, extra freight, luggage, etc. They should only bring a change of clothing. . ."

The optimism of Brigham led him to simplify the vicissitudes: "Fifteen miles a day will bring them through in 70 days, and after they get accustomed to it they will travle 20, 25, and even 30 with all ease, and no danger of giving out, but will continue to get stronger and stronger; the little ones and sick, if there are any, can be carried on the carts, but there will be none sick in a little time after they get started. There will have to be some few tents." [2]

As president of the Perpetual Emigration Fund, Brigham Young wrote a letter of instructions to President F. D. Richards at Liverpool: "In your elections of the Saints who shall be aided by the Fund, those who have proven themselves by long continuance in the Church shall be helped first, whether they can raise any means of their own or not; . . . if they have not a sixpence in the world. But be wary of assisting any of those who come into the Church now, during these troublesome times for Britain, whose chief aim and intention may be to get to America." [3]

President Young's letter and announcement were published in the *Millennial Star* of December 22, 1855. In a long editorial in the same issue, Franklin D. Richards, who was editor of the paper as well as

[2] Published in *Millennial Star* of Dec. 22, 1855 (XVII, pp. 813-14).
[3] *Ibid.*, 814-15.

President of the European Mission, endorsed the project and amplified its advantages:

"The plan about to be adopted by the P.E. Fund Company, of substituting handcarts for ox-teams in crossing the plains, has been under consideration for several years. The plan proposed is novel, and, when we allow our imaginations to wander into the future and paint the scenes that will transpire on the prairies next summer, they partake largely of the romantic. The plan is the device of inspiration, and the Lord will own and bless it. . .

"More speedy measures must be devised for strengthening Zion, . . . The system of ox-trains is too slow and expensive, and must give way to the telegraph line of handcarts and wheelbarrows. It would be much more economical both in time, labor, and expense, if, instead of spending several weeks to obtain and accustom to the yoke, a lot of wild ungovernable cattle, impairing the health of many of the brethren by excessive labor and fatigue, and bringing disease and death into the camps by long delays on the miasmatic banks of the Missouri River, on the arrival of a company of Saints on the frontier they could have the necessary handcarts ready and load them, and be 200 or 300 miles on their journey, with the same time and labor that would otherwise be expended in getting started.

"It is only to those who have traveled the plains with ox-teams, that the advantages of doing without them will appear in all their force. They alone can realize what it is to get up on a sultry morning, spend an hour or two in driving up and yoking unruly cattle, and while impatiently waiting to start on the dusty, wearisome road, in order to accomplish the labors of the day in due time, hear the word passed around that some brother has an ox missing, then another hour, or perhaps half a day, is wasted and finally, when ready to start, the pleasantest time for travelling is past, during which a company with handcarts would have performed the greater part of an ordinary day's journey. There being few animals in a handcart company, there will be less to tempt the cupidity of the Indians – a large share of that most laborious and harrassing duty – guarding – can be dispensed with, and the time occupied with sleep and refreshments, with songs of rejoicing and prayer.

"The anxieties of mind about losing cattle by stampedes, poisonous water, and exhaustion will be avoided. It may be safely considered that the extra time and labour of a company that will be required to get started with an ox-team and take care of the cattle, aside from that spent in actual travelling, will enable that same company, with a handcart to every five persons, loaded with five or six hundred pounds, on starting, to accomplish two-thirds of the journey and besides it will reduce the cost of emigration from Britain to two-thirds of what it is at present at most, and after the first year probably to one half. This greatly decreased amount of indebtedness on the part of the emigrating Saints will be much to their pecuniary advantage after their arrival in Utah."

One object of the Perpetual Emigration Fund Company, from its commencement, had been to bring the expense of the emigration down to the means of the greatest possible number. Another had been, to select mechanics and persons best calculated to build up and strengthen new settlements in Zion. A third reason had been to cut the time consumed in the long journey from Europe to Utah, thereby giving the emigrant added time for labor on his arrival in Zion. The handcart plan seemed to promote all of these objectives, President Richards observed.

"Many men have travelled the long and weary journey of 2000 miles from the Missouri to California on foot, and destitute, in order to obtain a little of the shining dust. . . The Mohammedan will perform a long and weary pilgrimage of months and even years and make every sacrifice that human nature can endure, to kiss the tomb of his prophet, and bring away a relict from the holy city of Mecca. The Roman Catholic will endure severe penance with the hope of saving his soul from purgatory. The Hindoo devotee will suffer self-inflicted tortures of the most excruciating nature to obtain the favor of his imaginary deity. . . Then shall not saints who have revelations of heaven . . . be ready to prove by their works that their faith is worth more than the life of the body – the riches of the world? . . ."

The plan was given official recognition when the Presidency of the Church, on October 29, 1855, issued to the membership the "Thirteenth General Epistle."

After stating that the P.E. Fund in 1855 had assisted some thirteen hundred persons, nearly one-fourth of the season's immigration, the Epistle made a strong appeal for donations, and urgently requested repayment by those who had been assisted by the Fund. The Epistle continued:

"The P.E. Fund is designed to deliver the honest poor, the pauper, if you please, from the thraldom of ages, from localities where poverty is a crime and beggary an offense against the law, where every avenue to rise in the scale of being to any degree of respectable joyous existence is forever closed, and place them in a land where honest labor and industry meet a suitable reward, where the higher walks of life are open to the humblest and poorest. . .

"Let all things be done in order, and let all the Saints who can, gather up for Zion and come while the way is open before them; let the poor also come, whether they receive aid or not from the Fund, let them come on foot, with handcarts or wheelbarrows; let them gird up their loins and walk through, and nothing shall hinder or stay them. . .

"Let the Saints, therefore, who intend to immigrate the insuing year, understand that they are expected to walk and draw their luggage across the plains, and that they will be assisted by the Fund in no other way. . . If this project is once fairly tested, and proves as successful as we have no doubt it will, the main expense of the immigration will be avoided, consequently thousands more than heretofore can receive assistance."[4]

Franklin D. Richards further encouraged the Saints with an editorial in his *Millennial Star* of March 1, 1856: "When ancient Israel fled from bondage into the wilderness, they had not even the privilege of taking provisions for their journey, but had to trust to the good hand of the Lord for their daily bread. If the Saints in these lands have not seen such times, the future will reveal them.

"The Lord can rain manna on the plains of America just as easily as He did on the deserts of Arabia, or as he sent quails into the camp of the Saints on the

---

[4] *Millennial Star,* Jan. 26, 1856, (XVIII, pp. 52, 54).

Mississippi river in 1846. Ancient Israel travelled to
the promised land on foot, with their wives and little
ones. The Lord calls upon modern Israel to do the
same." [5]

Among the Saints in Britain, enthusiasm for emigra-
tion became almost unbounded. One of the missionaries,
W. H. Kimball, wrote to Richards from London on
November 8, 1855:

"The fire of emigration blazes throughout the Pastorate to such an extent that the folks are willing to
part with all their effects, and toddle off with a few
things in a pocket handkerchief. . .

"Verily there is power in Mormonism. People who
once felt they would rather die than leave 'happy
England,' who used to sing 'Happy Land,' and 'Britons
Never Shall be Slaves,' who looked upon other countries with supreme contempt, . . . now perceive
that they have been in bondage, in darkness, and in
Babylon, and sing with joyful hearts –

> There is a land beyond the sea
> Where I should like to be;
> And dearer far than *all the rest,*
> Is that bright land to me. . .

"There are in the Pastorate about 300 who can raise
from two to three pounds per head, and are longing to
go home. They are those who have been on hand all the
day long to assist in the good work, and are worthy to
go to Zion. I want to know, brother Franklin, if you
can't get up a water party for them, an excursion across
the 'pond,' without a 'return ticket.' " [6]

---

[5] *Ibid.,* 138.
[6] *Ibid.,* xvii (1855) 765.

From the Worcestershire Conference, on December 28, 1855, Elder N. T. Porter wrote to President Richards: "As the season of emigration draws near, the appeals of the Saints become more incessant for deliverance, and many are begotten unto a lively hope, by the introduction of handcarts, as a cheaper mode of conveyance, while they are waiting with ready hands to try the experiment."[7]

From Belfast, Ireland, Elder John D. T. McAllister wrote on December 31, 1855: "The Priesthood and members feel alive in 'Mormonism,' and, from the oldest to the youngest, all feel Zionward, and are, at the present time, rejoicing in the anticipation of *pulling* or *pushing* a hand-cart to their home in the west. Tobacco smokers have resolved to quit, and put their savings thereby in the P.E. Fund, and those who have quit tea-drinking will also put their savings in the same."[8]

From Swansea, Wales, Dan Jones wrote in March, 1856: "Respecting emigration, I beg to assure you that I would not wish to see a greater desire for that than is evidently pervading every class, in every locality. 'Do help *me* to get to Zion,' 'When shall I go home?'; 'Oh, do try to help me off this time,' are so often reiterated in my hearing, . . . that they tingle in my ears.

"Some 130 emigrated per ship "Caravan" last month, a liberal portion of them contemplating to complete, in the States, their outfit for crossing the plains this summer; in addition to which, I have now on my books about 550 names of applicants for passage in the ship which sails next, with a fair prospect of timely making up the even 600. Of these, about 350 intend going

---

[7] *Ibid.*, XVIII (1856) 92.
[8] *Ibid.*, 47.

through to Utah by the swift-sure Handcart Train, and about 100 by the old 'slow and sure' ox-trains. . . I find that from among the *'poor Mormons'* in Wales some £3600 have rotated through my hands to yours during the last year, towards emigration deposits with you, and for the various funds." [9]

The new plan having been conceived, proclaimed, and accepted, the next problem was its execution.

The emigrants were to be sent out from Liverpool in sailing vessels, especially chartered for the purpose. Recent British and American Passenger Acts had required an increase in the amount of provisions that ships must supply; and this had caused a corresponding increase in passenger rates. On the first ship sent out under the new Acts the fare was 4 pounds, 5 shillings for adults; 3 pounds and 5 shillings for children, and 10 shillings for infants. The scale of provisions now fixed by law for each adult or two children weekly, was:

3½ lbs. Bread	2 lbs. Potatoes	2 oz. Salt
1 lb. Flour	1¼ lbs. Beef	½ oz. Mustard
1½ lbs. Oat Meal	1 lb. Pork	¼ oz. Pepper
1½ lbs. Rice	1 lb. Sugar	1 gill Vinegar
1½ lbs. Peas	2 oz. Tea	

3 quarts of water daily, and 10 gallons daily to every 100 for cooking.

The new Acts also required each ship to be provided with "Medical Comforts," as follows for each two hundred adults:

14 lbs. Arrowroot	2 gallons Lime Juice
25 lbs. Sago	½ gallon Brandy

---
[9] *Ibid.*, 242-44.

20 lbs. Pearl Barley	2 doz. milk, in pints
30 lbs. Sugar	1 doz. Beef Soup, in lbs.
12 lbs. Marine Soap	3 doz. Preserved Mutton, in ½ lbs.[10]

The *Millennial Star* published instructions on January 12, 1856, for the season's Mormon emigration. All applications for passage to America were to be accompanied by a deposit of one pound for each person over one year old. Passengers would furnish their own beds, bedding, and cooking utensils. The P.E. Fund Emigrants were to be sent subject to the regulations of the Company existing at the time of embarkation, and after landing in America were to be forwarded in charge of Agents of the Church from place to place until their arrival in Utah. All P.E. Fund passengers were required to sign the following bond:

"We, the undersigned, do hereby agree, and bind ourselves to the Perpetual Emigrating Fund Company, in the following conditions, viz.– That, in consideration of the aforesaid Company emigrating or transporting us, and our necessary luggage, from (Name of Country) to Utah, according to the rules of the Company, and the general instructions of their authorized Agents:

"We do severally and jointly promise, and bind ourselves, to continue with, and obey the instructions of, the Agent appointed to superintend our passage thither, that we will receipt for our passages previous to arriving at the port of disembarkation in the United States at the point of outfit on the Missouri river, prior to arriving in the G.S.L. Valley, and at any intermediate stopping place the Agent in charge may think proper to require it;

---

[10] *Ibid.*, 25.

"And that on our arrival in Utah, we will hold ourselves, our time, and our labour subject to the appro-
priation of the Perpetual Emigrating Fund Company,
until the full cost of our emigration is paid, with interest
if required." [11]

Those passengers who were able to pay a portion of
the expenses were to deposit the amount with the Fund
before leaving Britain and this would be credited them
upon the final settlement in Utah.

A circular with further regulations was published
February 23, 1856. It announced that Iowa City, Iowa,
would be the point of outfit for the handcart travelers,
and that railroad travel to that point would be on the
Northern Route, via Chicago or Rock Island. A
through passage to Utah would be provided by the
P.E. Fund Company to all those desiring it, at the
rates of 9 pounds for persons over one year old, and
4 pounds and 10 shillings for children under one year.
The regulations continued:

"The P.E.F. Emigrants will use Handcarts in crossing the Plains, in which they will convey their provisions, tents, and necessary luggage, according to
instructions contained in the 'Thirteenth General
Epistle of the First Presidency.' There will of course
be means provided for the conveyance of the aged, infirm, and those unable from any cause to walk, . . .

"If the Saints do not appreciate the wisdom of taking
the smallest practicable amount of luggage, they will
before they have hauled it far on the plains. . .

"The mode now proposed to the Saints for travelling
up to Zion so nearly resembles that of ancient Israel in
the wilderness, that it must elicit the peculiar favour

---

[11] *Ibid.,* 26.

and blessing of the Lord upon it. The gathering poor, if they are faithful, have a right to feel that the favour of God, angels, and holy men is enlisted in their behalf. The present plan is peculiarly the Lord's, and it will have our special prayers and most untiring efforts for its success. The Lord, through His Prophet, says to the poor, 'Let them come on foot, with handcarts or wheel barrows; let them gird up their loins and walk through, and nothing shall hinder them." [12]

Although the plan met with general approbation, it was considered by some to be too hard. Some such were encouraged, while others were rebuked for lack of faith. One lady writing to John Jaques from New York said that it is asking too much to journey with handcarts and she did not care to attempt it. To her he wrote:

"You have looked upon the journey all in a lump. Recollect that you will only have to perform one day's travel at a time, and the first 200 or 300 miles from Iowa City to Florence, the handcarts will travel through partly settled country and be lightly loaded, for they will not take their full load for the Plains till they get to Florence. This first part of the journey will just get the Saints used to travelling, without a great deal of toil all at once. . .

"You talk of staying a little while in New York or St. Louis, till you can buy a wagon. How know you that you will ever have enough to buy a wagon? How can you expect the Lord to give you means to buy a wagon, when He has provided you a cart?" [13]

Those missionaries returning home to Zion were to

[12] *Ibid.*, 122-24.
[13] Printed in *Millennial Star*, XVIII (1856) 369-72.

be the captains and guardians of the emigrants. To them, President Richards addressed the following editorial on February 2, 1856:

"We take this occasion to remind the Elders in these lands, who are expecting to go home during the coming season of emigration, that their mission is not done when they are released from their present fields of labor, nor yet when they leave the shores of Great Britain. . . It will devolve on you to aid those who emigrate the coming season, to accomplish the task which lies before them. The poor have particular demands upon you. . . On your arrival in the United States . . . be in readiness to render any assistance or assume any responsibility which those having charge of the emigration may see fit to place upon you. . .

"Traveling across the plains with teams has always been trying to the patience and perseverance of the unexperienced, and traveling with handcarts cannot be expected to be any less so. . . To toil along with handcarts through a journey of 1000 miles over the 'desert plain,' and rugged mountains, through streams and kanyons, will be no easy task even for those who are accustomed to the fatigues and hardships of mountain life and the Saints who are willing to do it, with their aged and little ones, for the Gospel's sake, the Lord will make the objects of His special care and blessing. None of the emigrating Saints have ever crossed the plains who have had greater demands on the shepherds of their flock, than those who will travel in the handcart companies the coming season. . .

"It is our constant desire not to mislead the Saints concerning the difficulties of the journey to Utah. We wish them calmly to make up their minds that it is not an easy task, and to start with faith, trusting in Israel's God for success, and seek of Him continually, by prayer and supplication." [14]

These instructions were followed, and no company of emigrants was without its missionary leaders.

The first of the regular P.E.F. passengers for the 1856 season set sail from Britain on March 23 and the last on May 25. Of the first company the *Millennial Star* reported on April 5, 1856:

"The ship 'Enoch Train,' Captain Henry P. Rich, cleared on Saturday the 22nd ult., hence for Boston, with 534 souls of the Saints on board, of whom 19 were from the Swiss, 4 from the Cape of Good Hope, and 2 from the East India Missions, all under the presidency of Elder James Ferguson, Edmund Ellsworth, and Daniel D. McArthur. . .

"This is the first shipload of Emigrants for Utah by the P.E. Fund this season. The day was delightfully pleasant, and all things connected with the clearing of this Company seemed peculiarly auspicious. Her Majesty's Officers had a word of admiration to express at the excellence of the arrangements which marked the embarkation of this first company who expect to cross the plains with hand-carts. The Elders on board seemed to feel the responsibility that rests upon them, and the whole was rendered particularly pleasing and cheerful by the performances of the Band that goes out from Birmingham, which will be a means of much comfort to the journeying Saints." [15]

On board, the Saints were organized under a pres-

14 *Ibid.,* 73-75.
15 *Ibid.,* 217.

idency of three Elders for the company, and into five wards with a captain over each. They were called to prayer, morning and evening, by the sound of the bugle, and meetings were held at regular intervals.

Upon reaching Boston, on April 30, a successful and generally pleasant voyage was reported. Four births and two deaths had occurred on board the vessel. Upon reaching port, the company, by resolution, expressed appreciation to the Captain of the ship for his kindness and consideration. He responded in a letter to the leaders of the Saints, thanking them for "the spirit of kindness manifested by you all during the present voyage, tending to the health and comfort of the passengers under your charge. If such rules and regulations could be followed by all emigrant ships, we should have less, far less sickness and distress at sea. Cleanliness is part of your religion, and nobly you have carried it out." [16]

The company passed inspection without difficulty on May 1, and the next day entrained for New York City, whence they traveled westward to Iowa.

The second shipload of Saints, destined for handcraft travel, crossed the Atlantic with 707 passengers aboard. They left Liverpool on April 19 and had a generally good voyage, though they experienced two weeks of rough sailing. Elder Dan Jones reported:

"The 'S. Curling,' though called a mammoth of her species, with her 700 passengers and luggage, crew, and withal 2,000 tons of iron in her bowels, rocked like a crow's nest on a lone sapling in the gale, . . .

"Notwithstanding the roughness of this wintry pas-

[16] *Ibid.,* 353-56.

sage, we continued to be quite a devotional people. At
5 a.m. each day the bugle called the men out to clean
their wards, and then to retire on deck while the ladies
were dressing for morning prayers, at a quarter to six
o'clock. At dusk the bugle called all hands to prayer
again, by wards, and it pleased me much to see, by
the almost universal willingness to go below, that the
call was duly appreciated, nor was the scene less interesting to see seven hundred Saints on their way to Zion,
pent up in so small a space, all bow the knee, and, with
their hearty Amen, lift their hearts in aspirations of
praise to Him who deserves our all . . .

"Our evenings, after meetings until bedtime, were
spent in singing the songs of Zion; after which the
men retired on deck, while the females retired to a
better place . . .

"Two wards at a time have a half hour for cooking
breakfast, three quarters for dinner, and half an hour
for supper, reversing alternately, and the intervals
between meals for baking, &c. This dispenses with the
throng around the galley, and each knows his turn by
seeing the number of his ward over the door . . .

"The passengers were all remarkably clean, as well
as the ship, which commanded the admiration of all.
In proof of the latter I would say, that I had made a
wager with Captain Curling, upon leaving Liverpool,
that the lower decks would be whiter than his cabin
floor, and the Quarantine Doctor decided in my favour . . .

"24th. Concluded a contract with the Railway, to
take about 400 to Iowa City direct, fare $11, under
14 half-fare, and under 6 years free, with 100 lbs of
luggage free; $3.50 per cwt for freight; to leave Mon-

day, 11 a.m. Got the privilege from our ever kind Captain Curling, to remain on board until that time."[17]

Six infants died and two were born on the voyage. The good order of the passengers and their general conduct brought favorable comment from the officials at Liverpool, and from officials and newspapermen at the American port. These two shiploads being the first emigration by the northern route, the leaders of the Church and of the emigration were anxious to create a favorable impression upon transportation officials and the general public.

Concise and valuable data is given in the following report:

LATTER-DAY SAINTS' EMIGRATION REPORT, NOVEMBER 30, 1855, TO JULY 6, 1856

Ship	Pres. of the Company	Date of sailing	Port of disembar- kation	P. E. Fund	Ordi- nary	Totals
Emerald Isle	P. C. Merril	Nov. 30	N.Y.	—	350	350
John J. Body	Canute Peterson	Dec. 12	" "	34	478	512
Caravan	Daniel Tyler	Feb. 19	" "	—	457	457
Enoch Train	J. Ferguson	Mar. 23	Boston	431	103	534
S. Curling	Dan Jones	Apr. 19	"	428	279	707
Thornton	J. G. Willie	May 4	N.Y.	484	280	764
Horizon	Ed. Martin	May 25	Boston	635	221	856
Wellfleet	J. Aubray	June 1	"	—	146	146
Miscellaneous	Ships	. .	. .	. .	69	69
	Totals	.	. .	2012	2383	4395

"Of this number, as the table shows, 2012 are P.E. Fund Passengers, of whom 333 were ordered out by their friends in Utah, also 788 members, of many years standing in the church, have been forwarded to Utah under the P.E.F.Co.'s arrangements, and 28 are Elders returning home from missions. We have not the means

---

[17] *Ibid.,* 427-30.

of ascertaining definitely, but the approximate number of those who started from here with the intention of going through to the Valley this season, about 2397, which will leave 1998 who have located for the present in various parts of the United States, in order to obtain means to complete their journey whenever circumstances will permit.

"The numbers of natives of the various countries may be classified as follows: From the United Kingdom of Great Britain and Ireland: English, 2611; Scotch, 367; Welsh, 667; Irish, 54; American, 19; from the French Mission (Channel Islands), 9. The total number from the Scandinavian Mission is 615, of which there are: Danes, 502; Swedes, 67; Norwegians, 46. The total number from the Swiss and Italian Mission is 50: from the Swiss Cantons, 19; from Piedmont, Italy, 31. There are also 2 from the East India Mission, and 1 from Germany – making a grand total, as per table, of 4395 souls." [18]

There was nothing of especial interest in the sailings of the ships. All reached port safely, after voyages varying in length from 38 to 65 days. From the Atlantic ports the Saints were taken by railroad to Iowa City, Iowa, at a contract price of from ten to eleven dollars per person.

One noticeable thing, that proved to be lamentable as matters subsequently turned out, was the late sailing of two shiploads of the emigrants. Various causes contributed to this result, and responsibility is hard to place. Throughout January and February, President Richards had continually urged the necessity of getting off early. The winter's severity, with hard times and

[18] *Ibid.,* 542.

high prices, sharpened the Saints' desire to emigrate.
Many of these, carried away with the idea of gathering
to Zion that season, left their various employments
even before arrangements had been made for their
transportation. The result was that some of them were
left to choose between the alternatives of remaining
in Great Britain during the winter to starve or go to
the poor house, or else run the risk of a late journey
across the plains. They chose the latter course, in which
the presidency of the British Mission, seeing no better
way out of the difficulty, acquiesced, and chartered the
ships, "Horizon" and "Thornton." Procuring the boats
depended greatly upon winds and weather, and upon
conditions of commerce.

President Richards wrote in the *Millennial Star* of
April 5, 1856: "As the Emigration will be somewhat
late this season in getting off from Liverpool, Pastors
and Presidents are especially requested to counsel the
Saints and aid them in the disposition of their effects
that they may not be left destitute, or be thrown out
of their homes longer before their embarcation than
necessary. We hope to give each shipload about three
week's notice of their embarcation.

"The scarcity of ships for the more northern of the
American ports has caused a considerable rise in the
prices of passage, which is an additional reason why
the Elders should help the Saints to make the best
disposition of their effects, and wisely observe that they
do not act too hastily and thereby, as some have, dis-
pose of their goods and leave themselves destitute. We
cannot expect to know the scarcity or plentitude of
ships any great length of time before securing one, as

this depends upon fluctuations of commerce, and also upon the winds." [19]

Brigham Young, upon learning of the late departure of the last emigrants was greatly concerned, and wrote Orson Pratt, new President at Liverpool: "The mail has just arrived (July 31). The emigration are all late, owing, I suppose to the difficulty in obtaining ships. It would be much better when it can be accomplished to have the emigrants shipped earlier in the season. They should be landed early in May, and not much, if any after the first of that month, in Boston or New York. You will please to attend to this matter in the season there of." [20]

Thus far, we have considered the emigration as a whole. But, since the Saints did not reach Iowa City simultaneously, and as their subsequent journey is the part of particular interest in our present story, we shall proceed to treat the Handcart Companies individually.

[19] *Ibid.,* 218.
[20] *Ibid.,* 651.

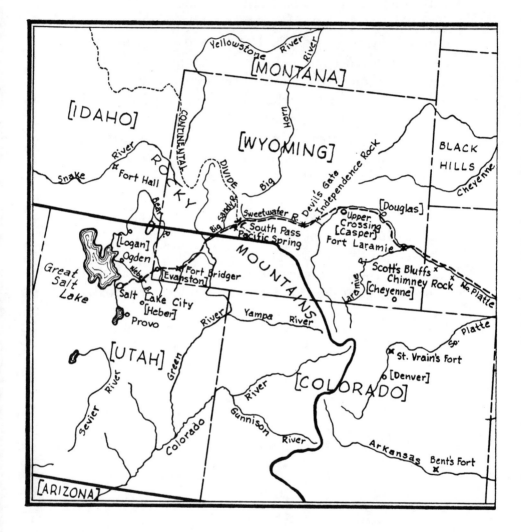

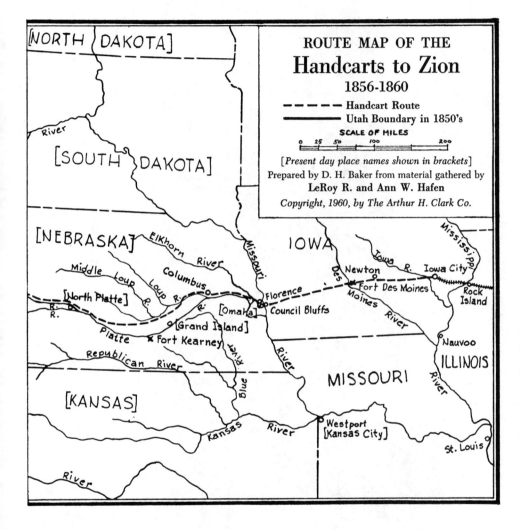

ROUTE MAP OF THE
Handcarts to Zion
1856-1860

-------- Handcart Route
———— Utah Boundary in 1850's

SCALE OF MILES

[*Present day place names shown in brackets*]
Prepared by D. H. Baker from material gathered by
LeRoy R. and Ann W. Hafen
Copyright, 1960, by The Arthur H. Clark Co.

Mormon Handcart Emigrants Passing through Iowa

From a contemporary print.

The First Handcart Companies 1856

Before starting these crusaders on their long march across the prairies and mountains, let us pause to examine the unique vehicle that is to be their friend or burden, as they push westward to Zion.

The handcarts used by the different companies varied in size and construction, but the general pattern was uniform. The carts resembled those used by porters and street sweepers in the cities of the United States. They were constructed with little or no iron.[1] The axles of many consisted of a single pole of hickory, without iron skeins. Some of the wheels were hooped with thin iron tires, others were not. Many of the carts, made in a hurry and of unseasoned wood, shrank, warped, and cracked as they were drawn across the dry plains through the summer heat.

J. Rogerson, a veteran of the handcart emigration, gives the following description: "The open handcart

---

[1] Upon being requested for suggestions relative to the construction of handcarts, C. R. Dana wrote to F. D. Richards from Manchester, England, on Feb. 7, 1856: "Supposing that a suitable person should be sent to the Iowa for that purpose, he should in the first place seek out some good timber adjacent to a saw mill, and near the outfitting point. He should select hickory for axle-trees, red or slippery elm for hubbs, white oak for spokes and rims to the wheels, white ash for fills or shafts, and for making cribbs or beds. I am of the opinion that the axle-trees should be sawed two and a half by three and a half inches.

"The oak for the rims should be sawed into boards about three quarters of an inch thick, and ripped into strips three inches wide, or two and a half was made of Iowa hickory or oak, the shafts and side pieces of the same material, but the axles generally of hickory. In length the side pieces and shafts were about six or seven feet, with three or four binding cross bars from the back part to the fore part of the body of the cart; then two or three feet space from the latter bar to the front bar or singletree for the lead horse or lead man, woman or boy of the team.

"The carts were the usual width of the wide track wagon. Across the bars of the bed of the cart we generally sewed a strip of bed ticking or a counterpane. On this wooden cart of a thimbleless axle, with about a 2½ inch shoulder and 1 inch point, were often loaded

might possibly do. The timber for them should grow on low ground, as that kind is much easier to bend, and very tough. The axle-trees, hubbs, and spokes should be first prepared, so that they could have time to season.

"When the hubbs are prepared, the spokes driven and tenoned, the rims should then be mortised, or bored, to receive the spokes. The inside corners of the rims should also be rounded off to prevent the sand from gathering and remaining on them. . . I am confident that carts could be built that would be *substantial, light,* and *easy to draw;* and I will venture to say that they need not cost more than four or five dollars each; for there would be no necessity for any planing, or any polishing, only the arms or spindles at the axle-trees, and a very little about the shafts." *Millennial Star,* XVIII (1856) 127-28.

The carts of the Fourth and the Fifth companies were made in great haste, due to the lateness of the season. John Chislett, who came in the Fourth Company, says of their construction:

"They had to be made on the camp-ground. They were made in a hurry, some of them of very insufficiently seasoned timber, and strength was sacrificed to weight until the production was a fragile structure, with nothing to recommend it but lightness. They were generally made of two parallel hickory or oak sticks, about five feet long, and two by one and a half inches thick. These were connected by one cross-piece at one end to serve as a handle, and three or four similar pieces nearly a foot apart, commencing at the other end, to serve as the bed of the cart, under the centre of which was fastened a wooden axle-tree, without iron skeins. A pair of light wheels, devoid of iron, except a very light iron tire, completed the "divine" handcart. Its weight was somewhere near sixty pound."– "Mr. Chislett's Narrative," in T. B. H. Stenhouse, *The Rocky Mountain Saints* (New York, 1873), 314.

400 or 500 pounds of flour, bedding, extra clothing, cooking utensils and a tent. How the flimsy yankee hickory structure held up the load for hundreds of miles has been a wonder to us since then.

"The covered or family cart was similar in size and construction with the exception that it was made stronger, with an iron axle. It was surmounted by a small wagon box 3 or 4 feet long with side and end pieces about 8 inches high. Two persons were assigned to the pulling of each open cart, and where a father and son of age and strength were found in one family, with smaller children, they were allotted a covered cart, but in many instances the father had to pull the covered cart alone." [2]

The majority of the Saints who were to form the first two companies had crossed the Atlantic in the "Enoch Train." One hundred and four passengers from the "S. Curling" also were allotted to the first two companies. The remainder from this ship were to constitute Handcart Company Number 3.

Church agents had been dispatched early in the spring to Iowa City, there to make arrangements to receive the P.E.Fund emigrants, and procure equipment and supplies to send them on their journey. Saints left behind in Britain were glad to read a report in the *Millennial Star* of May 3, 1856:

"We have a very cheering letter from Elders G. D. Grant and W. H. Kimball who were at Iowa City March 20. They state that the weather had been very bad, and the lakes and rivers were still a block of ice. Cattle had been offered at seventy dollars per pair,

---

[2] Josiah Rogerson, in the *Salt Lake Tribune,* Jan. 4, 1914.

and they had purchased flour at $3.20 per hundred, and the prospect was that, as spring opened, there would be a still further decrease in the price of provisions. They had contracted for 100 hand-carts of excellent quality, at about two guineas each [$10]. There were good prospects for work. Common labourers could get from three to four shillings per day, and mechanics' wages were in proportion. . . Under the wise and judicious management of Elders Taylor and Spencer, we believe that nothing will be wanting to make the handcart operation a successful one." [3]

Upon arrival at Iowa City, terminus of the railroad, on May 12, emigrants from the "Enoch Train" found much to be done and endured, through nearly four weeks of waiting, before they could commence their farther journey to Zion.

Archer Walters, a carpenter from England, had brought his wife and five children – ages six to eighteen years. He was soon set to work building handcarts. But Walters was perturbed at the living conditions for his children. With twenty people crowded into each tent, sickness multiplied in the camp. When deaths occurred, Walters made the coffins. On June 4, with a few boards, he fashioned his first for a child. Two days later he made another little one, and this was but the beginning.[4]

The first two companies that were to make the great experiment with handcart travel to Zion, were organized in early June.

[3] *Millennial Star,* XVIII (1856) 281.

[4] Walters' diary, published serially in *The Improvement Era* (Salt Lake City), vol. XXXIX and XL.

Edmund Ellsworth, thirty-seven-year-old returning missionary, was selected to lead the first company. He was a native of New York state, had joined the Latter-Day Saints Church in 1840, and in 1842 had married Elizabeth, eldest daughter of Brigham Young. In 1852 he had taken a second wife, Mary Ann Dudley. Now, having finished his two-year mission in Britain he was returning home to his two wives and six children. Exactly one month after arrival in Salt Lake City, he was to marry two of the girls of his handcart company.[5]

To lead the second handcart company, Daniel D. McArthur, age thirty-six, was chosen. Like Captain Ellsworth, he too was a returning missionary and was a native of New York state. He had become a member of the Mormon Church at the age of eighteen, had experienced the persecutions in Missouri and Illinois, and had migrated to Utah in '48. He had married in 1841.[6]

By the time the first handcart company was ready to set out from Iowa City, passengers from the "S.

---

[5] Edmund Lovell Ellsworth was born in Paris, Oneida County, New York, on July 1, 1819. The handcart girls he married were Mary Ann Bates, 22; and Mary Ann Jones, 20. His four wives bore him 42 children and these gave him many grandchildren. In 1880 he moved to Arizona with his two youngest families. He died at Show Low, Arizona, on Dec. 29, 1893.– Andrew Jenson, *Latter-Day Saints Biographical Encyclopedia* (Salt Lake City, 1936), IV, pp. 700-701; and data from the elaborate genealogical chart of his grandson, Dr. Orville Ellsworth, of Brigham Young University, Provo, Utah.

[6] Daniel Duncan McArthur was born in Holland, New York on April 8, 1820. He married first in 1841, and later lived with three wives. After completing his handcart journey he became one of the first settlers in Utah's Dixie, making his home in St. George, where he became Stake President and important leader in the community. He twice made the long journey back to the Missouri River to pick up poor Saints and bring them to Utah in ox trains. As a military man he participated in the Ute and Navajo troubles and in the "so-called Buchanan War."– Jenson, *Biographical Encyclopedia,* I, pp. 336-37.

Curling" arrived at the outfitting depot. Some of these were placed in the Second Company, now about ready to go; others remained to form the Third Company.

The first two handcart caravans left Iowa City two days apart; were closely associated throughout the journey; and would arrive at Salt Lake City on the same day. A report of their historic departure was sent to Britain by Elder Daniel Spencer, who had been dispatched from England early in the spring to look after the emigration at Iowa City.

"L.D.S. Camp near Iowa City, June 22, 1856. It will give you much joy to learn that the handcart experiment is now being fairly and so far, most successfully tested. Captain Edmund Ellsworth left here on the 9th with 274 souls, accompanied by Elders Oakley and Butler as assistants.

"Captain D. D. McArthur left on the 11th with 221 souls, accompanied by Elders Crandall and Leonard as assistants. These numbered in all 497 souls, embraced 104 of the "S. Curling's" company, and their fit out was, together, 100 handcarts, 5 wagons, 24 oxen, 4 mules, 25 tents, and provisions to Florence. Brother Ferguson visited their camps 35 miles out, and accompanied them during a portion of a morning's march. He reports that though their first two days travel were good marches for strong men, considering the sandy roads, he never visited a camp of travelling Saints so cheerful and universally happy." [7]

The companies were organized with about five persons to a handcart, and approximately twenty individuals to a tent. The occupants of each tent were

---

[7] *Millennial Star,* Aug. 2, 1856 (XVIII, p. 489).

under a president, or tent captain; and five tents were supervised by the captain of a "hundred."

"The duty of the company captain," writes Joseph Argyle, Jr., who pulled a cart in the first company, and whose father was a tent captain, "was to look after everything in general to see that the company was provided with all provisions that they were able to carry and to assist in all that would aid for the betterment of the company. The tent captain was expected to give all his time and attention to his company, to make sure that all allotments of one pint of flour for each person were given every twenty-four hours and to equalize as nearly as possible all labor, or to act as the father over his family."[8] Each person was allowed seventeen pounds of baggage, including clothing, bedding, and utensils.

"When the brethren came to weigh our things," writes Mary Ann Jones, who was to become a wife of Captain Ellsworth after arrival in Utah, "some wanted to take more than the allotted portion and put on extra clothes; thus many who were real thin became suddenly stout and as soon as the weighing was over, put their extra clothes back on the handcarts. But that did not last long. In a few days we had to have all weighed again and many were found with much more weight on the carts than allowed. One old sister carried a teapot and colander on her apron string all the way to Salt Lake. Another carried a hat box full of things, but she died on the way."[9]

Since the journey from Iowa City to Florence,

[8] Kate B. Carter (Compiler), *Heart Throbs of the West* (Daughters of Utah Pioneers Publication, 1939), I, p. 84.

[9] *Ibid.*, VI, pp. 358-59.

Nebraska, a distance of some 275 miles, was through partly settled country, the travelers were able to obtain some supplies from the farmers en route.

The first company set forth from Iowa City in the late afternoon of June 9, made three or four miles and camped. Several oxen strayed and the next day the caravan halted while the animals were recovered.

Archer Walters, the English carpenter previously referred to as making coffins and handcarts, kept a revealing diary. From it we extract some details of the trip over this first stretch of the journey:

"June 11th, 1856. Journeyed 7 miles. Very dusty. All tired and smothered with dust and camped in the dust or where the dust blowed. Was captain over my tent of 18. . .

"June 15th. Got up about 4 o'clock to make a coffin for my brother John Lee's son named William Lee, aged 12 years. Meetings as usual and at the same time had to make another coffin for Sister Prator's child. Was tired with repairing handcarts the last week. . .

"16th. Harriet [his wife] very ill. Traveled 19 miles and after pitching tent mended carts.

"17th. Traveled about 17 miles; pitched tent. Made a little coffin for Bro. Job Welling's son and mended a handcart wheel. . .

"21st. Traveled about 13 miles. Camped at Indian Creek. Bro. Bower died about 6 o'clock; from Birmingham Conference. Went to buy some wood to make the coffin but the kind farmer gave me the wood and nails. It had been a very hot day and I was never more tired, but God has said as my day my strength shall be. . .

"22nd.   Got up at break of day and made the coffin for Bro. James Bowers by 9 o'clock . . .

"26th.   Traveled about 1 mile. Very faint from lack of food. We are only allowed about ¾ of a lb. of flour a head each day and about 3 oz. of sugar each week. About ½ of a lb. of bacon each week; which makes those that have no money very weak. Made a child's coffin for Sister Sheen – Emma Sheen aged 2½ years.

"July 1st.   Traveled about 15 miles. Walked very fast, – nearly 4 miles an hour. Bro. Brown's family and some young sisters with Bro. Ellsworth going first which causes many of the brothers to have hard feelings. . . ½ lb of flour each; 2 oz of rice; which is very little and my children cry with hunger and it grieves me and makes me cross.

"July 2nd.   Brother Parker's little boy, age six, was lost. The father went back to hunt him.

"July 3rd.   [Walters and several others started out early and traveled ten miles in the wrong direction.] 11 o'clock Brother Butler who had charge of the mule teams came with the mules and wagons to fetch us. Got to camp when they were getting up. Laid down about an hour and started with the camp.

"July 4th.   About 20 miles. Tired out. Tied my cart behind the wagon and got in. . .

"July 5th.   Brother Parker brings into camp his little boy that had been lost. Great joy through the camp. The mother's joy I can not describe.

"July 8th.   Traveled a round about road 20 miles. Crossed the river Missouri and camped at the city of Florence. Very tired; glad to rest. Slept well." [Here he is to work for five days repairing handcarts.] [10]

---

[10] Walters' diary, *op. cit.*

In the Second Handcart Company was another good
diarist, Twiss Bermingham, a graduate of Dublin University. At age twenty-four, with his wife Kate and
three small children, he had headed for Zion by handcart. From his journal we take some items about their
trip to Florence.

"Iowa City, Iowa, 11th June.   Left town with the
handcarts. Travelled 8 miles. Camped at 9 mile house.

"12th June.   Travelled 12 miles. Started at 9½
o'clock and camped at 1 o'clock. Very hot day and
windy. The dust flew so thick that we could not see
each other 1 yard distant. Before we left, I was appointed President of a tent.   .   .

"16th.   Travelled 15 miles. Day very hot. Bro.
Laurenson fainted under his cart.   .   .

"21st.   Travelled 14 miles. A child died this morning and was buried under a tree." [A German sister
fainted on the road on the 25th, and Sister Laurenson
fainted on the 28th.]

"30th.   This day Brother Arthur stopped at a Town,
himself and his family as he could not draw his handcart any further.   .   .

"July 1st.   Storm, thunder and lightning raged fear-
fully all night. Blew up part of our tent and wet all
our clothes through. Lay all night in our wet clothes
until morning with water running under us.   .   .

"July 3rd.   Started at 5 o'clock and camped at 7¼,
after a long and tedious journey of 25 miles. Some of
the Brethren fainted on the road and were carried into
camp in the ox-team. I nearly fainted myself from exhaustion, but plucked up courage and never let go the
handcart.   .   .

"7th. After 10 miles, 2 families gave out, being frightened at getting nothing for 3 days but Indian corn stirabout. They stopped at a farm house to work for 2 dollars per day and food. . .

"8th. Camped at the Mormon camp at Florence City at 7½ o'clock. The company generally very fatigued. Found some of Brother Ellsworth's company lying insensible on the road. This day we traveled through a beautiful country and passed Council Bluffs, which put me in mind of the mountains of Killarney, Ireland. . . At about 5 o'clock we reached the River Missouri, over which we were ferried by a small steamer." [11]

As the companies pushed across Iowa the sand and dust began to grind the wooden axles of the carts. Fortunately Joseph Argyle, a member of the first company and a tinner by trade, had with him a box of block tin. Captain Ellsworth asked him to use the tin and wrap the cart axles. Working morning, noon, and night at the encampments, he completed the task and wrapped every axle.[12]

The incident of the Parker child lost on July 1st, which is mentioned in both the Walters and Bermingham diaries, is given elaboration in the recollections of the Parker family. Robert and Ann Parker were traveling in McArthur's Company with their four children: Max, 12; Martha Alice, 10; Arthur, 6; and Ada, 1 year old. One day little Arthur sat down to rest,

---

[11] Diary of Twiss Bermingham. The original diary is in possession of a grandson, Rutledge Bermingham Barry of New York City. It was published in the American Legion Magazine and republished in Eliza M. Wakefield (ed.), *The Handcart Trail* (privately printed, 1949).

[12] Argyle's account in *Heart Throbs*, I, p. 84.

unnoticed by the other children. A sudden storm came up, and the company hurriedly made camp. Finding that Arthur was not with the children, an organized search was begun. It continued a second day, but without success.

"Ann Parker pinned a bright shawl about the thin shoulders of her husband and sent him back alone on the trail to search again for their child. If he found him dead, he was to wrap him in the shawl; if alive, the shawl would be a flag to signal her. Ann and her children took up their load and struggled on with the company, while Robert retraced the miles of forest trail, calling, and searching and praying for his helpless little son. At last he reached a mail and trading station where he learned that his child had been found and cared for by a woodsman and his wife. He had been ill from exposure and fright. But God had heard the prayers of his people.

"Out on the trail each night Ann and her children kept watch and, when, on the third night, the rays of the setting sun caught the glimmer of a bright red shawl, the brave little mother sank, in a pitiful heap in the sand. . . Ann slept for the first time in 6 days." [13]

Of the arrival of the first caravans at Florence, J. H. Latey wrote on August 14, 1856: "The first and second companies of emigrants by hand carts, under the care of Captains Edmund Ellsworth and Daniel D. McArthur, assisted by Elders J. Oakley, William Butler, Truman Leonard, and S. W. Crandall, piloted by Elder

---

[13] Camilla W. Judd's account in Kate B. Carter (Compiler), *Treasures of Pioneer History* (Salt Lake City, Daughters of Utah Pioneers, 1956), v, pp. 240-42.

Joseph France, who acted as agent and commissary, arrived in Camp on the 17th of July, in fine health and spirits, singing as they came along, Elder J. D. T. McAllister's noted hand cart song – 'Some must push and some must pull.' etc. One would not think that they had come from Iowa City, a long and rough journey of from 275 to 300 miles, except by their dust-stained garments and sunburned faces. My heart is gladdened as I write this, for methinks I see their merry countenances and buoyant step, and the strains of the handcart song seem ringing in my ears like sweet music heard at eventide or in a dream. The first company had among its number the Birmingham Band, and though but young performers, they played really very well – far superior to anything to be found this far west. In giving you this description of the feelings of the first companies, I give you in effect the feelings of the whole. This is the bright side of the picture, and is of those who may really be called Latter-day Saints; who have in continual remembrance the covenants they have made; who obey counsel, and may really be called Saints of the Most High God. There are others – for I have seen both sides of the picture – who are apt to forget the God who has delivered them from their Gentile chains and task masters, and are allured by fine promises and high wages; others there are whose faith is not of that nature to stand the trials they are called upon to undergo, and back out from five to fifty in a company of 300; but the mirth of the one kind does not interfere with the gloom of the other; or, vice versa, each one does what suits him best." [14]

The "Handcart Song," referred to above, can not be

---

[14] *Millennial Star,* XVIII (1856) 637.

ranked as great poetry, but it expresses the spirit of
the people. It became a source of encouragement to
them, and was often sung by the emigrants. The author-
musician, J. D. T. McAllister, had recently returned
from his British mission and had served at Iowa City
in disbursing equipment and supplies to the handcart
emigrants.[15] The first stanza and chorus are:

THE HANDCART SONG

Ye Saints that dwell on Europe's shore
Prepare yourselves with many more
To leave behind your native land
For sure God's Judgments are at hand.
Prepare to cross the stormy main
Before you do the Valley gain,
And with the faithful make a start
To cross the plains with your handcart.

Chorus

Some must push and some must pull
As we go marching up the hill,
As merrily on the way we go
Until we reach the Valley, oh! [16]

The two handcart caravans remained about two
weeks at Florence, recuperating their strength, repairing the carts, and preparing for the thousand-mile
journey ahead. Quite a large number dropped out

[15] John Daniel Thompson McAllister, a native of Delaware, migrated to
Utah in 1851. He was musically inclined; played in the brass band and took
part in dramatics, and frequently sang in the Mormon Tabernacle in Salt
Lake City. He was a prominent Church official, being President of the St.
George Stake from 1877 to 1888.— Jenson, *Biog. Ency.,* I, pp. 334-36.

[16] The complete song is given in Appendix L. Authorship has been claimed
for various persons, which results largely from the fact that several handcart songs were composed and sung. For the words of some of these, see
also Appendix L. There was some variation in the wording of this most
famous one, which has as its chorus "Some must push and some must pull,"
etc.

here to await easier transportation. The First Company set out on July 20 and the Second, four days later. Let us roll along with Archer Walters in the Ellsworth Company.

"July 20th, 1856. Preparing to start. Traveled about 7 miles.

"21st.   Traveled about 18 miles. Harriet better.

"22nd.   Passed over ferry at Elk Horn. Storm.   .   .

"26th.   Passed over the ferry – Luke Fort [Loup Fork]. Traveled about 6 miles. As soon as we crossed it looked very dark and black. We had not got far and it began to lightning and soon the thunder roared and about the middle of the train of handcarts the lightning struck a brother and he fell to rise no more in that body. By the name of Henry Walker, from Carlisle Conference, aged 58 years. Left a wife and children. One boy burned a little named James Stoddard; we thought he would die but he recovered and was able to walk, and Brother Wm. Stoddard, father of the boy was knocked to the ground and a sister, Betsy Taylor, was terribly shook but recovered. We then went 2 miles to camp. All wet through.   .   .   I put the body with the help of others, on the handcart and pulled him to camp and buried him without a coffin for there were no boards to be had.   .   .

"28th.   Traveled about 18 miles. Harriet much better; for such we feel thankful.

"29th.   Traveled about 15 miles. Met a company coming from California. A child born in camp. Sister Doney. My birthday.   .   .

"August 3rd.   Rested but mended handcarts. Got shell fish out of the creek for we was very hungry. Only ¾ lbs. of flour; 1½ oz. of sugar; a few apples.

"6th.   Saw thousands of buffalo. Four was killed. So thick together that they covered four miles at once. Camped by Buffalo Creek. Traveled 10 miles.

"7th.   Thousands of buffalo. Traveled 25 miles. Camped late at night. Had to dig for water and it was very thick. Our hungry appetites satisfied by the buffalo. Got up soon to repair handcarts.

"8th.   Rose soon to repair carts. Traveled about 15 miles. Camped by the side of Platte River. Repaired handcarts. Harriet getting around nicely and I feel thankful. My wife very ill-tempered at times. An old brother lost named Sanderson. Many went in all directions but could not find him.

"9th.   Found the old Brother Sanderson on a hill about 6 o'clock. Brought him into camp on a mule. Traveled about 15 miles after repairing handcarts until 12 o'clock.

"10th.   Traveled 14 miles. All or most of the people bad with the diarrhea or purging,– whether it was the buffalo or the muddy river water.

"11th.   Traveled about 17 miles. Four men sent to shoot buffalo. Harriet much better. Very weak myself. I expect it is the short rations; three-fourths lb of flour per day. It is but little but it is as much as the oxen teams that we have could draw from Florence. Forded over two creeks. Met a man coming from California by himself; going to the states. One of our cows died. Buffalo killed.

"12th.   Rested while some of the brethren with Captain Ellsworth went and shot two more buffalo and we dried the meat.   .   .

"17th.   Crossed over some creeks.   .   .   Brother

Missel Rossin, Italian, found dead by the side of the road. . .

"19th. Traveled 19 miles. Camped by the Platte. A nice camping ground. Buffalo chips to burn. . .

"21st. Traveled 18 miles. Camped 4 miles past Chimney Rock, Platte River. Sandy road the last 3 or 4 days. . .

"23rd. Traveled 16 miles. Camped by Platte River. Harriet getting well, thank God, and not been in the wagon to ride. Our allowance of flour tonight was 1 lb. a head. For this I was thankful for I never was so hungry in my life. Captain Ellsworth shot a cow. Very thankfully received.

"24th. [Sunday]. Rested from travels but had to repair handcarts, meeting at night. Received the Sacrament. Spoke at the meeting. Brother Ellsworth spoke some time and said we had made great improvement. That last week there had been less quarreling and those that had robbed the handcarts, or wagons, unless they repent their flesh would rot from their bones and go to Hell.

"25th. Traveled about 19 miles. Saw many Indians. Camped about 19 miles from Fort Laramie. Handcart axle tree broke on the road. Plenty of wood. Quite a treat after burning so many buffalo chips.

"26th. Traveled about 19 miles. Camped 3 miles from Fort Laramie. Tucked away [traded] a dagger for a piece of bacon and salt and sold one for One dollar and one-fourth. Bought bacon and meal and Henry and me began to eat it raw we were so hungry. Forded the river. Sister Watts got hurt by the wagon. My wife thinks she would have fell when half way over the river. Bro. John Lee came to her assistance.

"27th. Traveled about 18 miles. Had bacon and meal porridge for supper; the best supper for many weeks. A camp of Indians passed us.

"28th. Camped at a nice place called Horseshoe Creek. Mother and Sarah washed clothes. . .

"30th. Traveled 22 miles. Met some Californians and they told us that the wagons were waiting at Deer Creek for us.

"31. Very poorly, faint and hungry. Traveled to Deer Creek, 22 miles. Brother Stoddard from Carlisle Conference, about 54 years old, died in the wagon on the road. More provisions given out.

"September 1st. Rested from travels. I mended carts. Meeting about flour and paying for extra that was brought in the wagons, 18¢ per lb. Harriet getting quite well and walks all the way.

"2nd. . . . Walter Sanderson, aged 56 died. . .

"7th. Traveled 26 miles. Bro. Nipras died. Left on the road.

"8th. 11 miles. Had dinner at Devils Gate. . .

"13th. Traveled 28 miles. Camped at Paciffick Springs. Tucked a blanket with a brother from the valley. . .

"14th. Traveled 3 miles. Camped to mend hand-carts and women to wash. Sister Mayer died." [17] [Last entry in diary. He died two weeks after arriving in Salt Lake Valley. He had paid his way to Zion.]

As the handcart pioneers trudged across the treeless plains of western Nebraska the women and children gathered buffalo chips to feed the fires for cooking their meals. Carts were formed into a circle at night,

---

[17] Walters' diary, *op. cit.*

with the tents pitched in the center, and a guard put on watch.

"Some may recoil at the thought of a supper cooked in water dug from a buffalo wallow and with buffalo chips, but it tasted good to us," wrote Mary Ann Jones, future wife of Captain Ellsworth. "We once came across an immense herd of buffalo and it looked as if the whole prairie was moving. We waited more than an hour for them to cross the road before we could go on.

"One day we were stopped on the Platte River by a large band of Indians, who demanded food. They were in war paint and were very hostile. Captain Ellsworth talked to them and told the brethren to pray while he talked. He gave them some beads and they let us go. . . I never left my handcart for a day, and only rode over two rivers. We waded streams, crossed high mountains and pulled through heavy sand, leaving comfortable homes, father, mother, brother and sister to be where we would hear a prophet's voice and live with the Saints of Zion." [18]

As Captain McArthur's Second Handcart Company sets out from Florence – four days behind the First Company – we again utilize the Bermingham diary:

"24th July. Left Florence. Traveled 7 miles.

"25th. Traveled 20 miles, to Elkhorn River, where we found a camp of Indians, many of whom came to meet us and were very friendly. The chief took my cart and drew it into camp about ¼ mile and although a tall strong looking man, it made the perspiration run

---

[18] Kate B. Carter (Compiler) *Heart Throbs of the West* (Salt Lake City, Daughters of Utah Pioneers Publication, 1944), VI, p. 359.

down his face until it dropped on the ground. . .

"26th.   Crossed Elkhorn River by means of a very roughly constructed ferry. For the conveyance of us over, the company had to pay $6. Travelled 15 miles without any water until we came to the Platte River, where the water was a joyful sight. . .

"27th.   Camped all day on the north bend of the Platte. Took a dose of castor oil which sickened me very much and kept me cantering for a long time.

"28th.   Rather weak this morning and terribly annoyed by two boils, one on my jaw about as big as a pigeon egg and another on the calf of my leg which torments me very much when drawing the handcart.

"29th.   Boils very sore this morning but must draw on the cart still. With such sores at home I would lie upon two chairs and never stir until they were healed. Started early this morning and traveled 20 miles. . .

"31st.   Left Loup-Fork and traveled 20 miles without water. I was so exhausted with my sores and the labour of pulling that I was obliged to lie down for a few hours after arriving in camp before I could do anything. Kate was also so tired and fatigued out that she was glad to get lying down without any supper and I was not able to cook any for ourselves so we were obliged to do with a bit of bread and a pint of milk. This is the quantity of milk we have been allowed morning and evening since we left Florence. Sometimes it is less. Rather little for 5 persons. . .

"3d August.   Sunday.   Started at 5 o'clock without any breakfast and had to pull the carts through 6 miles of heavy sand. Some places the wheels were up to the boxes and I was so weak from thirst and hunger and being exhausted with the pain of the boils that I was obliged to lie down several times, and many others had to do the same. Some fell down. I was very much grieved today, so much so that I thought my heart would burst – sick – and poor Kate – at the same time – crawling on her hands and knees, and the children crying with hunger and fatigue. I was obliged to take the children and put them on the hand cart and urge them along the road in order to make them keep up. About 12 o'clock a thunder storm came on, and the rain fell in torrents. In our tent we were standing up to our knees in water and every stitch we had was the same as if we were dragged through the river. Rain continued until 8 o'clock the following morning."

[There were no diary entries from August 4 to 12 inclusive].

"16th. This morning an old woman belonging to our company was bitten by a rattlesnake in the leg and before half an hour her leg swelled to four times its thickness. She was administered to by the Elders and we started again, but unfortunately as we were starting another old woman was run over by one of the wagons. The front wheel went over her thighs and the back wheels over her shins, and singular to say, although the wagon was laden with 32 cwt. of flour, not one of her bones was broken.[19] This day we had the most severe day's journey we had since we started and travelled over 20 miles of heavy sand hills or bluffs. Besides having to ford many streams. All seemed to be fully worn out when they got into camp.

"17th. Sunday. In camp all day. Spent the day mending my boots, and Kate was washing. This day, a German sister died. . .

---

[19] For an interesting and fuller description of these incidents see Captain McArthur's account in Appendix B.

"24th.   Sunday.   Camped all day at Chimney Rock.
Spent the day mending my clothes and baking and
cooking while Kate was washing and mending the children's clothes. On the 22d while here on the road travelling we were overtaken by a very heavy thunder-
storm which wet us all to the skin, but as soon as it
was over we went at it again and made a journey of
7 or 8 miles before we camped and then we had to lie
on the wet grass all night, and go to bed supperless,
there being no firewood to cook, the buffalo chips
being wet. We had to ford 20 streams this week.   .   .

"28th.   After travelling 12 miles through sand, came
to Fort Laramie where after crossing the river and
getting some wet trousers and petticoats we remained
all night. Passed many camps of Indians, all peace-
able.   .   .

"4th Sept.   Crossed Muddy Creek and travelled 20
miles and late in the evening forded the Platte again
for the last time. For five days we were not in camp
for an hour after night and we were always up at
daybreak preparing to start at 5. We met the wagons
at Deer Creek which were sent with flour from the
Valley to meet us. There were 5 wagons, one for each
Company and each wagon had 1000 lbs. of flour in
them. Two started for the Valley with our Company.
German boy's father died.

"5th.   Very wet today. Could not start it rained so
much. Snow four feet deep on the mountains all around
us.   .   .

"21st.   From the 5th to the 21st nothing particular
occurred save meeting of some wagons of flour from
the valley for which we will have to pay at the rate
of 18¢ per lb. when we get to the city   .   .   .   Travelled at the rate of about 25 miles per day. Two days

we travelled 32 miles each. Camped last night at Fort Bridger where we remained until 10 o'clock today. We are now 113 miles from the city." [No further entries in diary].[20]

Another sampling of accounts from the Second Handcart Company. John and Nancy McCleve, natives of Ireland, took their seven children across the plains with this caravan. Sharing the tent with them was a German family, none of whom could speak English. It comprised Mr. and Mrs. Elliker and their eight children. Mr. Elliker and four children died on the journey. John McCleve was buried two days before the party reached Salt Lake City.[21]

An impressionistic picture of the handcarts in action, is given by Thomas Bullock who, with sixteen other missionaries bound for Britain and several en route to fields elsewhere, met the two first handcart caravans on September 18. He sent his report to the *Millennial Star,* from Florence on October 28.

"We were very agreeably surprised by suddenly coming upon the advance train of handcarts, composed of about 300 persons, travelling gently up the hill west of Green River, led by Elder Edmund Ellsworth. As the two companies approached each other, the camp of missionaries formed in line, and gave three loud Hosannahs with the waving of hats, which was heartily led by Elder P. P. Pratt, responded to by loud greetings from the Saints of the handcart train, who unitedly made the hills and valleys resound with shouts of gladness; the memory of this scene will never be forgotten

20 Bermingham diary, *op. cit.*

21 Carter, *Heart Throbs,* VI, pp. 356-58. For further data on the Elliker family, see the account by Wesley Bauer in Carter, *Treasures of Pioneer History,* V, pp. 244-46.

by any person present. . . They were very cheerful and happy, and we blessed them in the name of the Lord, and they went on their way rejoicing. The same day we met a company of hand-carts, led by Elder D. McArthur." [22]

The first two handcart companies reached Salt Lake Valley together on September 26. Despite the hard labor and the difficulties experienced by these travelers, the completion of their journey was hailed in Utah as the successful culmination of a cherished project and experiment, and so was celebrated with enthusiasm in Salt Lake City.

Wilford Woodruff, one of the Counsellors of President Young, describes the reception: "One of the most interesting scenes that was ever witnessed in our Territory, was the arrival of two of the handcart companies on the 26th inst. Having heard the night previous that they were camped between the two mountains, President Young and Kimball, and many citizens, with a detachment of the Lancers, and the brass bands, went out to meet and escort them into the city. They met the companies at the foot of the Little Mountain. Elder E. Ellsworth led the first company, and Elder Daniel D. McArthur the second.

"After the meeting and salutations were over, amid feelings which no one can describe, the escort was formed, a party of Lancers leading the advance, followed by the bands, the Presidency, the Marshal, and citizens; then came the companies of handcarts, another party of Lancers bringing up the rear. . . I must say my feelings were inexpressible to behold a company of men, women, and children, many of them aged and

---

[22] *Millennial Star,* XVIII (1856) 811-12.

infirm, enter the city of the Great Salt Lake, drawing
100 handcarts, (led by Brother Ellsworth, who assisted
in drawing the first handcart) with which they had
travelled some 1,400 miles in nine weeks, and to see
them dance with joy as they travelled through the
streets. . . This sight filled our hearts with joy and
thanksgiving to God. . . As I gazed upon the scene,
meditating upon the future result, it looked to me like
the first hoisting of the floodgate of deliverance to the
oppressed millions. We can now say to the poor and
honest in heart, come home to Zion, for the way is
prepared . . .[23]

The *Deseret News* reported the reception of the hon-
ored companies by the welcoming party: "Ere long the
anxiously expected train came in sight, led by Captain
Ellsworth on foot, and with two aged veterans pulling
the front cart, followed by a long line of carts attended
by the old, middle aged and young of both sexes.

"When opposite the escorting party, a halt was
called, and their Captain introduced the new comers
to President Young and Kimball, which was followed
by the joyous greeting of relatives and friends, and an
unexpected treat of melons. While thus regaling, Captain D. D. McArthur came up with his handcart company, they having traveled from the east base of the
Big Mountain. . .

"The procession reached the Public Square about
sunset, where the Lancers, Bands and carriages were
formed in a line facing the line of handcarts; and after
a few remarks by President Young, accompanied by
his blessing, the spectators and escort retired and the
companies pitched their tents, at the end of a walk,

---

[23] *Ibid.,* 794-95.

and pull upwards of 1300 miles. This journey has been performed with less than the average amount of mortality usually attending ox trains; and all, though somewhat fatigued, stepped out with alacrity to the last, and appeared buoyant and cheerful.

"And thus has been successfully accomplished a plan, devised by the wisdom and forethought of our President, for rapidly gathering the poor, almost entirely independent of the wealth so closely hoarded beyond their reach." [24]

Still another honor awaited Captain Ellsworth. Two days after arriving in the Valley, when the weary travelers had been regaled and provisioned by the Bishops and the sisters, a mighty multitude assembled in the old Bowery to hear a report from the Captains.

"My heart was in the enterprise," confided Ellsworth, "and I showed the Saints that if it was a hard journey they were called upon to pass through, and even should they lay down their bodies in the earth before they arrived in Great Salt Lake City, it was better to do so, keeping the commandment of God in gathering, than to wear out their bodies in the old countries; and so the Saints in that country feel now. . .

"I have had to labor with the people incessantly to keep faith in them, . . . by showing them that there was honor attached to pulling handcarts into the valley; by saying, 'I have walked 1300 miles, old and decrepit as I am, with these crooked legs of mine, and there is honor in that, brethren and sisters, far more than in having to be carried in a wagon to the valleys of the mountains.' . . .

[24] *Deseret News.*

"When we came to the large streams that had to be crossed, such as the Platte, it seemed almost too much for human nature, for men, women, and children to wade through a broad stream nearly two feet deep, and some would tremble at it; but the most, as they were requested, boldly entered and went through freely, . . .

"The brethren and sisters felt wonderfully tender of the children on the commencement of the journey, asking, 'What shall we do with them?' and saying that they must get into the wagons. I said, 'Let them stick by the hand-carts, and pull off their heavy shoes so that they can go along light footed, and the journey will be accomplished easily by them; their feet will become tough and the mothers who will take this course will see the utility of it before the journey is accomplished.' But some were so tender of their children that they nearly killed them by keeping on their heavy stockings and shoes . . .

"Some of the brethren wrote letters to their wives, immediately after starting in the handcart train, but I believe they have all had to bring their letters in their pockets; we have passed the ox-teams, and everything that started with us." . . .[25]

In conformity with church policy, Captain Ellsworth saw to it that an official record was kept of his company's travel, day by day. He appointed A. Galloway to serve as the keeper of the Journal. This valuable record is presented in full in Appendix A. The captain of the Second Company, D. D. McArthur, also gave a report, which is presented in Appendix B.

---

[25] *Ibid.*

The Welsh Company

The Third Company of handcart emigrants, made up almost entirely of Welshmen, had crossed the Atlantic in the "S. Curling," and rode the train most of the way to Iowa City – part of the time in cattle cars.[1] Upon arrival there, and finding the handcarts not yet ready, the Saints helped construct and finish them.[2] The company of 320 persons and 64 handcarts was organized with Edward Bunker as captain – a 34-year-old veteran in military and church service.

Like the captains of the other companies, Edward Bunker was a returning missionary, having been laboring in Great Britain for nearly four years. As leader of a handcart trek he had one distinguishing qualification. He had walked the long road from Fort Leavenworth to San Diego, California, with the Mormon Battalion, in 1846. A native of Maine, he had joined the Latter Day Saints Church in 1845, and had married in February, 1846. After his march with the Battalion he had returned to his wife and new baby at Winter Quarters, Nebraska, and in 1850 emigrated to Utah.

Of his experience with the handcarts Captain Bunker afterwards wrote in his brief Autobiography:

---

[1] Priscilla M. Evans (in Kate B. Carter, *Heart Throbs*, VI, p. 354), says they traveled in cattle cars.

[2] Daniel Spencer, Church emigration agent at Iowa City, wrote on June 22, 1856: "Since we have taken the making of the handcarts into our own hands it is getting along beyond our best calculations. Brother Webb has been most faithful and successful in charge of this department."– *Millennial Star*, XVIII (1856) 490. Previously the carts had been built under contract.

"We landed in New York, at Castle Garden, thence by rail to St. Louis, then by steam boat up the Mississippi River to Iowa City, which place we reached in the month of June, 1856. Here the company were fitted out with handcarts. I was given charge of a Welsh company and left Iowa City June 28, 1856. We procured our provisions and teams to haul our supplies at Council Bluffs. After leaving Iowa City we encountered some heavy rain and wind storms which blew down our tents and washed away our handcarts. I got a heavy drenching which brought on a spell of rheumatism that confined me to my bed a portion of the journey. I had my councilors Bros. Grant, a Scotchman and a tailor by trade, and Mac Donald, a cabinet maker, neither of whom had had much experience in handling teams. Both were returned missionaries. The Welsh had no experience at all and very few of them could speak English. This made my burden very heavy. I had the mule team to drive and had to instruct the teamsters about yoking the oxen. The journey from the Missouri River to Salt Lake City was accomplished in 65 days. We were short of provisions all the way and would have suffered for food had not supplies reached us from the valley. However, we arrived safely in Salt Lake City October 2, 1856." [3]

Of the trek across Iowa Priscilla M. Evans, one of the emigrants, writes: "People made fun of us as we walked, pulling our carts, but the weather was fine and the roads were excellent and although I was sick and

---

[3] See the "Autobiography of Edward Bunker," MS., Brigham Young University Library. Bunker was later to become the principal founder of Bunkerville, Nevada, my home town. He finally moved to Mexico and died there in 1901, leaving three wives and twenty-two children.

we were very tired at night, still we thought it was a glorious way to go to Zion.

"We began our journey with a handcart for each family, some families consisting of just a man and wife, and some had quite large families. Each handcart had one hundred pounds of flour, that to be divided up and we were to get more from the wagons as required. At first we had a little coffee and bacon, but that was soon gone and we had no use for any cooking utensils but a frying pan." [4]

The company arrived at Florence on July 19 and was detained there while their carts were repaired. They set out again on July 30. From Scott's Bluffs, Nebraska, David Grant, assistant captain of the company, wrote back to England on August 30:

"It is with pleasure that I spend a few moments in writing to you, after travelling today twenty miles, and helping to pull a handcart the most of the way. If you come to Utah next year, a few items of information from me may be useful to you. It is one month today since we left Florence, formerly called Winter Quarters, and we are almost five hundred miles from it. I have travelled the same road three times with horse and ox teams, but never made the trip in so short a time before. We have averaged twenty miles a day for the past week, and are determined to average that or more every day until we reach Great Salt Lake City, where the Prophets and Apostles of our God live.

"The Saints are getting more and more of the spirit of Zion upon them as they approach nearer to it. I will give it as my opinion that the Saints will cross the Plains with handcarts for years to come, because

---

[4] Carter, *Heart Throbs,* VI, p. 354.

of the utility of the plan, considering the circumstances by which the Saints are surrounded. There are twenty persons and four handcarts to each tent. Each adult person has seventeen and each child ten pounds of luggage, which consists of bedding and wearing apparel; extra of this they haul their cooking utensils.

"The provisions are hauled in a wagon, and rationed out to the company every other day, as follows – to each adult or child per day, one pound of flour, with tea or coffee, sugar, and rice. We have for the use of the company, eighteen cows that give milk, and have killed three fine buffaloes, and eaten as we had need. Besides that which I have enumerated, we have with us beef cattle enough to last through to Utah, using one of them a week. This is so healthy a country, that our appetites are very good, and we send our allowances home without much trouble. There are some very old brethren and sisters that walk every day. One sister, that has walked all the way from Iowa City, is seventy-three years old. There are in the company those still more advanced in years, who ride in the wagons.

"If there were settlements every hundred and fifty or two hundred miles on the road, from which companies could get supplies, they could carry their provisions on their handcarts, and dispense with the provision wagons, which greatly retard our progress. We travel together in peace and harmony, and when we camp, are not molested by wolves in sheep's clothing. Elder Bunker has proved himself a father to his people, and I know that the Holy Spirit has been with and aided him in leading them all the time. I am happy to say that we have been united in all things since we left Iowa City, and am glad in having such a man to lead us as our Captain." [5]

The reactions of some of the emigrants were not so favorable. Mrs. Evans recalled: "The flour was self-rising and we took water and baked a little cake. After the first few weeks of traveling this little cake was all we had to eat and after months of traveling we were put on half rations and at one time, before help came, we were out of flour for two days. During this hard journey I was expecting my first baby and it was very hard to be contented on so little food. My husband had lost a leg in his early childhood and walked on a wooden stump, which caused him a great deal of pain and discomfort. When his knee, which rested on a pad, became very sore, my husband was not able to walk any farther and I could not pull him in the little cart, being so sick myself, so one late afternoon he felt he could not go on so he stopped to rest beside some tall sagebrush. I pleaded with him to try to walk farther, that if he stayed there he would die, and I could not go on without him. The company did not miss us until they rested for the night and when the names were checked we were not among the company and a rider on a horse came back looking for us. When they saw the pitiful condition of my husband's knee he was assigned to the commissary wagon and helped dispense the food for the rest of the journey. I hated to see him suffer so but it was with relish that I ate his little cake when he was too miserable to care for food.

"Our company was a Welsh company of 300; there were about a dozen in our tent. There were only about six who could not speak the Welsh language, myself among that number. There were in our tent a man with

[5] *Millennial Star*, XVIII (1856) 767.

one leg (my husband) ; two blind, Thomas Giles being
one of them; a man with an arm gone; and a widow
with five children. The man with the one arm went
back to Wales in the spring as he had left his family
there. There were five mule teams and wagons to haul
the tents and flour. We were allowed to bring but 17
pounds of clothing. . . We were more favored than
those who came later as we had no snow and the
weather was quite pleasant. One incident will show
some of the trouble we had. We had no grease for the
wheels on the handcarts and one day they killed an old
buffalo and my husband and John Thain, a butcher,
sat up all night to boil some to get some grease to
grease the handcarts, but it was so old and tough there
was not a speck of grease in it." [6]

One of the blind men, mentioned above, Thomas D.
Giles, was later to become widely known as the Blind
Harpist. With a wife and baby girl and two boys,
aged seven and nine, he pulled his handcart westward.

"Soon after starting across the plains, the baby
became ill and died. She was buried beside the trail
and the company moved onward. A few weeks later,
his wife died. She also was buried beside the trail. The
two boys, because of their father's condition, were sent
back to join another company which included a group
of Welsh emigrants.

"Near Fort Bridger, Elder Giles himself became
seriously ill. After holding the company for two days,
Captain Bunker ordered the camp to move on, leaving
two of the men to bury the sick man when he died. It
was expected that death would come in a matter of
hours.

---

[6] Carter, *Heart Throbs,* VI, pp. 355-56. Mrs. Evans' first baby was born
less than three months after her arrival in Salt Lake Valley.

"Remarkable faith and the frequent administrations of the Elders who attended him kept the patient alive until evening when Parley P. Pratt the Apostle, who had known Brother Giles in Wales, reached the camp. Elder Pratt gave Brother Giles a remarkable blessing. In it he made these promises: that he should instantly be healed and made well, that he should rejoin his company and arrive safely in the Salt Lake Valley; that he should there rear a family; and that because of his faithfulness he would be permitted to live as long as he wanted. These blessings were all fulfilled in their entirety.

"Elder Giles rejoined his company, reached the Valley October 2, 1856, remarried, and lived to bless and name seven of his grandchildren. His death occurred November 2, 1895, after he had expressed a desire to go." [7]

Ellenor Roberts, a Welsh girl, was married to Elias Lewis under a shade tree at the Iowa outfitting camp. When loading their handcart they had to discard some of their precious belongings. Although the journey was a weary one they were cheerful and tried to be happy.

"As the journey continued, food became very scarce and many of their priceless possessions were traded for food. One of these was Ellenor's wedding ring, which was exchanged for flour.

"Elias and Ellenor walked the entire distance. Ellenor was always very proud and particular about her shoes. She always kept them shiny and clean. When they reached the Missouri River she took them off, set

---

[7] *Ibid.,* x, pp. 325-26. After arrival in Utah Elder Giles specialized in music; he played the harp and sang hymns and popular songs. He traveled about the state giving concerts and playing for dances. His harp is in the Daughters of Utah Pioneers Museum in Salt Lake City.

them on the bank of the river, and when she got on the other side she discovered she had left them. She walked the rest of the journey bare-footed." [8]

Hopkin and Margaret Mathews left Wales in April, 1856, with their children, one of whom was Mary, age nine. They crossed the ocean in the "S. Curling," and upon arrival at the frontier outfitting point were assigned to Captain Bunker's Company. A granddaughter of Mathews writes:

"Grandfather was stricken with rheumatism in his feet and legs and often had to be put in the cart. Mary walked all the way every day and cried at night with weariness and hunger. Her mother tried to comfort the children by promising them a little piece of bread.

"A young man with a team and wagon overtook a group of girls who were walking ahead and persuaded a young woman to go with him. She took Mary with her. They rode for a long distance and then Mary became frightened and started to cry. In the meantime the parents were frantic when they found the girls had disappeared and declared they would not go on until the girls were found. The young woman finally persuaded the man to take them back to camp where they arrived long after dark.

"After the company arrived in Salt Lake City the Mathews family moved to Ogden where they remained until the spring of 1859 when they moved to Providence, Cache Valley. Here Mary met George W. Marler, and later married him in the Endowment House in Salt Lake City. Mother passed away May 9, 1931, at the age of eighty-four years." [9]

---

[8] *Ibid.,* VI, p. 357.

[9] Gertrude Marler Ault in Carter, *Treasures of Pioneer History,* V, p. 248.

Ann Morris Butler, a widow, and her two children, Elizabeth, age 14, and William R., age 5, were members of the Third Handcart Company. The daughter contracted cholera.

"At one point along the way Ann became completely exhausted from nursing her daughter through this illness and asked the captain if she might ride in a wagon for a short way, but he refused. This was the one time she became thoroughly discouraged and feared she would have to stay behind with her children and die on the plains. However, a sister-in-law took their load into her cart With just a feather bed in her cart and an umbrella for shade, Ann and the children plodded on. The road had been sandy and rough, but suddenly it became smooth and she was able to pull the cart. Shortly after a halt was called while a broken wheel was repaired. She exclaimed, 'Thank God, now I can doctor my daughter.' By the next morning they were feeling much better and able to keep up with the company." [10]

Samuel Brooks, keeper of a lighthouse on the Welsh coast, was one who joined the Mormon Church and set his face toward Zion. Upon reaching Iowa City, he and his wife Emma with their three children – Mary, age 14, George, 12, and little crippled Frank, 5, – became members of the Third Handcart Company.

"When they set out," writes Juanita Brooks, "the father and mother pulled the cart, while the two older children pushed behind and little Frank rode on top of the load. The mother was small and of a quick nervous temperament, and the hard work and long hours proved too much for her. She sickened and died

---

[10] *Ibid.,* 249. Contributed by Elizabeth Ann Shirts Ford.

after a brief illness, and was buried in the cemetery at Florence, Nebraska.

"Now the fourteen-year-old Mary must step into her place and pull the cart, and George must give all his strength to pushing, for little Frank must ride all the way. Their rations were short; the work grew more strenuous as they neared the mountains. Their father tried to comfort them with the promise that after they reached Zion there would be plenty of food and they would not be hungry any more.

"The company arrived in Salt Lake City on October 2, 1856, with Samuel Brooks and his daughter Mary still pulling the cart. During the last several days he found it hard to keep going, but had sustained himself with the thought that it would soon be over. The relief at the end of the journey was overshadowed by illness; he was taken away from the public tent, evidently so that he could be better cared for. The children did not know where he was taken or by whom, when he died, or where he was buried. They were told only that he was dead, as much a victim of the long trek as though he had died on the way." [11]

Captain Bunker's Company was welcomed into Salt Lake Valley on October 2. The first three companies of 1856 had safely arrived in Utah. From Salt Lake City, on October 7, Elder S. W. Richards reported to the Saints in Britain: "The companies with hand-carts have been wonderfully successful thus far. . . One fact is established – that the Saints can cross the Plains almost without means, and only for the mighty waters that intervene, Israel would indeed come 'like doves to their windows, and like clouds before a storm.' " [12]

---

[11] *Ibid.*, 447-48.
[12] *Millennial Star,* of Jan. 17, 1857, XIX, p. 42.

A HANDCART PIONEER FAMILY

Sculpture by Torleif S. Knaphus, in the Church Museum, Temple Square, Salt Lake City. Photograph, courtesy of the Latter-day Saints Church Historian's office.

THE ORIGINAL HANDCART OF ARCHER WALTERS

The best original example now in existence, although some parts are missing and some replaced. Photograph by courtesy of the Daughters of Utah Pioneers.

THE MISSOURI RIVER AND COUNCIL BLUFFS

A sketch by Frederick Piercy, reproduced from James Linforth's *Route from Liverpool to Great Salt Lake Valley*, 1855. Courtesy of the Utah State Historical Society.

BRIGHAM YOUNG

A portrait by Frederick Piercy, reproduced from Linforth's *Route from Liverpool to Great Salt Lake Valley*, 1855. Courtesy of the Utah State Historical Society.

DEVIL'S GATE, A LANDMARK OF TRAGEDY ON THE HANDCART ROUTE
Courtesy of the Utah State Historical Society.

MORMON MISSIONARIES IN ENGLAND, 1855-1856, WHO ARRANGED FOR THE HANDCART MIGRATION, AND SEVERAL WERE LEADERS OR PARTICIPANTS IN THE RESCUE OF THE SNOWBOUND HANDCART EMIGRANTS

Top: Edmund Ellsworth, Jos. A. Young, Wm. H. Kimball, Geo. D. Grant, Jas. A. Little, Philemon Merrill.

Center: Edward Bunker, Chauncey G. Webb, Franklin D. Richards, Daniel Spencer, Daniel W. Jones, Edward Martin.

Lower: James Bond, Spicer Crandall, W. C. Dunbar, James Ross, Daniel D. McArthur.

Photograph taken in England in 1855. Courtesy of the Latter-day Saints Church Historian's Office.

HANDCART EMIGRANTS REACHING CAMP

Painting by C. C. A. Christensen, a sub-captain of the seventh handcart company. The original hangs in the offices of the Latter-day Saints' Church Historian, by whose courtesy it is reproduced here.

SALT LAKE CITY, IN 1853 FROM THE NORTH

A sketch by Frederick Piercy, reproduced from James Linforth's *Route from Liverpool to Great Salt Lake Valley*, 1855. Courtesy of the Utah State Historical Society.

BOWERY, MINT, AND PRESIDENT'S HOUSE, IN SALT LAKE CITY

From an illustration in Captain Stansbury's *Exploration and Survey of the Valley of the Great Salt Lake of Utah,* 1853.

Tragedy Stalks the Trail

The Saints who were to cross the plains in the last two handcart companies of 1856 were unduly late in sailing from England. The "Thornton," with 764 Mormons aboard, left Liverpool on May 3; and the "Horizon," carrying 856 Saints, did not sail until May 25. The former group, after a fair voyage to New York and a train trip westward by way of Albany, Buffalo, and Chicago, reached Iowa City on June 26; the second company arrived at the outfitting point twelve days later.

A multiplicity of causes explain the belated arrival. The unexampled clamor for passage to Zion, the difficulty in procuring ships and in making necessary arrangements, and various disappointments and miscalculations account for the failure to meet the planned schedule for departures. As matters eventuated, the lateness of sailings and subsequent delays that would occur at Iowa City and at Florence were to be nothing less than tragic.

Church agents at Iowa City, who had worked hard and successfully to equip and send off the first three handcart companies, now had to struggle frantically to provide for an unexpectedly large body of late arrivals. Most of these 1620 emigrants were poor Saints who had elected to travel in handcarts; some were to go by ox train. All had to be equipped and supplied.

For the Perpetual Emigration Fund travelers, more than 250 handcarts and dozens of tents were required. Whether the failure to have the carts ready for the Saints upon their arrival was due to lack of timely advice from England concerning the number needed (mail service then being very slow); to inability to get the required help or materials for construction; or to belief that the Saints could better afford to help make the carts than to pay for their being made, can hardly be determined. In any event, few foresaw the fatal consequences of the situation. Chauncey G. Webb, who superintended the making of the carts at Iowa City, put every available man to work on construction of the vehicles; the women made the tents.

From the "Thornton" passengers the Fourth Handcart Company was organized. These Saints, who had reached Iowa City June 26, set out on their trek July 15. The Fifth Company, with passengers from the "Horizon," who arrived at the outfitting point on the eighth of July, departed on the twenty-eighth.[1] The first group had been detained nineteen days, the second, twenty days – precious time that could have seen them far along their perilous journey.

James G. Willie,[2] returning missionary who had

---

[1] This company traveled as far as Florence in two divisions, one under Edward Martin, and the other under Jesse Haven. They were to be consolidated under Captain Martin on leaving the Missouri River.– Jaques' narrative published in the *Salt Lake Herald* in 1878 and reprinted in Orson F. Whitney, *History of Utah* (Salt Lake City, 1892), I, pp. 559-64.

[2] James Grey Willie was born November 1, 1814, at Murell Green, Hampshire, England. He came to America when 21, was married and joined the L.D.S. Church in 1842. Ten years later he returned to England as a missionary. Upon his release he came home, captaining the Fourth Handcart Company. In 1859 he moved to Cache Valley, Utah, where he was active in community enterprises. He died in 1895.– Carter, *Treasures of Pioneer History*, V, pp. 250-52.

been president of the Saints on the "Thornton's" voyage, became Captain of the Fourth Handcart Company. Edward Martin,[3] who was also returning from a British mission and had fathered the "Horizon's" passengers, was to be Captain of the Fifth Company. Inasmuch as the two companies were so closely related and were to share the same ordeals, we shall treat their stories together – at least, the early portion of their trip.

Willie's company comprised 500 persons. They had 120 handcarts, 5 wagons, 24 oxen, and 45 beef cattle and cows. Martin's party consisted of 576 souls, with 146 carts, 7 wagons, 30 oxen, and 50 cows and beef cattle. Behind them were to travel two ox trains – Captain W. B. Hodgett's 33-wagon company carrying 185 passengers with 187 oxen, cows, and beef cattle; and Captain John A. Hunt's train of 50 wagons, with 297 oxen, beef cattle, and cows, and carrying 200 emigrants.[4]

John Chislett, one of the sub-captains of the Fourth Company, says that the company was divided into groups of 100 persons each, with a sub-captain over each of these. He writes: "The third hundred were principally Scotch; the fifth, Scandinavians. The other hundreds were mostly English. To each hundred there were five round tents, with twenty persons to a tent; twenty hand-carts, or one to every five persons; and one Chicago Wagon, drawn by three yoke of oxen, to haul provisions and tents. Each person was limited to seventeen pounds of clothing and bedding. . .

---

[3] Edward Martin was born in Preston, Lancashire, England, November 18, 1818. After joining the Mormon Church and coming to America he became a member of the Mormon Battalion in the Mexican War. Upon his return from a mission in England he became Captain of the Fifth Handcart Company. He died in Salt Lake City, August 8, 1882. *Ibid.*, 261-62.

[4] Solomon F. Kimball, "Belated Emigrants of 1856," in *The Improvement Era*, XVII, pp. 5-7.

"The strength of the company was equalized as much as possible by distributing the young men among the different families to help them. Several carts were drawn by *young girls* exclusively; and two tents were occupied by them and such females as had no male companions." [5]

The Martin Company was similarly organized. The road across Iowa was good; and the journey, though made through heat and dust, was accomplished without unusual difficulties. A few dropped out en route, to await more propitious traveling, or to forsake the project entirely.

The journey to Florence, 277 miles, was made in a little less than four weeks, Willie's Company reaching there August 11, and Martin's on the twenty-second. Here each company was delayed for repairs.

J. H. Latey, writing from Florence, August 14, and reporting the arrival of Willie's Company, says: "The companies stay here longer than they otherwise would in consequence of their carts being unfit for their journey across the Plains; some requiring new axles, and the whole of them having to have a piece of iron screwed on to prevent the wheel from wearing away the wood." [6]

These emigrants impressed the representative of the *Council Bluffs Bugle,* who wrote in this paper of August 26:

"A few days since, in company with Colonel Babbitt, Secretary of Utah, and several citizens of this place,

---

[5] "Mr. Chislett's Narrative," in Stenhouse, *The Rocky Mountain Saints* (New York, 1873), 314-15. Chislett names the sub-captains of the various hundreds as follows: "first, Millen Atwood; second, Levi Savage; third, William Woodward; fourth, John Chislett; fifth, [Jacob A.] Ahmensen."

[6] *Millennial Star,* XVIII, p. 638.

we visited Florence, N.T. and there found encamped about 500 of the 'faithful,' all in good health and spirits. . . we learned that the train had been but three weeks in coming from Iowa City, and that all were healthy, cheerful, and contented.

"Having seen several handcart trains pass through this city and cross the ferries at Elkhorn and Loup Fork, we could not help but remark the enthusiasm which animated all classes and ages. . . We saw the butcher dealing out a splendid beef to the crowd and were informed that the allowance was one half pound each, one pound of flour per day, and the usual quantities of molasses, sugar, etc. Many, however, have private supplies, which enable them to live very comfortably.

"It may seem to some that these people endure great hardships in traveling hundreds of miles on foot, drawing carts behind them. This is a mistake, for many informed me that after the first three days travel, it requires little effort for two or three men or women to draw the light handcart with its moderate load of cooking utensils and baggage.

"It is, also, a fact, that they can travel farther in a day and with less fatigue than the ox teams.

"These trains are composed of Swedes, Danes, Germans, Welsh, Scotch, and English, and the best evidence of their sincerity is in the fact that they are willing to endure the fatigues and privations of a journey so lengthy. . .

"This is enthusiasm – this is heroism indeed. Though we cannot coincide with them in their belief, it is impossible to restrain our admiration of their self-sacrificing devotion to the principles of their faith." [7]

---

[7] Reprinted in *ibid.*, 667.

It was not without some hesitation that these companies left Florence at so late a date. Chislett, of Willie's Company, writes:

"The elders seemed to be divided in their judgment as to the practicability of our reaching Utah in safety at so late a season of the year, and the idea was entertained for a day or two of making our winter quarters on the Elkhorn, Wood River, or some eligible location in Nebraska; but it did not meet with general approval. A monster meeting was called to consult the people about it.

"The emigrants were entirely ignorant of the country and climate – simple, honest, eager to go to 'Zion' at once. . . Under these circumstances it was natural that they should leave their destination in the hands of the elders. There were but four men in our company who had been to the Valley, viz.: Willie, Atwood, Savage, and Woodward; but there were several at Florence superintending the emigration, among whom elders G. D. Grant and W. H. Kimball occupied the most prominent position. These men all talked at the meeting just mentioned, and all, with one exception, favoured going on."

Levi Savage declared that they "could not cross the mountains with a mixed company of aged people, women, and little children, so late in the season without much suffering, sickness, and death. He therefore advised going into winter quarters without delay. Savage was voted down, the majority being against him. He then added: "Brethren and sisters, what I have said I know to be true; but seeing you are to go forward, I will go with you, will help you all I can, will work with you, will rest with you, will suffer with you, and, if necessary, I will die with you. May God in his mercy bless and preserve us." [8]

President F. D. Richards had been released from his European Mission; and after fulfilling the gigantic assignment of putting three thousand Saints onto ships, and settling related business, he, in company with other Elders, left Liverpool on July 26. They reached Florence, Nebraska, just in time to assist the Fifth Handcart Company and the two rear wagon trains to recruit here. Cyrus H. Wheelock, a member of the party, wrote on September 2, 1856:

"We arrived at this point on the 21st of August, having been 26 days on our journey from Liverpool. In less than an hour after our arrival on the camp ground we laid by our fine cloth, and mentally and physically engaged in practical Mormonism in assisting to complete the organization of the handcart and wagon companies for their journey over the Plains. The presence of brothers Franklin, Spencer, and my humble self, among them seemed like the magic of heaven. Their spirits and bodies seemed almost instantly refreshed and when we passed up and down the lines we were met with those hearty greetings that none but Saints know how to give and appreciate. All were in good spirits, and generally in good health, and full of confidence that they should reach the mountains in season to escape the severe storms. I have never seen more union among the Saints anywhere than is manifested in the handcart companies. And hundreds bear record of the truth of the words of President Young, wherein he promised them increasing strength by the way.

---

[8] Chislett, in Stenhouse, *op. cit.,* 316.

"The last handcart company under the Presidency of Elder Edward Martin, left here on the 25th of August and the last wagon company left this day." [9]

F. D. Richards, after getting the final companies upon their way from the Missouri River, wrote at Florence on September 3:

"The operations of the season are likely to turn out quite as favorably with regard to cost of outfit as we have at any time expected or hoped. But for the lateness of the rear companies everything seems equally propitious for a safe and profitable wind-up at the far end. From the beginning we have done all in our power to hasten matters pertaining to emigration, therefore we confidently look for the blessing of God to crown our humble efforts with success, and for the safe arrival of our brethren the poor Saints in Utah, though they may experience some cold.

"It certainly would warm your heart with melting kindness to pass along the line of a camp going by hand-carts, and receive the cordial shakes of the hand, with a fervent 'God bless you,' as I did when I visited Captain Edward Martin's train, several of whom expressed their thanks in a particular manner for being permitted to come out this year." [10]

Let us now, from Chislett's "Narrative," follow Willie's Company on its journey westward until help is received.

"We started from Florence about the 18th of August, and travelled in the same way as through Iowa, except that our carts were more heavily laden, as our teams

9 *Millennial Star,* XVIII, p. 682.
10 *Ibid.,* 682-83.

could not haul sufficient flour to last us to Utah; it was therefore decided to put one sack (ninety-eight pounds) on each cart in additional to the regular baggage. Some of the people grumbled at this, the majority bore it without a murmur. Our flour ration was increased to a pound per day; fresh beef was issued occasionally, and each 'hundred' had three or four milch cows. The flour on the carts was used first, the weakest parties being the first relieved of their burdens.

"Everything seemed to be propitious, and we moved gaily forward full of hope and faith. At our camp each evening could be heard songs of joy, merry peals of laughter, and bon mots on our condition and prospects. Brother Savage's warning was forgotten in the mirthful ease of the hour. The only drawbacks to this part of our journey were the constant breaking down of carts and the delays caused by repairing them. The axles and boxes being of wood, and being ground out by the dust that found its way there in spite of our efforts to keep it out, together with the extra weight put on the carts, had the effect of breaking the axles at the shoulder. All kinds of expedients were resorted to as remedies for the growing evil, but with variable success. Some wrapped their axles with leather obtained from bootlegs; others with tin, obtained by sacrificing tin-plates, kettles, or buckets from their mess outfit. Besides these inconveniences, there was felt a great lack of a proper lubricator. Of anything suitable for this purpose we had none at all. The poor folks had to use their bacon (already totally insufficient for their wants) to grease their axles, and some even used their soap, of which they had very little, to make their carts trundle somewhat easier. In about twenty days, however, the flour being consumed, breakdowns became less frequent, and we jogged along finely. We traveled from ten to twenty miles per day, averaging fifteen miles. The people felt well, so did our cattle, and our immediate prospects of a prosperous journey were good. But the fates seemed to be against us.

"About this time we reached Wood River (a few miles above Grand Island, Nebraska). The whole country was alive with buffaloes, and one night – or, rather, evening – our cattle stampeded. Men went in pursuit and collected what they supposed to be the herd; but, on corralling them for yoking next morning, thirty head were missing. We hunted for them three days in every direction, but did not find them. We at last reluctantly gave up the search, and prepared to travel without them as best we could. We had only about enough oxen left to put one yoke to each wagon; but as they were each loaded with about three thousand pounds of flour, the teams could not of course move them. We then yoked up our beef cattle, milch cows, and, in fact, everything that could bear a yoke – even two-year-old heifers. The stock was wild and could pull but little, and we were unable, with all our stock, to move our loads. As a last resort, we again loaded a sack of flour on each cart. . .

"It was really hard for the folks to lose the use of their milch cows, have beef rations stopped, and haul one hundred pounds more on their carts. Every man and woman, however, worked to their utmost to put forward towards the goal of their hopes." [11]

While trudging up the Platte the Fourth Handcart

---

[11] Chislett, in Stenhouse, *op. cit.,* 317-18. See also the account of George Cunningham in Carter, *Treasures of Pioneer History,* v, pp. 252-56.

Company was overtaken by President Richards and the party of missionaries who had left Florence after seeing the last of the season's emigrants leave that point. They were traveling in carriages and light wagons pulled by horses and mules. After camping with Willie's company and giving them encouragement, the officials hurried on toward Salt Lake City, promising to send back supplies with all possible dispatch.[12] Chislett continues:

"We reached [Fort] Laramie about the 1st or 2nd of September, but the provisions, etc., which we expected, were not there for us. Captain Willie called a meeting to take into consideration our circumstances, conditions, and prospects, and to see what could be done. It was ascertained that at our present rate of travel and consumption of flour the latter would be exhausted when we were about three hundred and fifty miles from our destintion. It was resolved to reduce our allowance from one pound to three-quarters of a pound per day, and at the same time to make every effort in our power to travel faster. We continued this rate of rations from Laramie to Independence Rock.

"About this time Captain Willie received a letter from Apostle Richards informing him that we might expect supplies to meet us from the valley by the time we reached South Pass. An examination of our stock of flour showed us that it would be gone before we reached that point. Our only alternative was to still

---

12 The members of the party were: Franklin D. Richards, George D. Grant, William H. Kimball, Joseph A. Young, Cyrus H. Wheelock, Chauncey G. Webb, James Ferguson, John D. T. McAllister, William C. Dunbar, Nathan H. Felt, John Van Cott, Dan Jones, and James McGaw.–*Deseret News,* Oct. 8, 1856.

further reduce our bill of fare. The issue of flour was then to average ten ounces per day. . .

"We had not travelled far up the Sweetwater before the nights, which had gradually been getting colder since we left Laramie, became very severe. The mountains before us, as we approached nearer to them, revealed themselves to view mantled nearly to their base in snow, and tokens of a coming storm were discernable in the clouds which each day seemed to lower around us. . .

"Our *seventeen pounds of clothing and bedding* was now altogether insufficient for our comfort. Nearly all suffered more or less at night from cold. Instead of getting up in the morning strong, refreshed, vigorous, and prepared for the hardships of another day of toil, the poor Saints were to be seen crawling out from their tents haggard, benumbed, and showing an utter lack of that vitality so necessary to our success.

"Cold weather, scarcity of food, lassitude and fatigue from over-exertion, soon produced their effects. Our old and infirm people began to droop, and they no sooner lost spirit and courage than death's stamp could be traced upon their features. Life went out as smoothly as a lamp ceases to burn when the oil is gone. At first the deaths occurred slowly and irregularly, but in a few days at more frequent intervals, until we soon thought it unusual to leave a campground without burying one or more persons.

"Death was not long confined in its ravages to the old and infirm, but the young and naturally strong were among its victims. . . Many a father pulled his cart, with his little children on it, until the day preceding his death. I have seen some pull their carts in the morning, give out during the day, and die before next morning. . .

"Each death weakened our forces. In my hundred I could not raise enough men to pitch a tent when we camped, and now it was that I had to exert myself to the utmost. I wonder I did not die, as many did who were stronger than I was. When we pitched our camp in the evening of each day, I had to lift the sick from the wagon and carry them to the fire, and in the morning carry them again on my back to the wagon. When any in my hundred died I had to inter them; often helping to dig the grave myself. In performing these sad offices I always offered up a heartfelt prayer to that God who beheld our sufferings, and begged him to avert destruction from us and send us help.

"We travelled on in misery and sorrow day after day. Sometimes we made a pretty good distance, but at other times we were only able to make a few miles progress. Finally we were overtaken by a snowstorm which the shrill wind blew furiously about us. The snow fell several inches deep as we travelled along, but we dared not stop, for we had a sixteen-mile journey to make, and short of it we could not get wood and water.

"As we were resting for a short time at noon a light wagon was driven into our camp from the west. Its occupants were Joseph A. Young and Stephen Taylor. They informed us that a train of supplies was on the way, and we might expect to meet it in a day or two. More welcome messengers never came from the courts of glory than these two young men were to us. They lost no time after encouraging us all they could to press forward, but sped on further east to convey their

glad news to Edward Martin and the fifth handcart
company who left Florence about two weeks after us,
and who it was feared were even worse off than we
were. As they went from our view, many a hearty 'God
bless you' followed them.

"We pursued our journey with renewed hope and
after untold toil and fatigue, doubling teams frequently, going back to fetch up the straggling carts,
and encouraging those who had dropped by the way
to a little more exertion in view of our soon-to-be improved condition, we finally, late at night, got all to
camp – the wind howling frightfully and the snow
eddying around us in fitful gusts. But we had found a
good camp among the willows, and after warming and
partially drying ourselves before good fires, we ate our
scanty fare, paid our usual devotions to the Deity and
retired to rest with hopes of coming aid.

"In the morning the snow was over a foot deep. Our
cattle strayed widely during the storm, and some of
them died. But what was worse to us than all this was
the fact that five persons of both sexes lay in the cold
embrace of death.

"The morning before the storm, or, rather, the morning of the day on which it came, we issued the last
ration of flour. On this fatal morning, therefore, we
had none to issue. We had, however, a barrel or two
of hard bread which Captain Willie had procured at
Fort Laramie in view of our destitution. This was
equally and fairly divided among all the company.
Two of our poor broken-down cattle were killed and
their carcasses issued for beef. With this we were informed that we would have to subsist until the coming
supplies reached us. All that now remained in our

commissary were a few pounds each of sugar and dried apples, about a quarter of a sack of rice and a small quantity (possibly 20 or 25 lbs.) of hard bread. . .

"Being surrounded by snow a foot deep, out of provisions, many of our people sick, and our cattle dying, it was decided that we should remain in our present camp[13] until the supply train reached us. It was also resolved in council that Captain Willie with one man should go in search of the supply train and apprise the leader of our condition, and hasten him to our help. When this was done we settled down and made our camp as comfortable as we could. As Captain Willie and his companion left for the West, many a heart was lifted in prayer for their success and speedy return. They were absent three days – three days which I shall never forget. The scanty allowance of hard bread and poor beef, distributed as described, was mostly eaten the first day by the hungry, ravenous, famished souls.

"We killed more cattle and issued the meat; but, eating it without bread, did not satisfy hunger, and to those who were suffering from dysentry it did more harm than good. This terrible disease increased rapidly amongst us during these three days, and several died from exhaustion. . . The recollection of it unmans me even now – those three days! During that time I visited the sick, the widows whose husbands died in serving them, and the aged who could not help themselves, to know for myself where to dispense the few articles that had been placed in my charge for distribution. Such craving hunger I never saw before, and may God in his mercy spare me the sight again. . .

"The storm which we encountered, our brethren

[13] This camp was on the Sweetwater, at what later became known as St. Mary's Station.

from the Valley also met, and, not knowing that we were so utterly destitute, they encamped to await fine weather.[14] But when Captain Willie found them and explained our real condition, they at once hitched up their teams and made all speed to come to our rescue. On the evening of the third day (October 21) after Captain Willie's departure, just as the sun was sinking beautifully behind the distant hills, on an eminence immediately west of our camp several covered wagons, each drawn by four horses were seen coming towards us. The news ran through the camp like wildfire, and all who were able to leave their beds turned out en masse to see them. A few minutes brought them sufficiently near to reveal our faithful captain slightly in advance of the train. Shouts of joy rent the air; strong men wept till tears ran freely down their furrowed and sun-burnt cheeks, and little children partook of the joy which some of them hardly understood, and fairly danced around with gladness. Restraint was set aside in the general rejoicing, and as the brethren entered our camp the sisters fell upon them and deluged them with kisses."

The Salt Lake boys, mounted on harnessed mules and with axes in hand, were soon dragging wood from the hills. Fires warmed the camp and cooked food allayed starvation. But help had come too late to save all. Nine died that first night.

Chislett continues: "I was installed as regular commissary to the camp. The brethren turned over to me flour, potatoes, onions, and a limited supply of warm

---

[14] This camp was below the mouth of Willow Creek, a small Sweetwater affluent that runs through present South Pass City. See entry of Oct. 19 in the Journal of the relief train, Appendix D.

clothing for both sexes, besides quilts, blankets, buffalo robes, woolen socks, etc. I first distributed the necessary provisions, and after supper divided the clothing, bedding, etc. where it was most needed. That evening, for the first time in quite a period, the songs of Zion were to be heard in the camp, and peals of laughter issued from the little knots of people as they chatted around the fires. The change seemed almost miraculous, so sudden was it from grave to gay, from sorrow to gladness, from mourning to rejoicing. With the cravings of hunger satisfied, and with hearts filled with gratitude to God and our good brethren, we all united in prayer, and then retired to rest.

"Among the brethren who came to our succour were elders W. H. Kimball and G. D. Grant. They had remained but a few days in the Valley before starting back to meet us. May God ever bless them for their generous, unselfish kindness and their manly fortitude. They felt that they had, in a great measure, contributed to our sad position; but how nobly, how faithfully, how bravely they worked to bring us safely to the Valley — to the Zion of our hopes!" [15]

Kimball and about half of the rescue party stayed with the Willie Company to help it move westward; while Grant, with the other half of the Salt Lake wagons, pushed on to find Martin's Company and the two rear wagon trains.

Let us now return to Florence and follow the Fifth Handcart Company until help reaches it.

On August 27 the company left from Cutler's Park camp, two and one-half miles west of Florence. They

---

[15] Chislett, in Stenhouse, *op. cit.*, 319-26.

pushed along the road to the Platte River and up that stream for two weeks, making good time and encountering no unusual difficulties.

"After toilsome and fatiguing travel," writes Mrs. Elizabeth Jackson in her pamphlet, "we reached [Fort] Laramie on the 8th of October. Here we rested for a short time. Our provisions by this time had become very scant, and many of the company went to the Fort and sold their watches and jewelry for provisions." [16]

One hundred buffalo robes had been purchased by F. D. Richards at Laramie, and these were eagerly secured by the members of the company.

"Hitherto," continues Mrs. Jackson, "although a ration of a pound of flour had been served out daily to each person, it was found insufficient to satisfy the cravings of hunger. Shortly after leaving Fort Laramie it became necessary to shorten our rations that they might hold out, and that the company be not reduced to starvation. The reduction was repeated several times. First, the pound of flour was reduced to three-fourths, then to one-half of a pound, and afterwards to still less per day. However we pushed ahead."

Grass for the stock also became scarcer, and the oxen began to weaken. On the nineteenth of October they reached the last crossing of the North Platte, near Red Buttes and a little west of present Casper, Wyoming. Here the two wagon trains in the rear caught up with Martin's Company and helped the emigrants and their

---

[16] "Leaves from the Life of Elizabeth Horrocks Kingford Jackson" (pamphlet). John Jaques, in Whitney, *op. cit.*, 560, says the commandant at the fort sold them supplies at reasonable prices – biscuit at 15½ cents per pound, bacon at 15 cents, rice at 17 cents, etc. Apparently, but little food was purchased.

handcarts across. The river was wide, the current strong, the water exceedingly cold. The company was barely over when snow and sleet began to fall, accompanied by a piercing north wind. Winter had come upon them suddenly in a fury.

Josiah Rogerson of Martin's Company says: "The crossing of the North Platte was fraught with more fatalities than any other incident of the entire journey. . . More than a score or two of the young female members waded the stream that in places was waist deep. Blocks of mushy snow and ice had to be dodged. The result of wading of this stream by the female members was immediately followed by partial and temporary dementia from which several did not recover until the next spring." [17]

Mrs. Jackson adds, in reference to this crossing: "Some of the men carried some of the women on their back or in their arms, but others of the women tied up their skirts and waded through, like the heroines that they were, and as they had gone through many other rivers and creeks. My husband (Aaron Jackson) attempted to ford the stream. He had only gone a short distance when he reached a sandbar in the river, on which he sank down through weakness and exhaustion. My sister, Mary Horrocks Leavitt, waded through the water to his assistance. She raised him up to his feet. Shortly afterward, a man came along on horseback and conveyed him to the other side. My sister then helped me to pull my cart with my three children and other matters on it. We had scarcely crossed the river when we were visited with a tremendous storm of snow, hail, sand, and fierce winds."

[17] Account of Josiah Rogerson, in the *Salt Lake Tribune,* Jan. 14, 1914.

Back at Deer Creek (present Glenrock, Wyoming), two days before, the company, because of the growing weakness of the emigrants and teams, had reduced baggage to ten pounds per adult, five pounds for children under eight. Blankets, other bedding, and clothing were thus thrown away to lighten the load. Now, with the bitter cold, those wraps were desperately needed, for almost four hundred winter miles stretched between them and shelter in Salt Lake City.

After effecting the crossing of the Platte on the nineteenth, the company pushed on a little farther before encamping. "I was detailed," says Rogerson, "to wheel the dying Aaron (Jackson) on an empty cart with his feet dangling over the end bar, to camp. After putting up his tent, I assisted his wife in laying him in his blankets. It was one of the bitter cold, bleak, frosty nights near the Black Hills and notwithstanding the hard journey the day before, I was awakened at midnight to go on guard again till six or seven in the morning.

"Putting jacket or coat on (for both sexes had for weeks past lain down at night in the clothing we had traveled in during the day), and passing out through the middle of the tent, my feet struck those of poor Aaron. They were stiff and rebounded at my accidental stumbling. Reaching my hand to his face, I found that he was dead with his exhausted wife and little ones by his side all sound asleep. The faithful and good man Aaron had pulled his last cart. I did not wake his wife, but whispered the fact to my mother. After reaching my hand to the side of the tent and feeling it heavy and weighted with snow, I said, 'Mother, the snow has come.' What a chill seemed to fill the whole tent as I whispered those five words." [18]

Mrs. Jackson tells the story: "About nine o'clock I retired. Bedding had become very scarce so I did not disrobe. I slept until, as it appeared to me, about midnight. I was extremely cold. The weather was bitter. I listened to hear if my husband breathed, he lay so still. I could not hear him. I became alarmed. I put my hand on his body, when to my horror I discovered that my worst fears were confirmed. My husband was dead. I called for help to the other inmates of the tent. They could render me no aid; and there was no alternative but to remain alone by the side of the corpse till morning. Oh, how the dreary hours drew their tedious length along. When daylight came, some of the male part of the company prepared the body for burial. And oh, such a burial and funeral service. They did not remove his clothing – he had but little. They wrapped him in a blanket and placed him in a pile with thirteen others who had died, and then covered him up with snow. The ground was frozen so hard that they could not dig a grave. He was left there to sleep in peace until the trump of God shall sound, and the dead in Christ shall awake and come forth in the morning of the first resurrection. We shall then again unite our hearts and lives, and eternity will furnish us with life forever more.

"I will not attempt to describe my feelings at finding myself thus left a widow with three children, under such excruciating circumstances. I cannot do it. But I believe the Recording Angel has inscribed in the archives above, and that my suffering for the Gospel's

---

[18] Quoted in Carter, *Heart Throbs,* VI, p. 368.

sake will be sanctified unto me for my good. My sister became sick. So severe was her affliction that she became deranged in her mind, and for several days she ate nothing but hard frozen snow." [19]

The snow continued to fall for three days. Deaths multiplied until a burying squad was appointed to prepare graves at night for those who died during the day.

"A few days after the death of my husband," says Mrs. Jackson, "the male members of the company had become reduced in number by death and those who remained were so weak and emaciated by sickness, that on reaching the camping place at night, there were not sufficient men with strength enough to raise the poles and pitch the tents. The result was that we camped out with nothing but the vault of Heaven for a roof and the stars for companions. The snow lay several inches deep upon the ground. The night was bitterly cold. I sat down on a rock with one child in my lap and one on each side of me. In that condition I remained until morning."

About twelve miles above the last crossing of the Platte, the company was snowed in and came to a standstill. John Bond, a twelve-year-old boy was in the Hodgett wagon train stalled beside the Fifth Handcart Company. He later wrote a graphic account of his experiences:

"Day after day passes and still no tidings of help coming from the westward. The bugle is sounded again by John Wadkins to call all the Saints together for prayers to ask the infinite Father to bring food, medicines and other things necessary for the sick and needy.

---

[19] Mrs. Jackson's pamphlet, *op. cit.*

After prayers, all are ordered to bed. I had been to many of the meetings previously but this time I saw sister Scott cooking a nice pot of dumplings just before the bugle sounded. She hid the dumplings under the wagon, being a zealous woman, and went to prayer meeting, but I did not go this time, I stood back and looked for the dumplings, found them and being so hungry I could not resist the temptation, sat down and ate them all." [20]

Deaths continued in the camp. Some died, says Bond, "lying side by side with hands entwined. In other cases, they were found as if they had just offered a fervent prayer and their spirit had taken flight while in the act. . . Some died sitting by the fire; some were singing hymns or eating crusts of bread."

Concerning the burials, Bond reports: "Captain Martin stood over the grave of the departed ones with shotgun in hand, firing at intervals to keep the crows and buzzards away from hovering around in mid air."

Sister Sirman, whose husband was near death and whose two sons were suffering with frozen feet,[21] appealed to Captain Martin, "Do you think that the relief party will come soon with food, clothing and shoes?"

Bond recalls that the Captain's answer was, "I almost wish God would close my eyes to the enormity of the sickness, hunger and death among the Saints. Yes, Sister Sirman, I am as confident as that I live that the President (Brigham Young) will and has dispatched

---

[20] John Bond, *Handcarts West in '56* (privately issued in mimeograph form, 1945), 23.

[21] Bond, *ibid.*, 25, says that in 1912 he met one of the boys, John Sirman, in Blackfoot, Idaho. One leg had been amputated as a result of the freezing in 1856.

the relief valley boys to us and I believe that they are
making all the haste they can, that they are bringing
flour, clothing, shoes, etc."

A day or two later, while young Bond was in front
of the Scott wagon he saw Sister Scott looking into the
West. All at once she sprang to her feet and screamed
at the top of her voice, "I see them coming! I see them
coming! Surely they are angels from heaven!"

And so it was. On the twenty-eighth of October,
when despair had almost overwhelmed the camp, the
messengers of rescue came. Joseph A. Young (son of
President Young), Daniel W. Jones, and Abel Garr
rode into camp amid the tears and cheers of the emigrants.[22] These men were an express from the advance
relief company from Salt Lake, bringing the glad
word that assistance, provisions, and clothing were
near, that ten wagons under Captain George D. Grant
were encamped at the abandoned houses of an old
trading fort near Devil's Gate.[23]

These couriers later reported: "We found the Martin Company in a deplorable condition, they having
lost fifty-six of their number since crossing the North
Platte, nine days before. Their provisions were nearly
gone, and their clothing almost worn out. Most of their
bedding had been left behind, as they were unable to
haul it, on account of their weakened condition. We
advised them to move on, every day just as far as they

---

[22] They had been sent from Grant's encamped wagon party near Devil's
Gate on Oct. 27. See entry of that date in the Journal of the First Rescue
Party, Appendix D.

[23] There is a good brief account of these events by J. Jaques in *Millennial
Star*, XIX, pp. 254-55. See also Daniel W. Jones, *Forty Years Among the
Indians* (Salt Lake City, 1890), 62-75.

could, as that was the only possible show they had to escape death." [24]

Joseph Young and his companions pushed on to the Hunt wagon train, ten miles farther east. After finding this rear company, back near the Platte Crossing, and urging it to push westward, Jones and Garr turned back towards Devil's Gate. They overtook the Martin Company, now on the move, slowly ascending a long muddy hill.

"A condition of distress," writes Jones, "here met my eyes that I never saw before or since. The train was strung out for three or four miles. There were old men pulling and tugging their carts, sometimes loaded with a sick wife or children – women pulling along sick husbands – little children six to eight years old struggling through the mud and snow. As night came on the mud would freeze on their clothes and feet. There were two of us, and hundreds needing help. What could we do? We gathered on to some of the most helpless with our riatas tied to the carts, and helped as many as we could into camp on Avenue Hill. This was a bitter, cold night and we had no fuel except very small sage brush. Several died that night. Next morning, Brother Young having come up, we three started for our camp near Devil's Gate." [25]

Upon arrival at the encampment of the relief party, and apprising them of the desperate plight of the emigrants, Captain Grant and most of the rescuers hitched up their teams and moved eastward, leaving part of the men at the trading houses with most of the supplies. On the last day of October Grant's rescue party met

---

[24] S. F. Kimball, in *Improvement Era*, XVII, p. 204.
[25] D. W. Jones, *op. cit.*, 68-69.

Martin's Company at Greasewood Creek, sixteen miles east of Devil's Gate. They gave every possible immediate assistance, and helped the handcart sufferers move along toward the supply depot.

On November 1, amid falling snow, camp was made near Independence Rock, only five miles east of Devil's Gate.

"There was a foot or eighteen inches of snow on the ground," wrote John Jaques, "which, as there were but one or two spades in camp, the emigrants had to shovel away with their frying pans, or tin plates, or anything they could use for that purpose, before they could pitch their tents, and then the ground was frozen so hard that it was almost impossible to drive the tent pegs into it. Some of the men were so weak that it took them an hour or two to clear the places for their tents and set them up." [26]

The next day the desperate company arrived at Devil's Gate fort. On November 3, Captain Grant sent an express – Joseph A. Young and Abel Garr – to Salt Lake Valley. In preparing for the journey, says John Jaques, "Joseph A. put on three or four pairs of woolen socks, a pair of moccasins, and a pair of buffalo hide over-shoes with the wool on, and then remarked, 'There, if my feet freeze with those on, they must stay frozen till I get to Salt Lake.'" [27]

In his dispatch to Brigham Young, Captain Grant said: "It is not much use for me to attempt to give a description of the situation of these people, for this you will learn from your son Joseph A. and br. Garr, who are the bearers of this express; but you can imagine

[26] Quoted in Whitney, *op. cit.,* I, p. 562.
[27] *Ibid.,* 562. See Joseph A. Young's report after reaching Salt Lake City, Appendix F.

between five and six hundred men, women and children, worn down by drawing handcarts through snow and mud; fainting by the wayside; falling, chilled by the cold; children crying, their limbs stiffened by cold, their feet bleeding and some of them bare to snow and frost. The sight is almost too much for the stoutest of us; but we go on doing all we can, not doubting or despairing.

"Our company is too small to help much, it is only a drop to a bucket, as it were, in comparison to what is needed. I think that not over one-third of Mr. Martin's company is able to walk. This you may think is extravagant, but it is nevertheless true. Some of them have good courage and are in good spirits; but a great many are like children and do not help themselves much more, nor realize what is before them.

"I never felt so much interest in any mission that I have been sent on, and all the brethren who came out with me feel the same. We have prayer without ceasing, and the blessing of God has been with us.

"Br. Charles Decker has now traveled this road the 49th time, and he says he has never before seen so much snow on the Sweet Water at any season of the year. . .

"Br. Hunt's company are two or three days back of us, yet br. Wheelock will be with them to counsel them, also some of the other brethren who came out.

"We will move every day toward the valley, if we shovel snow to do it, the Lord helping us.

"I have never seen such energy and faith among the 'boys,' nor so good a spirit as is among those who came out with me. We realize that we have your prayers for us continually, also those of all the Saints in the Valley. . .[28]

---

[28] *Deseret News*, Nov. 19, 1856. The entire report is printed in Appendix E.

The Rescue

Having left Florence on September 4 with a good outfit, President Franklin D. Richards and party of missionaries and emigrant officials passed the handcart trains, and hurried on toward Salt Lake City. The mules ate up the miles, and brought the delegation through to the Valley in thirty days.[1]

HELP FROM SALT LAKE VALLEY

The Church authorities were much surprised to learn that so many Saints were far back on the trail. "We had no idea there were any more companies upon the Plains," said President Brigham Young "until our brethren arrived, presuming that they would consider their late arrival in America and not start them across the Plains until another year."[2]

It was Saturday, October 4, when Richards came with the news. That evening the leading officials assembled to consider the needs of the oncoming emigrants. President Young, a practical man, believed the situation was critical; it would require immediate and vigorous action. He learned the general location of the handcart companies and the late ox trains. With specific information on their numbers and supplies, he calculated what would be required for effective relief.

---

[1] The arrival of the party was reported in the *Deseret News* of Oct. 8, 1856. The full report of the trip is printed in Appendix c.

[2] Young's letter of Oct. 30, 1856, to Orson Pratt, printed in the *Millennial Star* of Feb. 14, 1857 (XIX, p. 99).

The Semi-annual Conference of the Mormon Church was about to convene. Some twelve thousand of the faithful had gathered into Salt Lake City from the scattered settlements, to hear the word of the Lord from the Prophet Brigham Young and the Apostles. News of the late departure of the Fourth and Fifth handcart companies had spread among the people; and as they assembled Sunday morning, in the first general meeting, the air was tense with expectancy.

The commanding figure of the fifty-five-year-old Mormon leader was always impressive as he rose from among the brethren on the stand to address the Saints. To his revering people, he was the mouthpiece of God.

"I will now give this people the subject and the text for the Elders who may speak to-day and during the conference," he announced. "It is this. On the 5th day of October, 1856, many of our brethren and sisters are on the plains with handcarts, and probably many are now seven hundred miles from this place, and they must be brought here, we must send assistance to them. The text will be, 'to get them here.' I want the brethren who may speak to understand that their text is the people on the plains. And the subject matter for this community is to send for them and bring them in before winter sets in.

"That is my religion; that is the dictation of the Holy Ghost that I possess. It is to save the people. This is the salvation I am now seeking for. To save our brethren that would be apt to perish, or suffer extremely, if we do not send them assistance.

"I shall call upon the Bishops this day. I shall not wait until tomorrow, nor until the next day, for 60 good mule teams and 12 or 15 wagons. I do not want to send oxen. I want good horses and mules. They are in this Territory, and we must have them. Also 12 tons of flour and 40 good teamsters, besides those that drive the teams. This is dividing my texts into heads. First, 40 good young men who know how to drive teams, to take charge of the teams that are now managed by men, women and children who know nothing about driving them. Second, 60 or 65 good spans of mules, or horses, with harness, whipple trees, neck-yokes, stretchers, lead chains, &c. And thirdly, 24 thousand pounds of flour, which we have on hand. . .

"I will tell you all that your faith, religion, and profession of religion, will never save one soul of you in the Celestial Kingdom of our God, unless you carry out just such principles as I am now teaching you. *Go and bring in those people now on the plains.* And attend strictly to those things which we call temporal, or temporal duties. Otherwise, your faith will be in vain. The preaching you have heard will be in vain to you, and you will sink to *Hell,* unless you attend to the things we tell you." [3]

Other leaders addressed the congregation. Elder Daniel Spencer, who had been in charge of the emigration at Iowa City, said: "The emigration is late, quite late. But it is useless for me to undertake to explain *why* it is so. They are late, but the faith of those that have been associated with them is that the God of heaven will control the elements, providing that you, my brethren and sisters, render them that assistance which He has given you ability to do." [4]

[3] Speech of October 5, reported in the *Deseret News,* Oct. 15, 1856.

[4] Spencer continued: "They were told when they came into Iowa that they could not go through; the people there tried to persuade them that it was impossible to carry out such an experiment, but they believed our words."– *Deseret News,* Oct. 15, 1856.

President F. D. Richards of the European Mission, who had managed the emigration from Britain, urged the necessity for help: "The Saints that are now upon the plains, about one thousand with handcarts, feel that it is late in the season, and they expect to get cold fingers and toes. But they have this faith and confidence towards God, that he will overrule the storms that may come in the season thereof, and turn them away, that their path may be freed from suffering more than they can bear.

"They have confidence to believe that this will be an open fall. . . On ship-board, at the point of outfit, and on the plains every time we spoke we felt to prophesy good concerning them. . . When we had a meeting at Florence, we called upon the Saints to express their faith to the people, and requested to know of them, even if they knew that they should be swallowed up in storms, whether they would stop or turn back. They voted, with loud acclamations, that they *would go on.* Such confidence and joyful performance of so arduous labors to accomplish their gathering, will bring the choice blessings of God upon them." [5]

President Young, more practical than some of his zealous fellow leaders, spoke again in the morning session: "I feel disposed to be as speedy as possible in our operation with regard to helping our brethren who are now on the plains. Consequently, I shall call upon the people forthwith for the help that is needed. I want them to give their names this morning, if they are ready to start on their journey tomorrow. And not say, 'I will go next week, or in ten days, or in a fortnight hence.' For I wish to start tomorrow morning.

[5] *Ibid.*

"I want the sisters to have the privilege of fetching in blankets, skirts, stockings, shoes, etc. for the men, women, and children that are in those handcart companies. . . hoods, winter bonnets, stockings, skirts, garments, and almost any description of clothing. . . I now want brethren to come forward, for we need 40 good teamsters to help the brethren on the plains. You may rise up now and give your names." [6]

At the regular Conference the next day (Monday, October 6), the theme was continued. President Young announced that the first business was to forthwith start assistance to those now on the plains. He called upon those who were willing to go, or to send teams, to come to the stand and report. If enough did not volunteer, he said, he would close the Conference, and he and Brother Kimball would start out with help.

Kimball, Young's first counsellor, having a humorous turn of mind, moved that the Conference adjourn and that he and President Young forthwith go to the aid of the emigrants. The question was put, and the assembly voted a unanimous, "NO!"

President Kimball then called on the blacksmiths in the congregation to retire; as they were wanted to shoe the horses and repair the wagons of those about to start to assist the brethren on the plains.[7]

Other speakers of the day interlarded their Gospel messages with urgings to help the incoming emigrants. Elder W. C. Dunbar, an actor, singer, and returned missionary, sang the "Handcart Song." Later, Captain Ellsworth of the first Company, sang "Handcarts Rolling."

---

[6] *Ibid.*

[7] Minutes of the Semi-annual Conference which convened on Oct. 6, 1856, reported in the *Deseret News,* Oct. 15.

The response for help was magnificent. Such sympathy and Christian brotherhood would be difficult to equal. Sixteen wagonloads of food and supplies were quickly assembled; and on the morning of October 7, sixteen good four-mule teams and twenty-seven hardy young men[8] headed eastward with the first installment of provisions. The gathering of more to follow, was pushed vigorously.

Only nine years removed from the stark desert it had settled upon with empty wagons and bare hands, the Mormon community was not yet one of surpluses. But the religious and human tie that bound the Saints in the Valley to those who soon might be freezing and starving on the Plains, transcended the instinct for personal safety.

Families of moderate means and the poorest individuals contributed from their meager stores. One lent a horse, one a wagon, one a tent; another, two bales of hay and a sack of barley. Some gave iron camp kettles, dutch ovens, brass buckets, tin cups and plates.

---

[8] These men were the real heroes of the rescue work. Several of them were missionaries who had accompanied F. D. Richards on the westward express, leaving Florence Sept. 4, passing the emigrants en route, and reaching Salt Lake City on October 4. Having preached the "gathering" and helped in starting the handcart emigrants on their journey they felt a special interest in, and responsibility to the handcart travelers. This advance rescue party comprised the following: George D. Grant, William H. Kimball, Joseph A. Young, Cyrus H. Wheelock, James Ferguson, Chauncey Webb, Robert T. Burton, Charles F. Decker, Benjamin Hampton, Heber P. Kimball, Harvey H. Cluff, Thomas Alexander, Reddick N. Allred, Ira Nebeker, Thomas Ricks, Edward Peck, William Broomhead, Abel Garr, C. Allen Huntington, George W. Grant, David P. Kimball, Stephen Taylor, Joel Parrish, Charles Grey, Amos Fairbanks, Daniel W. Jones, and Thomas Bankhead. This is the list as given by Kimball in *The Improvement Era*, XVII, p. 109. The six first named were of the Richards missionary company and had been in Salt Lake City but two days before they turned back to help the emigrants. For accounts of the rescue efforts see Appendices D, E, F, and G.

Women darned socks and shawls; patched underwear, trousers, and dresses; faced quilts, sewed together pieces of blankets; and took clothes from their own backs. Families brought out from their scant cellars sacks of flour, sides of home-cured bacon, bags of beans, dried corn, packages of sugar and rice.

Prayers at all public meetings and in private homes petitioned the Almighty to avert the storms, strengthen the rescuers, and spare the trapped emigrants. Gradually more wagon trains were assembled, loaded with contributed goods, and driven by dedicated men over the Wasatch Mountains, towards South Pass and the high plains beyond. By the end of October, two hundred and fifty teams were on the road to give relief.[9]

The advance train, first night out, camped at the foot of Big Mountain, and elected George D. Grant as Captain, with William H. Kimball and Robert T. Burton as assistants.[10] The next morning the train pushed on, and each day moved as far as possible. Stormy weather came, and the roads were difficult. They reached Fort Bridger on the twelfth; deposited some flour here and picked up some beef. No word of the emigrants. Three days later they reached Green River, fifty-six miles farther on; but still no news. From here they sent scouts ahead.

As the relief train reached the elevation of South Pass, where the continent divides to east and west drainages, the wagons were overtaken by a severe storm and cold weather. Snow continued for three days.

At Willow Creek, on the upper reaches of the Sweetwater, they halted to await better weather. Into this

---

[9] Letter of Wilford Woodruff, Journal History, Oct. 3, 1856, p. 3.
[10] The Journal of this train is printed in Appendix D.

camp, riding worn-out mules, came Captain J. G. Willie and Joseph Elder of the Fourth Handcart Company on the evening of October 20. They reported that the emigrants were freezing and starving. All would perish if help did not reach them soon.

Early next morning the rescue party pushed on, and by night arrived at the destitute encampment. They had come in time to save the lives of most of Willie's Company.

After giving emergency relief, the rescue train was divided into two parties. About half, under Captain Kimball, remained with Willie's Company to help it westward. The other half, led by Captain Grant, pushed eastward to meet the Martin Company and the rear wagon trains.

During the next five days, Grant's party traveled one hundred miles through deep snow and reached Devil's Gate. After encamping here, as related in the preceding chapter, the messengers – Young, Garr, and Jones – were sent ahead to find Martin's Company and the two rear wagon trains. Four days later on October 30, the express returned to Devil's Gate with news of the location and the desperate condition of the companies. Grant's party hurried forward, and about sixteen miles to the east met Martin's Handcart Company on Greasewood Creek. They helped to bury their dead, then led the handcart emigrants westward to the Devil's Gate fort, where they were to remain for several days.

Now let us journey with the handcart companies, from the time they receive the first relief, until they finally reach the Salt Lake Valley.

WILLIE'S COMPANY CARRIED TO SAFETY

The Fourth Handcart Company, with the aid of the rescue wagons and provisions, continued its westward trek. "We travelled but a few miles the first day," reports John Chislett, "the roads being very heavy. All who were unable to pull their carts were allowed to put their little outfits into the wagons and walk along, and those who were really unable to walk were allowed to ride. The second day we travelled a little farther, and each day Brother Kimball got the company along as far as possible to move it, but still our progress was very slow.

"Timely and good beyond estimate as the help which we received from the Valley was to our company generally, it was too late for some of our number. They were already prostrated and beyond all human help. Some seemed to have lost mental as well as physical energy. We talked to them of our improved condition, appealed to their love of life and showed them how easy it was to retain that life by arousing themselves; but all to no purpose. We then addressed ourselves to their religious feelings, their wish to see Zion; to know the Prophet Brigham; showed them the good things that he had sent out to us, and told them how deeply he sympathized with us in our sufferings, and what a welcome he would give us when we reached the city. But all our efforts were unavailing; they had lost all love of life, all sense of surrounding things, and had sunk down into a state of indescribable apathy.

"The weather grew colder each day, and many got their feet so badly frozen that they could not walk, and had to be lifted from place to place. Some got their fingers frozen; others their ears; and one woman lost her sight by the frost. These severities of the weather also increased our number of deaths, so that we buried several each day.

"A few days of bright freezing weather were succeeded by another snow-storm. The day we crossed the Rocky Ridge[11] it was snowing a little – the wind hard from the north-west – and blowing so keenly that it almost pierced us through. We had to wrap ourselves closely in blankets, quilts, or whatever else we could get, to keep from freezing. Captain Willie still attended to the details of the company's travelling, and this day he appointed me to bring up the rear. My duty was to stay behind everything and see that nobody was left along the road."

Chislett assisted, as best he could, those who lagged behind. But this rear group kept increasing in number until he had to leave them, and hurry on to the main camp for help.

"After some time I came in sight of the camp fires, which encouraged me. As I neared the camp I frequently overtook stragglers on foot, all pressing forward slowly. I stopped to speak to each one, cautioning them all against resting, as they would surely freeze to death. Finally, about 11 p.m. I reached the camp almost exhausted. I had exerted myself very much during the day in bringing the rear carts up the ridge, and had not eaten anything since breakfast. I reported to Captain Willie and Kimball the situation of the folks behind. They

---

[11] This difficult terrain, some 25 miles east of South Pass, was examined in 1955 by Paul C. Henderson, authority on portions of the Oregon Trail, and is described by him in *The Westerners New York Posse Brand Book,* III, pp. 33-34, 45.

immediately got up some horses, and the boys from the Valley started back about midnight to help the ox teams in. The night was very severe and many of the emigrants were frozen. It was 5 a.m. before the last team reached the camp. . .

"There were so many dead and dying that it was decided to lie by for the day. In the forenoon I was appointed to go round the camp and collect the dead. I took with me two young men to assist me in the sad task, and we collected together, of all ages and both sexes thirteen corpses, all stiffly frozen. We had a large square hole dug in which we buried these thirteen people, three or four abreast and three deep. . . Two others died during the day, making fifteen in all buried on that camp ground" [12]

This was on Willow Creek, a tributary of the Sweetwater, and about fourteen miles east of South Pass. From here an express was sent to the Salt Lake Valley. It arrived on October 31. On that day Wilford Woodruff, writing to George A. Smith, told of the arrival of the messengers:

"They bring bad news of that company; through starting so late in the season they have got caught in the snow storms and many have died. When the teams sent out at Conference, arrived at this camp, there had been 20 deaths, nineteen of them men, and while with them in one day there were 15 burials; and when the messengers left, there had been fifty-five deaths. They did not seem to be sick, but chilled through. Men would dig graves for their brethren and before night die themselves. . .

<hr />

[12] "Mr. Chislett's Narrative," in Stenhouse, *The Rocky Mountain Saints,* 326-29.

"At least 250 teams have been sent out to meet those companies and several tons of flour and great quantities of clothing. . . The presidency started east [on the 13th] to meet the emigration, but while on Canyon Creek President Young was taken so severely ill that the company were obliged to return." [13]

Chislett continues with his narration: "The day of rest on Willow Creek did the company good, and we started out next morning with new life. During the day we crossed the Sweetwater on the ice, which did not break, although our wagons were laden with sick people. The effects of our lack of food, and the terrible ordeal of the Rocky Ridge, still remained among us. Two or three died every day. . .

"Near South Pass we found more brethren from the Valley, with several quarters of good fat beef hanging frozen on the limbs of the trees where they were encamped. These quarters of beef were to us the handsomest pictures we ever saw. The statues of Michael Angelo, or the paintings of the ancient masters, would have been to us nothing in comparison to these *life-giving pictures.*

"After getting over the Pass we soon experienced the influence of a warmer climate and for a few days we made good progress. We constantly met teams from the Valley, with all necessary provisions. Most of these went on to Martin's company, but enough remained with us for our actual wants. At Fort Bridger [on November 2d] we found a great many teams that had come to our help. The noble fellows who came to our assistance invariably received us joyfully, and did all in their power to alleviate our suffering. May they

---

[13] Woodruff's letter in the Journal History, Oct. 31, 1856, p. 3.

never need similar relief! From Bridger all our company rode, and this day I also rode for the first time on our journey. The entire distance from Iowa City to Fort Bridger I walked and waded every stream from the Missouri to that point, except Elkhorn, which we ferried, and Green River, which I crossed in a wagon. During the journey from Bridger to Salt Lake a few died of dysentery, and some from the effects of the frost the day we crossed the fatal Rocky Ridge. But those who weathered that fatal day and night, and were free from disease, gradually regained strength and reached Salt Lake City in good health and spirits.

"When we left Iowa City we numbered about five hundred persons. Some few deserted us while passing through Iowa, and some remained at Florence. When we left the latter place we numbered four hundred and twenty, about twenty of whom were independent emigrants with their own wagons, so that our handcart company was actually four hundred of this number. Sixty-seven died on the journey, making *a mortality of one-sixth of our number*. Of those who were sick on our arrival, two or three soon died. President Young had arranged with the bishops of the different wards and settlements to take care of the poor emigrants who had no friends to receive them, and their kindness in this respect *cannot be too highly praised*. It was enough that a poor family had come with the handcarts to insure help during the winter from the good brethren in the different settlements." [14]

The Fourth Handcart Company arrived at Salt Lake City on November 9, 1856.

---

14 Chislett, in Stenhouse, *op. cit.,* 330-32.

WITH MARTIN'S COMPANY
TO THE VALLEY

We now return to Captain Edward Martin, and follow him from Devil's Gate to Zion. Within a few days after his company arrived at the Devil's Gate mail station, the remaining wagon emigrants came in, making some twelve hundred persons assembled here.

What to do next, became the problem. Snow storms and severely cold weather continued to harrass the beleaguered Saints. Present supplies were inadequate to provide so many people for long. Men and cattle continued to die.

It was decided that the handcart company, with the help from the rescue party and some wagons, should move on to find a sheltered place where wood was procurable. Loaded with the sick and dying, the wagons were to move along the Sweetwater and cross to a depression later to be known as Martin's Cove,[15] about two and one-half miles from Devil's Gate.

The handcarts moved on November 3 and reached the river, filled with floating ice. To cross would require more courage and fortitude, it seemed, than human nature could muster. Women shrank back and men wept. Some pushed through, but others were unequal to the ordeal.

"Three eighteen-year-old boys belonging to the relief party, came to the rescue; and to the astonishment of all who saw, carried nearly every member of that ill-

---

[15] A monument on the highway marks the place. The rounded wall of solid granite running along the north side of the Sweetwater here curves to make a cove. In the central part of the encircled area the winds of centuries have heaped up a huge dune of sand; but along the granite wall runs a sheltered ravine that is clear of sand. When we visited the place in 1956 a band of antelope was in the cove.

fated handcart company across the snow-bound stream. The strain was so terrible, and the exposure so great, that in later years all the boys died from the effects of it. When President Brigham Young heard of this heroic act, he wept like a child, and later declared publicly, 'That act alone will ensure C. Allen Huntington, George W. Grant, and David P. Kimball an everlasting salvation in the Celestial Kingdom of God, worlds without end.' " [16]

The fatigued Saints finally reached the wagons, encamped in the cove against the granite mountain, where they found some shelter through several freezing days. The thermometer reached eleven degrees below zero on November 6. [17] It was decided to store the merchandise from the wagon trains at Devil's Gate fort; and then, in the emptied wagons, to haul the sick and incapacitated members of the handcart company on to Salt Lake. Most of the handcarts would be abandoned.

After the freight from the two rear wagon trains was stored in the log cabins, a delegation was chosen to remain behind and guard the goods during the winter. Dan W. Jones, with two companions from the Valley and seventeen men from the emigrant trains, were assigned the gruelling task. [18]

---

[16] Kimball, in *The Improvement Era*, XVII, p. 288.

[17] The journal entry of that date in Appendix D.

[18] Jones writes: "There was not money enough on earth to have hired me to stay. I had left home for only a few days and was not prepared to remain so long away; but I remembered my assertion that any of us would stay if called upon. I could not back out, so I selected Thomas Alexander and Ben Hampton. I am satisfied that two more faithful men to stand under all hardships could not have been found."

The ordeal they endured during the long winter was terrible. Their cattle died; they ate the lean meat, and got hungry eating it. Finally they were reduced to eating rawhide. At first it made them sick. But Jones, a professional cook, devised a plan and evolved this recipe: "Scorch and scrape the

Hodgett's and Hunt's wagon trains, now relieved of their freight, moved on to Martin's Cove. Here the meager loads from the handcarts, and all the emigrants that the wagons could carry, were packed under the wagon covers. The stronger persons still had to walk, but pulling of handcarts was at an end; all these two-wheeled burdens were left behind. The party moved forward on November 9.[19]

Ahead of the company, there still stretched 325 miles of high, mountain desolation, mantled in snow. Another cold spell coated the Sweetwater with an ice sheet, thick enough to support wagons. As the train plowed slowly westward through the snow, the severe cold continued. Some persons had their fingers, toes, or feet frozen; others died.

Food supplies became dangerously low. No more help had yet come. And there was uncertainty as to when, or if, it *would* come. The continued storms, that slowed the emigrants, had halted the later rescue wagons headed toward them. Some of these had even started to turn back from the South Pass region, thinking that the emigrants must have taken up winter quarters somewhere – or had perished. But Redick N. Allred and others refused to turn back; they held their wagons at South Pass.

---

hair off; this had a tendency to kill and purify the bad taste that scalding gave it. After scraping, boil one hour in plenty of water, throwing the water away which had extracted all the glue, then wash and let it get cold, and then eat with a little sugar sprinkled on it. This was considerable trouble, but we had little else to do and it was better than starving.

"We asked the Lord to bless our stomachs and adapt them to this food. We hadn't the faith to ask him to bless the raw-hide for it was 'hard stock.' . . . We enjoyed this sumptuous fare for about six weeks, and never got the gout."– Jones, *Forty Years Among the Indians,* 72, 81-82.

[19] See Journal entry, Appendix D.

Ephraim Hanks, one of the greatest of Mormon scouts, also refused to turn back. Though compelled to leave his wagon load of supplies, he pushed on alone through the storms, with a saddle horse and a pack animal, hoping to meet the westbound handcarts. On the way, he providentially encountered buffalo and killed one.

"I skinned and dressed the cow;" he writes, "then cut up part of its meat in long strips and loaded my horses with it. Thereupon I resumed my journey, and traveled on till towards evening. I think the sun was about an hour high in the west when I spied something in the distance that looked like a black streak in the snow. As I got near to it, I perceived it moved; then I was satisfied that this was the long looked for hand-cart company, led by Captain Edward Martin. I reached the ill-fated train just as the immigrants were camping for the night. The sight that met my gaze as I entered their camp can never be erased from my memory. The starved forms and haggard countenances of the poor sufferers, as they moved about slowly, shivering with cold, to prepare their scanty evening meal was enough to touch the stoutest heart. When they saw me coming, they hailed me with joy inexpressible, and when they further beheld the supply of fresh meat I brought into camp, their gratitude knew no bounds. Flocking around me, one would say, 'Oh, please, give me a small piece of meat'; another would exclaim, 'My poor children are starving, do give me a little'; and children with tears in their eyes would call out, 'Give me some, give me some.' At first I tried to wait on them and handed out the meat as they called for it; but finally I told them to help themselves. Five minutes later both my horses had been released of their extra burden – the meat was all gone, and the next few hours found the people in camp busily engaged in cooking and eating it, with thankful hearts."

Hanks went about the camp administering to the sick. He continues: "Many of the immigrants whose extremities were frozen, lost their limbs, either whole or in part. Many such I washed with water and castile soap, until the frozen parts would fall off, after which I would sever the shreds of flesh from the remaining portions of the limbs with my scissors. Some of the emigrants lost toes, others fingers, and again others whole hands and feet; one woman who now resides in Koosharen, Piute Co., Utah, lost both her legs below the knees, and quite a number who survived became cripples for life." [20]

An express was sent to South Pass to get relief from the rescue company there. Four wagons, loaded with flour, hurried eastward. At five o'clock on the morning of November 12 they reached the handcart sufferers near Three Crossings on the Sweetwater.[21]

With food and with three days of good weather matters improved. The diarist could make this encouraging entry on the fourteenth: "No deaths in camp tonight." [22]

---

[20] From the Andrew Jenson interview with Hanks in June, 1891, and reproduced in S. A. Hanks and E. K. Hanks, *Scouting for the Mormons on the Great Frontier* (Salt Lake City, 1946), 135-36.

[21] Journal, Appendix D.

[22] *Ibid.*

On November 16, at Rocky Ridge, where Willie's Company had suffered its most terrible ordeal, Martin's Company was cheered by ten wagons of supplies from Salt Lake Valley. Two days later other teams with food and clothing reached them.[23] Among the men was William Kimball, who had taken the Willie Company into Salt Lake City (November 9) and was now back again with help for Martin's Company.

Although it was snowing on the nineteenth, all emigrants, now securely tucked under wagon covers, crossed South Pass safely. They met more supplies near Green River, and reached Fort Bridger on the twenty-third.

The Young and Garr express, which had left Devil's Gate on November 3, met the secondary relief trains en route and urged them to the rescue. Pushing on, Young and Garr had reached Salt Lake City at four a.m. on the morning of November 13.[24]

The wagon train carrying the Martin Handcart Company reached Bear River (modern Evanston, Wyoming) on November 25. Two days later it camped on the Weber, and on November 29 crossed Big Mountain. Here Joseph A. Young, his brother Brigham, Jr., and other young men were keeping the mountain roads open by packing the snow with moving animals.

On November 30, the emigrants, in relief wagons that now numbered 104, descended into Salt Lake

23 *Ibid.,* entries of Nov. 16, 18.

24 *Deseret News,* Nov. 19, 1856. Joseph A. Young's speech in the Tabernacle on Nov. 16 was published in the same issue. It is reprinted in Appendix F.

Valley.[25] The suffering of all was not yet over, indeed for some it was to continue throughout life.

Samuel and Margaret Pucell and their two daughters were in the Martin Company. On the way "Margaret became ill, so had to ride in the handcart part of the way. Her husband grew so weary and weakened from the lack of food that this additional burden caused him to slip and fall one day as he crossed a river. Having to travel in the cold, wintry weather with wet clothing he, too, became ill and died from hunger and exposure. His wife died five days later, leaving ten-year-old Ellen and fourteen-year-old Maggie orphans. . . Many died and many others suffered from frozen limbs, among them the Pucell girls, both having badly frozen feet and legs. . . When shoes and stockings were removed from the girls' feet, the skin came off. Although Maggie's legs were frozen, she would not allow them to do more than scrape the flesh off the bones, but Ellen's were so bad they had to be amputated just below the knees. . .

"The girls stayed in Salt Lake waiting for their wounds to heal. Later they lived in Parowan for awhile, then on to Cedar, where both married and reared families, although Ellen Pucell (Unthanks) went on her knee-stubs all her life." [26]

November 30 was a Sunday. The faithful Saints were assembled in the Tabernacle, with President Young presiding. Having been apprised of the imminent arrival of the belated emigrants, he spoke to the congregation:

---

[25] John Jaques' account in Whitney, *op. cit.,* 564.
[26] Wesley P. Bauer, in Carter, *Treasures of Pioneer History,* v, pp. 266-67.

"When those persons arrive I do not want to see them put into houses by themselves; I want to have them distributed in the city among the families that have good and comfortable houses; and I wish all the sisters now before me, and all who know how and can, to nurse and wait upon the new comers and prudently administer medicine and food to them. To speak upon these things is a part of my religion, for it pertains to taking care of the Saints. . .

"As soon as this meeting is dismissed I want the brethren and sisters to repair to their homes, where their Bishops will call on them to take in some of this company; the Bishops will distribute them as the people can receive them. . .

"The afternoon meeting will be omitted, for I wish the sisters to go home and prepare to give those who have just arrived a mouthful of something to eat, and to wash them and nurse them up. You know that I would give more for a dish of pudding and milk, or a baked potato and salt, were I in the situation of those persons who have just come in, than I would for all your prayers, though you were to stay here all the afternoon and pray. Prayer is good, but when baked potatoes and pudding and milk are needed, prayer will not supply their place on this occasion; give every duty its proper time and place. . .

"Some you will find with their feet frozen to their ankles; some are frozen to their knees and some have their hands frosted. . . we want you to receive them as your own children, and to have the same feeling for them. We are their temporal saviors, for we have saved them from death." [27]

---

[27] *Deseret News,* VI (Dec. 10, 1856) 320, cols. 1, 2.

President Young's suggestions were complied with. The newly arrived sufferers were taken in and cared for tenderly. During the winter it had only to be known that a person had come in the late handcart train, and he was given special consideration by all.

The 1856 handcart experiment was now history. Nearly two thousand Saints, long desirous of gathering to Zion, had been helped to their mountain home. Five Companies had crossed the plains. The First and Second arrived in Utah, September 26; the third, on October 2. These were pronounced successful. The Fourth Company arrived November 9; the Fifth and last, November 30. These last two migrations were terrible tragedies.

The death count in these has not been determined exactly. Captain Willie placed the number of deaths in his Company at 62; sub-captain Chislett, at 67. Of Martin's Company, Josiah Rogerson says: "The actual loss of life was between 135 and 150. Taking into consideration that we were the last company of that season and that we had three veterans of Waterloo between 75 and 80 years of age, and considering that more than half of our 622 members were from 35 to 55 years, it is hardly to be wondered at that our loss was so great." [28]

With the death of some two hundred and the maiming of others, we have in the fate of the two late handcart companies, the worst disaster in the history of Western migration. The early winter and its exceptional ferocity, the unduly late start from Britain and from the frontier outposts in America, the delays in

---

[28] Rogerson's account was published in the *Salt Lake Tribune,* Jan. 14, 1914.

procuring equipment, and the Saint's over-zealous faith
in a divine intervention to save them from the results
of their lack of caution and errors of judgment – all
these are acceptable reasons for the sad fate of these
western wayfarers.

In thinking of this tragedy, one is inclined to compare it with other similar ones. The Donner Party,
caught in the snows of the high Sierra Nevadas, just
ten years before, saw 40 die in a company of 87. John
C. Fremont, in the blizzards of the San Juan Mountains of Colorado in 1849 lost 10 of his 33 men, and
all of his 120 mules. The proportion of losses in both
of these instances was greater than in the late handcart
companies; but the number of deaths in the Mormon
caravans reached a much higher total.

These tragedies have been compared by Wallace
Stegner: "Perhaps their suffering seems less dramatic
because the handcart pioneers bore it meekly, praising
God, instead of fighting for life with the ferocity of
animals and eating their dead to keep their own life
beating, as both the Fremont and Donner parties did.
And assuredly the handcart pilgrims were less hardy,
less skilled, less well equipped to be pioneers. But if
courage and endurance make a story, if human kindness
and helpfulness and brotherly love in the midst of raw
horror are worth recording, this half-forgotten episode
of the Mormon migration is one of the great tales of
the West and of America." [29]

29 Wallace Stegner, "Ordeal by Handcart," in *Collier's,* July 6, 1956, pp.
78-85.

Handcart Companies of 1857

The tragic experiences of the belated handcart companies turned people against handcart travel. The success of the first three companies was forgotten in the sufferings of the fourth and fifth. The scheme as a whole was condemned, few thinking to blame the tragedy on the late start, which brought the emigrants into the grasp of an early and severe winter. The handcart plan was on the defensive now, and the Mormon leaders were at some pains to save it from condemnation.

Brigham Young, speaking in the Tabernacle on November 16, after Willie's company had come in, but before Martin's had arrived, emphasized the safe arrival of the first companies, explained the fate of the late ones, and concluded: "We are not in the least discouraged about the handcart method of travelling."[1]

The Fourteenth General Epistle of the Presidency of the Church, addressed to the Mormons throughout the world, gave official endorsement: "This season's operations have demonstrated that the Saints being filled with faith and the Holy Ghost can walk across the plains, drawing their provisions and clothing on handcarts. The experience of this season will of course help us to improve in future operations; but the plan has been fairly tested and proved entirely successful. . .

---

[1] Reported in the *Deseret News,* VI (Nov. 26, 1856), 298.

"[It] will in future enter largely into all our emigration operations. . . Our emigration MUST start earlier in the season, and the necessary arrangements MUST be made and completed by the time they arrive on the western frontier, and no company must be permitted to leave the Missouri River later than the first day of July.

"They must be provided with stronger handcarts, . . ."[2]

A dramatic and successful demonstration of the efficiency of handcart travel was needed. This might have the desired psychological effect and restore the humble vehicle to favor. Heber C. Kimball, President Young's First Counsellor, had suggested in the fall of 1856 that no elders be sent from Utah again "unless they take handcarts and cross the plains on foot."[3]

This scheme was now adopted, plans were perfected, and on April 23, 1857, a party of about seventy missionaries were ready to set out from Salt Lake City for the Missouri River in a handcart train. Clothing, bedding, and food supplies were to be transported on carts, and the company thus freed of the handicap of ox-drawn wagons.

---

[2] It then goes on to give these specific instructions as to construction of the cart: "The hub or nave of the cart wheels should be eight inches long and seven inches through the centre. The boxes at the shoulder should be two-and-a-quarter inches, and the point boxes one-and-a-half inches in diameter.

"If it should be considered best to have cast iron arms, they should be one-and-a-quarter inches thick at the shoulder and three-quarter inch at the point. The wooden axles should have iron or steel skeins, and the wheels should be bound with band iron one-quarter or three-eighths of an inch in thickness, with a dish of two inches, and track four feet apart. The timber must be of the best quality for toughness, and be well seasoned. In other respects they may be constructed as heretofore."

The Epistle was published in *Deseret News,* Dec. 10, 1856, and reprinted in *Millennial Star* of April 18, 1857 (XIX, pp. 241-53).

[3] Referred to by Pres. Young in his Tabernacle speech of Nov. 16 and published in the *Deseret News,* Nov. 26, 1856.

"We loaded our carts," Robert Gardner, one of the members, wrote in his diary, "and went to the Temple Square. After receiving instructions from Orson Hyde, President Young came and told us to start. We were escorted by the brass band to the Canal. It seemed that the whole city and a great many of the country folk followed us that far. 'God Bless You Brethren,' was heard from nearly every mouth. They then gave us three cheers and returned to the city." [4]

In Emigration Canyon the missionaries organized, with H. Herriman, President; W. H. Branch, Captain of the Company; Daniel McIntosh, Clerk; and five brethren as "Captains of Tens." On reaching the top of Big Mountain they halted, "took a farewell view of the valley," "gave three cheers, and started down the other side where snow was at times 15 feet deep." [5]

They reached Fort Bridger on May 1. The next day Philip Margetts recorded in his diary: "It was very difficult for me to travel as I had large blisters on my feet." But two days later he wrote: "I was very tired tonight, but I ran a foot race three hundred yards and won an oyster supper to be paid at St. Louis. Traveled 29 miles today." [6]

They forded Green River, two and one-half feet deep, on May 3, crossed South Pass on the sixth and descended to the Sweetwater, where they met twenty-five lodges of friendly Bannock Indians. Devil's Gate

---

[4] Gardner's diary, published in Carter, *Heart Throbs*, x, p. 290.

[5] *Ibid.*, 290.

[6] Margett's diary, published in Carter, *Heart Throbs*, vi, p. 398. The details of the trip here given are gleaned largely from the Gardner and Margett diaries. Three other diaries of the trip are in the Journal History, under date of June 10, 1857, pp. 20-49. These diaries are by George Goddard, Joseph W. Young, and Minor G. Atwood.

was reached on the tenth, and the North Platte River three days later. At Fort Laramie, on the twenty-first, they purchased some pork, crackers, sugar and molasses. The company was ferried across the Platte for $12. The next day John Wickey killed a deer, and the meat was divided amongst all.

On May 23 they passed Scott's Bluff, and the next day left the famous inverted funnel of Chimney Rock behind them. Twenty-eight miles, on May 26, brought them opposite Ash Hollow. The twenty-ninth, they met emigrants driving four thousand cattle to California.

"Mon., June 1. We started at 3 a.m. Traveled 4 miles and took breakfast. E. Richardson killed two buffalo. We sent five carts well manned to bring them in to camp. After dinner we traveled 21 miles. Tues. 2. At break of day, Charles Shumway and John Wimmer came into camp from Steward's Horse Train. The train had been doing their best to catch our handcart company but could not. So they sent these two men who rode all night in order to overtake us. We traveled 32¼ miles."[7]

At the Loup River they reached a new Mormon settlement, whose inhabitants took teams and helped the missionaries across the stream. Next day they passed the infant town of Columbus, Nebraska.

"June 10. Emptied our flour bag and ate all we had in camp. Then started for Florence. Arrived there about 11 o'clock. Felt like young lions and almost as savage in consequence of hearing of the assassination of our beloved P. P. Pratt. Work seems very scarce and poor prospects of selling our cart."[8]

---

[7] Gardner, in Carter, *op. cit.*, X, p. 292.

[8] Margett, in Carter, *op. cit.*, VI, p. 400.

Daniel Mackintosh, clerk of the company, summarized the trip: "We travelled with our handcarts across the Plains to Florence, Nebraska Territory, without horse, mule, cow, or any other animal to assist, drawing in them our provisions, bedding, cooking utensils, tents, &c., at which place we arrived in the full enjoyment of health, on the 10th inst, making the entire trip from point to point in forty-eight days; but out of the number we lay by to rest, repair carts &c., 7½ days, which would make the total number of travelling days 40½." [9]

A representative of the *Florence Courier* visited the Mormon camp and observed: "The bodies of the carts were tastefully painted to suit the fancy of the owners, and with such inscriptions on the sides as: 'Truth will Prevail,' 'Zion's Express,' 'Blessings follow Sacrifice,' 'Merry Mormons.' They had canvas covers, and were better looking vehicles in every respect than we had expected to see. From the accounts published in the leading journals throughout the country, the general impression on the mind of the public is that the handcart is the slowest and most laborious mode of conveyance that can be used. From the report of this party and of others, we are inclined to think it exactly the reverse. This party was but nineteen days in coming from Fort Laramie, a distance of 520 miles – an average of over 27 miles per day – some days they made 35 miles. This is certainly not slow traveling, and when we reflect upon the many inconveniences to which a traveller is subjected with his horses, mules, etc., we

---

[9] Mackintosh's letter written at New York City, June 27, 1857, published in *The Mormon*, and reprinted in *Millennial Star* of Aug. 8, 1857 (XIX, p. 511).

are inclined to think that for a California or Salt Lake trip we would give the handcart the preference.

"The members of the party were Elders going on missions to different parts of the world. They were feeling fine after their trip and expressed themselves to be on hand for a foot race or wrestling match with any one in Florence who might feel inclined to indulge. The party sold their wagons at auction at prices ranging from eight to twelve dollars. They cost forty dollars to build, in the Valley." [10]

From Florence the missionaries scattered to their various fields of labor, most of them going by boat to St. Louis. Eighteen traveled by train to New York City and thence voyaged to Britain.[11]

The great effort of 1856 to help the poor Saints in Europe to emigrate to Zion, had exhausted the Perpetual Emigration Fund, and had even piled up debts. As early as August 30, 1856, Brigham Young, as President of the P.E.F., had written to Orson Pratt, new President of the European Mission and manager of emigration, that the funds were all expended. There must be no more borrowing, he writes "and then paying out of the tithing money, as we have had to do under existing practice. . . We truly feel to assist the poor Saints to come home to Zion," he continues, "and think that we have proven this by our work; but it is not wisdom to absorb every other interest, pertaining to the building up of the kingdom of God, in gathering the poor, which is only one branch of it." [12]

In conformity with this policy, Pratt announced in

---

10 *Florence Courier,* reproduced in Journal History.

11 The *Millennial Star* of Aug. 1, 1857 (XIX, p. 489) names these eighteen missionaries.

12 Published in *Millennial Star,* Dec. 27, 1856 (XVIII, p. 821).

the *Millennial Star* of December 27, 1856: "This office will not send any P.E.Fund emigrants to Utah, during the year 1857. All the funds that the Company can command will be exhausted in discharging the heavy liabilities, incurred in sending out over two thousand souls, in the year 1856."

Persons who could finance their own transportation to Utah were encouraged to emigrate. Those who planned to go by handcart were to send in $12.50 each for railroad fare to Iowa City, and $15 each to pay for the handcarts and outfit for crossing the plains. These deposits were to be in Pratt's office by February 1, 1857.[13] The ship fare was in addition to these amounts.

About 2000 Saints sailed from Europe under Mormon auspices in the spring of 1857. Of these, 566 planned to travel through to Utah by handcarts, 311 by teams. The remainder, 1302, expected to stop in eastern United States or on the frontiers until they could earn sufficient to carry them on to Zion.[14]

In the meantime, important plans for improved

[13] *Ibid.*, 822. Pratt stated that for those wanting to travel by team the cost would probably be $275 for "one wagon with bows, yokes, and chains, four oxen, and one cow — perhaps two."

[14] The report published in *Millennial Star* of July 25, 1857 (XIX, p. 479), follows:

LATTER-DAY SAINTS EMIGRATION REPORT
From July 6, 1856, to July 1, 1857

Ship	President of the Company	Date of Sailing	Port of Disembarkation	P.E. Fund	Handcarts	Ordinary	Total
Columbia	J. Williams	Nov. 17	New York			223	223
G. Washington	J. P. Park	Mar. 28	Boston	1	142	674	817
Westmoreland	M. Cowley	Apr. 25	Philadelphia		424	120	544
Tuscarora	R. Harper	May 30	"			547	547
Miscellaneous ships	.	.	.	.		50	50
			Total		566	1614	2181

The numbers from the different countries are given.

transportation were developing in Utah. Brigham Young, and other Mormon leaders, had searched the possibilities of transport by way of the Colorado River, the Snake, the Missouri-Yellowstone. They had compared cost and efficiency of ox and mule freighting. They had even dreamed of a railroad line to and through the State of Deseret. But in the year of our Lord 1856, a line of stagecoaches for passengers and express, and a fast freight line with mules and light wagons, would seem most feasible.

Government mail service to Utah and to California, since the first days of settlement, had been slow, inefficient, and undependable. If the Mormons could procure the United States mail contract to Utah, establish stations along the road, and develop a big freight line, they would not only improve the letter mail service, but could also give aid to emigration of Saints from abroad.

During the winter of 1855-56 the Territorial Legislature, convened at Fillmore, discussed the project and incorporated a transportation company. Then, in a mass meeting at the Salt Lake Tabernacle on February 2, 1856, the project was thoroughly considered and out of the larger body came an organization known as the B.Y.Express and Carrying Company.[15]

Early in 1856, the Post Office Department, having become disgusted with the failures of the mail carrier on the Central Route, annulled his contract and advertised for new bids.[16] Here was the great opportunity for the new Carrying Company.

---

[15] Neff, *History of Utah,* 327-28.

[16] LeRoy R. Hafen, *The Overland Mail* (Cleveland, 1926), 60-62. W. M. F. Magraw received the contract for mail service from Independence, Mo., to Salt Lake City, in 1854, at a price of $14,440. per year. The mail was to be

"Under the advertisement of May 31, 1856, Hiram Kimball, of Utah, was found to be the lowest bidder, and accordingly a contract was entered into with him October 9, 1856. The service was to continue monthly with carriages or wagons, and the compensation was to be $23,000 per annum." [17] Kimball was merely an agent for the B.Y.Express Company and the Mormon leaders who were behind it.

As we have previously noted, the winter of 1856-57 was exceptionally severe. The mail from the east, which carried the unsigned Kimball contract, holed up at Devil's Gate until roads were passable. However, Governor Young, without waiting for the official notification, began preparations for the service. On March 24 the contract arrived, and Young plunged into the new venture with his characteristic vigor.

First, the Company proceeded to establish substantial stations along the overland road, places where grain and other supplies could be safely deposited, where hay could be cut and crops raised. Settlements to sustain the stage line and to assist emigrant trains were launched. Agents, supplies, and settlers were dispatched to strategic locations at once.

Genoa, Nebraska, 102 miles west of Florence, and Deer Creek, 98 miles west of Fort Laramie, Wyoming, were the earliest way stations established.

On May 11, 1857, settlers from Florence arrived at the site of Genoa. They immediately began to plow, and to plant corn and potatoes, buckwheat, and garden

---

carried in 4-horse coaches, going through in 30 days. During the first year Indian troubles caused losses, and the payment was raised to $36,000 for the year ending Aug. 7, 1855. The next year the contractor presented a similar claim, and Congress voted him $17,750 in relief, but ordered the contract annulled. Accordingly, on May 31, 1856, new bids were called for.
    [17] *Ibid.,* 61.

vegetables. They started a steam saw mill and a brick yard. The city laid out was patterned after the Mormon capital, with ten-acre blocks and a public square in the center. On the first of July the community's Historian reported that the new settlement had "97 men, 25 women, 40 children, 42 yoke of oxen, 20 cows, 6 horses, 20 hogs, two dozen chickens, 2 cats, and dogs aplenty." [18] The farm, south of the city, contained about seven hundred and fifty acres, bounded by the Beaver River, the Loup Fork, and a sod fence. The city was laid off on a beautiful eminence near the bluffs, with an enchanting view of distant groves of timber, a sea of grass and the winding rivers.

But the gigantic transportation project died almost at its birth. In June, 1857, Kimball's mail contract was annulled by the government. This unjustified action was doubtless the result of a malignant letter to the President of the United States by the previous mail contractor, a Mr. McGraw. In his letter, McGraw pictured the Mormons being in an "uncontrolled state of lawlessness in which murder, rapine and terrorism flourished and which had been superimposed upon a helpless society by a vicious, despotic, self-constituted theocracy at the head of which was Brigham Young." Judge W. W. Drummond also wrote an unjust letter of criticism. [19]

Cancellation of the Kimball mail contract in June was followed by the sending of a military force against the Mormons in July. This large government expedition, which finally turned into a fiasco, was to have

---

[18] Letter of Henry J. Hudson from Genoa, July 1, 1857, and published in *Millennial Star* of Sept. 19, 1857 (XIX, p. 607).

[19] These are quoted in full in Hafen, ed., *The Utah Expedition, 1857-1858* (Glendale, Calif., 1958), *Far West and Rockies Series,* VIII, pp. 361-66.

tremendous consequences upon Mormon immigration. It would affect handcart travel in 1857 and would blot it out for the year 1858.

With this wider background, let us resume our handcart narrative, bearing in mind that the treks of this year, 1857, were being conducted beside the wreckage of the B.Y.Express and Carrying Company, and in the shadow of an army of supplies and men advancing toward Zion to put down a supposed rebellion.

THE SIXTH HANDCART COMPANY

The emigrants who were to comprise the Sixth Handcart Company (under Captain Israel Evans) embarked on the "George Washington" at Liverpool on March 27, 1857. Fourteen returning missionaries and 803 converts were passengers. At three o'clock in the afternoon the Saints assembled on the upper deck for a general meeting and organization. A President of the Company – James P. Park – and two counsellors were chosen. The membership was then divided into five wards, with a leader selected for each.[20] Stirring songs of Zion were sung, one of which was written by Cyrus H. Wheelock:

> Ye elders of Israel come join now with me
> And seek out the righteous, where'er they may be:
> In desert, on mountain, on land, or on sea,
> And bring them to Zion, the pure and the free.
>
> *Chorus:*
> O Babylon, O Babylon, we bid thee farewell;
> We're going to the mountains of Ephraim to dwell.[21]

---

[20] *Millennial Star*, Apr. 11, 1857. The Counsellors to Pres. Parks were J. B. Martin and C. R. Dana; the leaders of wards were Israel Evans (destined to head the Sixth Handcart Co.), B. Ashby, J. Carrigan, D. B. Dille, and J. C. Hall.

[21] See Appendix K for the complete song.

A speedy voyage brought the ship to Boston in twenty-three days. The Saints were soon entrained and on their way to Iowa City, where they arrived before the emigration agents were quite ready for them.

James A. Little, now the church representative on the frontier, had recently returned from his British mission, having sailed from Liverpool on February 14 and arrived in Boston on March 2.[22] He had expected the first detachment to reach Iowa City about the tenth of May; but being apprised of their earlier arrival, he hurried preparations for their reception.

At St. Louis he gathered up the eleven tents (each to house twenty persons) and twenty-five wagon covers already finished by the manufacturers, wrote to Peter Schuttler, the wagon maker, to hurry his vehicles, and took the up-river steamer to Muscatine, Iowa (nearest port to Iowa City).

Since it was a cold and late spring, the gathering and driving of the oxen to Iowa City for the wagon company was delayed. Until fresh grass came, cattle could not be maintained there without undue expense. Mules, however, to be used on the wagons with the handcart companies, were useful for camp duties, and they could be fed on purchased hay, if need be.

Elder Little reached Iowa City on the evening of April 29. The emigrants arrived the next noon, with only their small luggage in hand. The tents and wagon covers were hurriedly set up, and on May 1 a supply of provisions and the general luggage were hauled in wagons to camp.[23] It was three weeks before all was in readiness for the trek westward.

---

[22] Little's letter of Mar. 3, 1857, from Boston, published in *Millennial Star*, April 11, 1857.

[23] Little's letters of April 25, 27, and May 2, written on the Mississippi steamer and at Iowa City, and published in *Millennial Star*, June 13, 1857.

The Sixth Handcart Company was organized at Iowa City, with Israel Evans as Captain. He was now returning from a four-year mission to England. Having been born in Ohio and a member of the Church since childhood, also a volunteer in the Mormon Battalion who had dug gold at Sutter's Mill in California, he was an experienced traveler.[24] The handcarts started rolling on May 22.[25]

Accompanied by a good four-mule team and wagon to haul extra provisions, the Company pushed across Iowa, making fifteen to twenty miles per day. They reached Florence on June 13.[26] After being delayed there for a week by storms and unfinished arrangements for the farther trip, they pushed out into the unsettled lands on June 20.[27]

Amos M. Musser writes: "The company numbers one hundred and forty-nine souls, (eighty of whom are females – twenty-one under eight and two over sixty years old, the eldest, a female, sixty-eight years old,) twenty-eight hand-carts, and an excellent four-mule team." He mentioned the problem of the storms which "swelled the small streams to an impassable depth."[28]

---

[24] Israel Evans was born Oct. 2, 1828, in Hanover, Columbia Co., Ohio, a son of David Evans and Mary Beck. As a boy he endured the persecutions in Missouri. He married Matilda A. Thomas on Jan. 1, 1849. He died at Lehi, Utah, on May 31, 1896.– Jenson, *Biographical Encyclopedia*, IV, p. 743.

[25] The date of starting is taken from the sketch of Hannah Pendlebury Jones, a member of Evans' Company, in Carter, *Treasures of Pioneer History*, V, pp. 279-30. Mrs. Jones lived in Nephi, Utah, and died there on Dec. 1, 1912.

[26] Letter of Joseph W. Young, written at New York City on June 29, published in *The Mormon*, and reprinted in *Millennial Star* of Aug. 8, 1857. Benjamin Ashby was assisting Capt. Evans, according to Young.

[27] J. A. Little's letter of July 12, 1857, from Florence, published in *Millennial Star* of Aug. 22, 1857 (XIX, p. 541).

[28] Letter written from the Plains west of Florence on July 16, 1857, published in *The Mormon*, and reprinted in *Millennial Star* of Sept. 26, 1857.

Annie B. Thornley, a member of this Company, remembered one incident in particular – "she lost her sunbonnet soon after the company started on the long journey to Utah, and was compelled to continue bareheaded over one thousand miles." [29]

James Reeder, his wife Honor Welch Reeder, and their five-year-old son were with one handcart. James sickened and died, and was buried on the plains. Honor plodded on with her son and cart. Six weeks after arrival in the Valley she gave birth to a baby girl who lived to maturity. [30]

Robert L. Fishburn, a young man of twenty-three, teamed with three young ladies in taking a handcart to Zion. Apparently he and one of the girls worked well together, for a year after arrival they decided to team up permanently. This girl was Eliza Priscilla Noble. [31]

The Company came through safely, and apparently with little difficulty, to Salt Lake City. Wilford Woodruff reported on September 11th: "Brother Israel Evans' hand-cart company arrived at 2 p.m. in very good condition. 154 souls, 31 carts." [32]

On the sixteenth of September the *Deseret News* gives a brief account of the Sixth Handcart Company's march to Zion: "On the 12th Israel Evans and Benjamin Ashby arrived with the 1st Handcart Company

---

[29] Carter, *Heart Throbs*, VI, p. 401.

[30] Carter, *Treasures of Pioneer History*, V, p. 458. Honor Reeder married James Gallyer in 1859, and lived in Murray, Utah.

[31] *Ibid.*, 280-81.

[32] His letter of Sept. 12, published in *Millennial Star*, XIX (1857), 766. No roster of this company has been found, and the reports as to number of persons and of carts vary somewhat. The *Deseret News*, VII, p. 188, carried a report that the company would arrive at Deer Creek on the 8th inst. "There are 30 handcarts, 2 teams, and some 150 persons in the company; they are very lively and making good progress."

[of 1857] ; and Jesse Martin with the first wagon company, . . . All in excellent spirits, time and condition." *Typed in Brethren Family File — 6-24-02*

THE SEVENTH COMPANY

The Seventh Handcart Company was made up of Scandinavian Saints, most of whom had sailed from Copenhagen April 18, 1857, on the steamship "L. N. Hvidt" to Britain; and from Liverpool, April 25, on the "Westmoreland." Aboard the latter were 504 converts and four returning missionaries. Mathias Cowley was president of the company.[33]

When five young Danish couples were married on the boat at Liverpool, a holiday spirit developed which lasted for several days.[34] The ship landed on May 31 at Philadelphia, where the Saints were received by Angus M. Cannon in the absence of Elder John Taylor. Necessary arrangements were quickly made, and on June 2 the company entrained for the west, going by way of Baltimore and Wheeling. There was much sickness en route; three children and one man died on the crowded trains.[35]

Upon arrival at Iowa City on June 9, the emigrants were taken to the camp grounds, about three miles from town. Here large round tents, held up by a center pole, and capable of holding about twenty persons, awaited them. About 330 of the Scandinavian Saints were to go by handcart; some would travel in wagons.

---

[33] *Millennial Star,* May 16, 1857 (XIX, pp. 313-14). Elders Henry Lunt and Olaf W. Liljenquist were his counsellors.

[34] Anna S. D. Johnson, "The Seventh Handcart Company," in *The Relief Society Magazine,* XXXV (1948), pp. 449ff; and J. M. Tanner, *Biography of James Jensen.*

[35] Journal History, Sept. 13, 1857, pp. 12-22.

Three days were allowed to prepare for the hand-cart trek. In Denmark the emigrants had understood that the fifteen pounds allowed per person was for clothing alone; but now they learned that this was to cover everything. So feather beds, dishes, books, and some clothing had to be left behind.[36]

The company was equipped with 66 handcarts, and 4 mule-drawn wagons. It was organized with James P. Park as Captain, and eight sub-captains, each in charge of eight or nine handcarts. Captain Park, a Scotsman, could not understand Danish, so had to communicate through an interpreter, O. N. Liljen-quist. The arrangement was considered not satisfactory, so Christian Christiansen, who had planned to go by wagon, consented to serve as their Captain. Elder Christiansen, who spoke both Danish and English, was a native of Denmark who had migrated to Utah, and recently had served as a missionary in the United States.

As the Scandinavians pushed across Iowa a regular routine was followed. At night the tents were pitched in a circle. The campfires, lighted outside, served to cook the meals, while the smoke helped keep away the hungry mosquitoes. A whistle at five o'clock told all to rise and get breakfast. Immediately afterward, everyone assembled for a song, prayer, and instruc-tions.[37]

Frederick Hansen wrote: "Father worked on the left side of the cart, my brother John on the right, I worked

---

[36] Frederick Hansen, "The Great Handcart Train from Iowa City to Salt Lake City," in *Iowa Journal of History,* IX (1916), 408-16. Anders and Peter Christensen reluctantly gave up their violins.– Carter, *Treasures of Pioneer History,* v, p. 283.

[37] Hansen, in *Iowa Journal of History, loc. cit.*

in the middle, pulling on a rope about four feet long, one end of which was tied to the cart, to the other end a small stick was fastened for a handle. We made what some called a spike team. I always thought I had the easiest part, as I did not have to hold back going down hill." [38]

His mother was sick and rode most of the time in the wagon. He says that the handcart train had to turn out of the road for the United States mail. The pilgrims crossed the Des Moines River on a bridge. Upon approaching Council Bluffs the caravan was met by officers who forbade them to enter the city, saying the company had smallpox, which the emigrants denied. So the caravan passed west and south of the city and crossed the Missouri River on a steamboat ferry. Because of the mother's continued illness the Hansen family decided to drop out and remain a year or so before continuing their journey.

At Florence the company was reorganized. Under Captain Christian Christiansen, four sub-captains were appointed, each to be in charge of sixteen or seventeen handcarts. [39]

"On the third," wrote J. A. Little from Florence, "the Scandinavian handcart company arrived; quite a number of the company were out of health from the effects of their voyage, and change of diet." The next day a council was held to consider the condition of the party and it was "unanimously decided that it was wisdom for the companies to go on; and that all who

[38] *Ibid.,* 411.

[39] J. F. F. Dorius' account in Journal History, Sept. 13, 1857, pp. 12-22. Dorius says the assistants to the Captain were James P. Parks and Elder Rudd. The four sub-captains were C. C. A. Christensen, J. F. F. Dorius, Ole C. Olsen, and Carl C. N. Dorius.

were not able to walk in the handcart company should
remain, that they might not be a burden.

"On the 6th, the company of teams consisting of
thirty-one wagons, left here, and on the 7th the handcart company, consisting of 330 souls, with ten mules
and three wagons left here, all able to travel on foot." [40]

The first night out the company was inspected to see
if any were unfit to proceed. A Swede, Brother Hulberg, was advised to turn back because of his wife's
illness. But Brother Hulberg had his heart set on going
to Zion. He trailed along a little distance behind the
company for about fifty miles. When he was too far
from base to be sent back, he rejoined the company.
Much of the way he had pulled his two children and
even his wife on the cart, through his superior strength
and unquenchable desire to proceed. [41]

On reaching the Loup Fork, July 16, some Indians
familiar with the river crossing, were hired to help
the company ford the stream. Provisions and goods
were hauled across in the wagon, pulled by double
teams. The emptied handcarts were then taken across
by the strongest men; some women rode on horseback,

---

[40] Little's letter of July 12 from Florence, published in *Millennial Star* of
Aug. 22, 1857. Elder Little was superintendent of emigration on the frontier.
A. M. Musser, in his letter of July 16, 1857, says the company "numbered
about three hundred thirty souls, sixty-eight handcarts, three wagons, and
ten mules. Capt. Christianson, a Dane from the Valley, was deputed to
conduct them to Utah; they left on the 7th instant, in good spirits."

Of the year's emigration in general, Musser wrote: "By recapitulating, we
find that there are now on the plains one thousand two hundred and fourteen
souls, one hundred and fifty-seven wagons, six hundred and forty-six oxen,
twenty horses, eighteen mules, seventy-five cows, nineteen loose cattle, and
ninety-seven hand-carts; add to these the isolated emigrants in company with
brother Taylor and others, and you will have the sum total of our this
year's emigration; which, I believe, have been as well fitted out, and are
under as prosperous circumstances, as our emigrants have been in any
preceding year."–*Ibid.*, 620.

[41] J. M. Tanner, *op. cit.*, 26-27.

clinging to the almost naked Indians who guided the horses.[42]

In traveling up the Platte, relates James Jensen, he and his father were a wheel team, a younger brother and sister Karen were leaders, mother pushed from behind, a seven-year-old boy walked, and the sickly baby rode in the cart. When the little girl died, a grave was dug, and a sieve was placed over her face before earth covered the emaciated little body.[43]

At Wood River a sister, Anna Marie Sorenson, retired from the camp, and under some willows gave birth to a baby girl. In the morning she appeared with the baby in her apron, but the captain told her to ride in the wagon for a day or so. The baby survived, as well as the mother.[44]

The caravan reached Fort Laramie on August 9. Approaching now the country known as the Black Hills, they found the road more rough and hilly, wood more abundant, and the nights cool. But their supply of food dwindled, and had to be rationed.

One bit of aid came from an unexpected quarter. A detachment of the "Utah Expedition," the army going west to discipline the Saints, was traveling near the Danish handcart train. An ox, belonging to the soldiers, was disabled when a heavy wagon ran over and crushed its foot. The military captain came over to the hungry emigrants and said: "You may have the ox, I guess you need it." [45] The fresh meat was gratefully devoured.

---

[42] *Ibid.*, 28.

[43] *Ibid.*, 24-25.

[44] *Ibid.*, 31; and Carter, *Treasures of Pioneer History*, v, pp. 282-83. Other experiences of members of this company are given by Lucinda P. Jensen and Delia N. T. Harris in Carter, *Heart Throbs*, vi, pp. 401-404.

[45] Tanner, *op. cit.*, 38.

James Jensen tells of another meat offer; this, however, was not relished. An old man devoid of a sense of smell was walking some distance from the handcarts, when he saw an animal that might be suitable for food. Creeping cautiously upon it, he proceeded to lambaste it with his cane until it was lifeless. Then he threw the little striped animal over his shoulder and headed for the handcart caravan. As he approached, his friends retreated. The gift was vociferously declined, and even the giver was considered unbearable. With no change of clothing available, the kind man was ostracized. Happily, the company soon reached Deer Creek Station, where the emigrant's son was located. At this supply depot the unhappy man remained for the rest of the season and probably found new wearing apparel. By spring he was able and fit to go on to the Salt Lake Valley.

Jensen also tells of a personal experience with the prickly-pears that covered sections of the Wyoming high country. One dark night the sixteen-year-old boy was out in search of water, when he ran into an extensive bed of these cacti. His feet, covered only with canvas-soled socks, were soon filled with the sharp spines. When he could bear the pain no longer, he sat down to pull out the thorns; but he jumped up quicker than he sat; for he had squatted on a healthy bed of prickly pears. The impressions remained deep in his memory.

As the emigrants neared South Pass, the great divide between the Atlantic and Pacific drainage, they met wagons loaded with flour. By giving promises or some handcart equipment as security, they were able to purchase enough for their needs. At Fort Bridger further supplies were procured. And some miles out from Salt Lake City, they were met by friends laden with fresh bread, cake, and fruits.

The final stages of the journey furnished a test between the endurance of men and mules, both groups having been on short rations through the miles of heat and sand. Feed on the trail was especially scant this year for mules. Some 50,000 cattle were being driven to California along this route, besides the oxen of the huge freight trains of Johnston's army.

"When we came to the last steep hills of the mountain sides," continues Jensen, "our mules were so weak that the emigrants were obliged to help them over by the aid of ropes." The handcart travelers reached their destination in a better condition than did the mule teams, concludes Brother Jensen. However, he adds a sobering bit of information: "One out of every ten of our number died on the journey." [46]

The Seventh Handcart Company had made much faster time than had the Sixth one. In fact, Christiansen's Company arrived one day after Israel Evans' Company in Salt Lake City, though Evans had left Florence three weeks earlier than Christiansen.

Doubtless both companies received some sort of welcome, but available accounts give little evidence of it. The *Deseret News,* which generally reflects the spirit and the prevailing interest of the Utah people, was at this time crowded with news and speeches about the approaching United States Army, the annulment

---

[46] *Ibid.,* 34-40. Capt. Philip St. George Cooke, of Mormon Battalion fame, made a cavalry march in connection with the Utah Expedition during the late fall. He set out with 278 animals and upon reaching Fort Bridger had lost 134.

of the mail contract, and the consequent collapse of the great B.Y.Express Carrying Company.

All the space devoted to arrival of the handcart companies of 1857 was a brief statement under "Immigration" in the September 16 issue of the *Deseret News*. It ended with the generalization: "All in excellent spirits, time, and condition."

Renewed Emigration, 1859

With "Johnston's Army" encamped on the borders of Utah during the winter of 1857-58, and with the conflict unresolved and the future uncertain, foreign emigration to Zion was interrupted. In Europe the announcement was made:

"In view of the difficulties which are now threatening the Saints, we deem it wisdom to stop all emigration to the States and Utah for the present." But this note of hope, appended to the editorial, prepares the way for resumption of emigration:

"It will not be long until the way will again be opened, so that the Saints can gather to Zion according to the desires of their hearts. Continue to treasure up means, and add to what you already have, so that you may not be delayed when the way opens." [1]

By the time the difficulties were settled, in the summer of 1858, it was too late to resume emigration for that season. But for the following year plans could be made. In the fall of 1858 the word was sent abroad that the gathering to Zion could be resumed.

President Young penned a vigorous appeal: "Urge on the emigration so far as you have the power. Wherein the Saints are not able to come all the way through, let them come to the States, and then make their way through as soon as they can. We would like to strengthen at Genoa and Florence, and to make a

---

[1] *Millennial Star* of Oct. 17, 1857 (XIX, p. 668).

large settlement on Deer Creek, and the Black Hills, and would not object seeing about 10,000 Saints find their way to Utah the ensuing year, if they have the means and are disposed to come. But you must always remember to not run us in debt." [2] Such were the instructions to the President of the European Mission, Asa Calkin.

With the opening of the year 1859 the *Millennial Star* began a series of articles emphasizing the "Gathering." Since the Church could not furnish money for emigration, it was necessary to emphasize continually the necessity of self-exertion and economy. In the issue of January 29, Editor Calkin wrote:

"The Lord has again opened the door of emigration; and, for the same reason which has guided us heretofore, we now direct particular attention to the gathering, this most important part in the work of God. . . Some have expected to start for Zion 'in the due time of the Lord.' . . Others have rather anticipated being gathered in some very remarkably mysterious way." His final message was, that the gathering could be accomplished *only* by their own individual efforts.

"Behold, now is the accepted time – now is *your* day of salvation. . . If this period of temporal salvation now begun closes without your embracing it, you may never see Zion in the flesh." [3]

HANDCART EMIGRATION OF 1859

Only one handcart company was to cross the plains in 1859. The Saints that were to comprise this group sailed from England on April 11, in the "William

---

[2] *Ibid.,* XXI, p. 27.
[3] *Ibid.,* XXI, p. 141.

Tapscott." The president of the company, Robert F. Neslen, organized the 725 Saints on board into ten wards – five English, and five Scandinavians. Nine different languages were spoken by the passengers.

"In the matrimonial department," reported Neslen, "we did exceedingly well, as we had nineteen marriages, five couples of which were English, one Swiss, and thirteen Scandinavians – all of which were solemnized by myself." During the crossing there were two births, and one death.[4]

After a pleasant voyage of thirty-one days, the Saints landed at New York. On May 14 they took the steamer "Isaac Newton" to Albany, and thence traveled by train to St. Joseph, Missouri – the Hannibal and St. Joseph railroad having been completed to the Missouri River.[5] From the railhead they sailed to Florence, where they were to get their handcarts.

It was nearly three weeks before the carts were available and everything was arranged for the journey. During this period, reports William Atkin, "We often sang the handcart song. A young man by the name of Frank Pitman took great pleasure in singing our song. We would sit around the campfire, and he would sing it for anyone who would ask him, and it being new to most people, he was asked to sing it often."[6]

On June 6, Mathias Nielson, according to his diary, received his handcart, utensils, water-can, and some bedding – a blanket and a rug. A tent, he said, was provided for each ten persons. Two young women,

---

[4] *Ibid.*, 286, 400-401.

[5] *New York Herald*, May 15, 1859, and *Millennial Star*, XXI (1859), 407, 419.

[6] Atkin's account published in *The Union*, of St. George, Utah, in 1896, and reprinted in Carter, *Heart Throbs*, VI, pp. 380-94.

Caroline Chapel (English), and Albertine Berthelson (Swedish), were assigned to his cart. (He later married the English girl.) [7]

The preliminary start was made on June 9; the company traveled four miles and encamped. Here, where they laid over another day, organization of the company was completed, with George Rowley as captain.

Elder Rowley, born in England in 1827, was married and had three children when he first emigrated to Utah as a Mormon convert in 1854. At that time he had been unable to take his family with him. After spending more than two years in Utah, he returned to Britain to do missionary work and to get his family. His journey eastward from Salt Lake City had been with the Missionary Handcart Company that walked to Florence in the spring of 1857. Now, two years later, he was returning to Zion to make his home, bringing with him his wife and three sons, the youngest of whom was six years old. [8]

The company comprised 235 persons, with 60 handcarts, and six ox-drawn wagons to haul provisions and the sick. There was a sub-captain for each ten carts, and these subdivisions took turns at leading the caravan. Each cart had a cover of bed ticking stretched over three bows. [9]

On June 11, the emigrants began their trek in earnest, traveling sixteen miles that day. "The most of us were tired when we camped at night," admitted Atkin, "and

---

[7] Diary of Mathias Nielson, in Journal History, Sept. 4, 1859, pp. 8, 15-31.

[8] Biographical sketch of Rowley by Pearl R. Cunningham, in Carter, *Treasures of Pioneer History,* v, pp. 285-86. Rowley was blind during the forty years preceding his death in 1908.

[9] Frederick A. Cooper's account in Journal History, Sept. 4, 1859; and Nielson diary, *op. cit.*

some were already getting foot-sore. Again we asked our little brother Frank to sing the handcart song, but he very reluctantly replied . . . and there were less who joined in the chorus than before.

"The next day we made about 22 miles and a good many of our feet were sore and a number had their feet blistered, and we were all tired indeed. One brother, more hardy than many others, asked our little Frank to again sing the handcart song, and methinks I now see him stamp his little feet and wring his hands and yell at the top of his voice, saying, 'I will never sing it again,' and I think he kept his word." [10]

Writes Mrs. Helen E. Roseberry: "We had to carry provisions on the handcart to last a week, besides our bedding and clothing, two hundred pounds of flour for us to pull, so Roseberry and another man went and took one of the sacks back and told them we could not pull so much, we had too many children [a three-year-old daughter, and twins nine months old]. I had to walk and carry one of my babies and help pull the cart for many weeks, until my feet began to swell up so I had to ride some, but it was so crowded I would rather walk as long as I possibly could. I cannot tell all I suffered on that journey, but the Lord knows it." [11]

At the Elkhorn River camp on June 12 the hosts were swarms of big mosquitoes that pursued and pricked the unhappy emigrants. The next day the company reached Fremont, Nebraska. On June 22 they crossed the Loup Fork on a ferry. Provisions for ten

---

[10] Atkin's account, *op. cit.,* 380.

[11] "Autobiography of Helena Erickson Roseberry," MS., written at Smithville, Arizona, and dated Feb. 1, 1883. Copy supplied by a granddaughter, Mrs. Edith Young Booth of Provo, Utah.

days were distributed on the twenty-fourth – ten pounds
of flour, one pound bacon, and a little sugar and salt
for each person.[12]

The once promising Mormon town of Genoa was
almost deserted, with but a few dugouts and one small
house remaining. Here two men, each with an ox-
drawn wagon and two or three cows, asked to join the
company. Their purpose was soon apparent. They
milked their cows and peddled the milk to the hungry
emigrants. When they had obtained all available cash
in the company, they accepted jewelry and other
articles. The emigrants became disgusted at their
greediness.

At Wood River, where there were a few dugouts,
Atkin traded off some of his little valuables for an old
shotgun and some ammunition. These were to prove
helpful in hunting later, when food was at a premium.

On July 3, the company encountered a large band
of Sioux, the first Indians that most of the people had
ever seen. When the red warriors demanded food, the
frightened emigrants gave them three sacks of flour
and one of bacon from their scant supplies. At night
the Indians staged an impromptu dance, that did little
to allay the fears of the travelers.

"We hastened on our journey as soon as daylight did
arrive, hoping to be free from them, but lo, our troubles
were not at an end for we had not gone over a mile or
two when a number of the natives came just as fast as
they could ride, with their long hair floating in the air
behind them and shouting like demons, and they rode
up beside our carts and threw their lassoes to us and
showed us that they wanted us to tie them to our carts,

---

[12] Nielson's diary, *op. cit.*

and where there were young women at the carts they seemed determined to tie their ropes to the carts; and thus they followed us and tormented us for hours, and thus our first Indian experience was a terror to us in very deed." [13]

Nielson records that an Indian brought in some buffalo meat; and one offered him eight ponies for one of the girls helping to pull his handcart. The next day the Indian tugged at the cart for three miles over sandhills, but he had to leave without a white squaw.

The hard work in the outdoor air produced good appetites, and the allotted rations did not satisfy hunger. This was the year of the big "Pike's Peak or Bust" gold rush, which thronged the Platte Valley with argonauts. One party, well provided with horses and rifles, passed the caravan of carts, and killed a big buffalo.

"They took one quarter of it," says Atkin, "and covered the three-quarters carefully with the hide and put up a notice that read 'This is for the handcarts.' We found it in very good condition and it was divided out, giving us from one to two pounds each. This was the only good mess of fresh meat of this kind that we had obtained, for . . . we had neither horses nor other means to obtain it." [14]

The company passed Chimney Rock on July 22 and reached Fort Laramie on the twenty-seventh. Here an inventory of supplies revealed a grave shortage. The seventy pounds of flour per person for the intended seventy days of the trip, had been eaten up much faster than the schedule anticipated. The rations had to be

---

[13] Atkin's account, *op. cit.*, 382-83.

[14] *Ibid.*, 384.

sharply reduced. With one pint of flour for two persons, and then one pint for four, Atkin was thankful when he was able, with his shotgun, to bring down a sage hen.[15]

At Devil's Gate the last flour was distributed, eight pounds per man. Here two oxen died from drinking alkali water, and their meat augmented the food supply.[16]

There were many Indians in the Devil's Gate area. According to William Atkin, they greatly frightened and annoyed the emigrants. F. A. Cooper writes: "They had just had a great battle between two tribes. The victorious tribe were parading around with scalps suspended on sticks which they held high in the air. They had a number of prisoners. They invited a number of us boys to go to their camp that night to witness them torture to death their prisoners. However, we respectfully declined." [17]

One night, says Atkin, one of the guards, herding the oxen, smelled a dead animal. Dimly he "saw what he supposed to be a wild animal eating it, so he raised his gun and was about to fire when one of our brethren raised up. He was so near starved that he was glad to even get a bit of stale meat from a dead animal. The man who had the gun could hardly contain himself, in thinking how near he came to shedding the blood of one of our brethren." [18]

---

[15] *Ibid.,* 388.

[16] Nielson's diary, Aug. 12.

[17] Frederick A. Cooper, "Experiences in Crossing the Plains" (MS.). Cooper says of the food shortage at Devil's Gate: "Our provisions were found to be so very low that they were obliged to divide that which was left equally and started us on for life or death. There was but three pounds of flour each and nothing else."

[18] Atkin, *op. cit.,* 389.

"One day before we got to Green River," said Mrs. Ebenezer B. Beesley, "we were all literally on the verge of dying of starvation. Some of the people could go no farther, and we were in the heights of despair when we met some rough mountaineers. They felt very sorry for us and told us if we would come over to their camp they would give us some breakfast. I never tasted anything better in my life and it was cooked by squaws, too. They seemed to be living there with these men. The first thing they gave us was milk and whisky and we had to drink it out of gourds. Yes, I remember that so well. Then they gave us a sort of bread or cake that they cooked in kettles over the fire. Oh, it was all so good and there was plenty of it. Then when we were through we carried some back to the ones who were too sick to come with us. I remember one Scotch girl stayed there with them. One of the mountaineers offered her a home and her legs were in such a condition she could travel no farther, so she stayed. Yes, she never did get to Salt Lake and she left Scotland to come to Zion, too. She wasn't the only one who never reached the Valley." [19]

William Atkin gives another version of this incident and experience: "When the handcart people arrived at Big Sandy they were in a starving condition and here a scene transpired which I shall never forget. At this place was a mail station. There were three or four mountaineers and traders, a stage driver and mail agent at the station, being six or eight men in all, with more whiskey in them than good sound sense, and when the handcart people came to the stream and stopped to get water, two of those men stepped out of the house and

_____
[19] In Carter, *Heart Throbs,* VI, pp. 379-80.

yelled, "we want to get a wife; who wants to marry?"

"To our great surprise two of our young women stepped out and said they would marry them. One of these young women had a lover in our company, and they had always appeared affectionate and kind to each other, but alas! their starving condition seemed to drive all natural feelings away from them . . . so there were two weddings celebrated that day in their mountaineer style." [20]

When the handcart company reached Green River on August 22, there was grave disappointment at finding no supplies from Salt Lake City. The crossing of this stream was effected with much difficulty, the water being three feet deep and the current the swiftest encountered on the trip. It took four men to bring a handcart across. The women joined hands, and with one of the stronger men in the lead and one at the end of the string, crossed successfully. The day being warm, their clothes dried quickly. But hunger gnawed. An ox was killed, and every bit of the carcass was used. Some made soup of willow leaves and knuckle bones. [21]

"When we came to Green River," writes Mrs. Helena E. Roseberry, "I bought three pounds of flour and one pound of shorts for two pillows, which enabled me to keep my children from starving." [22]

They pushed on, almost famished. On the twenty-fourth, Sister Jarvis, an aged English lady, could walk no farther. She sat down beside the trail, "gave two or

---

[20] Atkin account, *op. cit.,* 390. Atkin says one of the girls later brought her husband to Salt Lake City and the other subsequently came to the city and ultimately to her handcart lover, who forgave and married her.

[21] Nielson diary.

[22] Mrs. Roseberry's autobiography, *op. cit.*

three heavy sighs," and died.[23] "We buried her by the wayside and traveled on but a short distance when another sister, her name was Shanks, came to my wife and said, 'Sister, the martyrdom of Joseph and Hyrum was nothing to compare to this,' and it was a very easy matter to see that she was very weak indeed, and unless she got immediate relief from some source she could not endure the hardships but a very short time." Presently she fell behind the train. The next day her body was found, mostly devoured by the wolves.[24]

"Twenty-four handcarts went on [from Green River] as fast as they could to meet the teams from Salt Lake with provisions," writes Mrs. Roseberry. "It was a happy time when they met the teams. If they had not brought provisions when they did, we would have starved." [25]

At Ham's Fork, on August 25, the provision wagons from the Valley rescued the handcart company. News of the emigrants' famished condition having reached the supply train, the mule-drawn wagons traveled night and day to bring food and assistance.

Most of the company reached Fort Bridger on August 28. Although their worst troubles were now over, a Danish woman, Anna Hansen, died that night, leaving a husband and five children.[26]

On August 30, Apostles John Taylor and Franklin D. Richards, who had been sent out from Salt Lake

[23] Nielson's diary, entry of Aug. 24; also Atkin's account, p. 392.

[24] Atkin's account, pp. 392-93. Her husband died on the 30th, the bite of a poisonous insect having contributed to his death.

[25] Mrs. Roseberry's autobiography.

[26] Nielson's diary, entries of Aug. 28 and 29. William Atkin, his wife, and their two little children remained ten weeks at Green River, where he found employment. In early November they came on to the Valley.

City by Brigham Young, met and camped with the handcart train at Yellow Creek, near present Evanston, Wyoming. By this time the spirit of the emigrants had revived considerably. Elders Taylor and Richards reported:

"The company were generally healthy, and some of the young people were very joyous and jubilant. There were among them many beautiful singers, who entertained us in the evening, around their camp-fires, with some of the late popular airs, and among the rest several amusing handcart songs, the chorus of which was –

> Some must push, and some must pull,
> As we go rolling up the hill:
> Thus merrily on the way we go,
> Until we reach the valley, O!

"And as they started next morning, they, in their prompt energetic action and uniform movements manifested a vivacity and life which comported very much with the spirit of their song. We had a very pleasant meeting with them, and gave them such counsel as their circumstances seemed to require. They had been met by five four-mule teams with provisions on Ham's Fork. With the aid of the mule teams and a horse team that went with us, and two yoke of cattle which we furnished, they were enabled to carry the aged and weary, and proceed comfortably." [27]

They now pushed on toward Zion. On Sunday after-

---

[27] Published in the *Deseret News* and reprinted in *Millennial Star*, XXI (1859), 727-29. Taylor and Richards investigated the reports that individuals had been left behind or lost from the handcart train. Accounts were conflicting, but apparently two persons had been lost and their bodies had been devoured by wolves. One was Mrs. Shank.

noon, September 4, the handcarts rolled down Emigration Canyon. News of the caravan's imminent arrival having reached the city, everyone turned out to welcome the train. The *Deseret News* reported:

"Immediately every horse and vehicle in the city was seemingly in motion, conveying those who were anxious to witness the egress of the company from the canyon in that direction. Within a few minutes of the designated time, the company arrived, escorted by two or three bands of music and a vast concourse of citizens of all grades and professions, and passing through the streets lined with anxious spectators, went to Union Square, accompanied by the thousands that joined the escort as they passed along. It was certainly a stirring scene, and such a one as has not been witnessed for some time past by this community, calling forth many expressions from the beholders, mostly of joy, but some of detestation that human beings would endure so much, leave their houses in foreign lands, traverse the seas, and cross the desert plains with handcarts, all for their religion. The liberality of the Saints was abundantly manifested on the occasion by the amount and variety of the provisions that were provided through the Bishops of the several Wards for the wayworn emigrants composing the company, who were thus made welcome." [28]

Womanlike, Mrs. Ebenezer Beesley, a nineteen-year-old bride from England who had walked all the way across the plains, had her own impressions of the Saints in Zion, companions on the way, and welcome at the end of the journey:

"It was September when we got here. I remember it

[28] *Deseret News,* reprinted in *Millennial Star,* xxi (1859), 719.

was a Sunday afternoon and the people were just coming out of the old Bowery. . . I never shall forget
how *clean* they looked. Oh, they all looked so fresh
and clean and nice. The women were all dressed in
calico dresses and wore sunbonnets. Oh, it was so
good! . . .

"The band came up Emigration Canyon to meet us
and escorted us to the city. We went down on the old
High School Square and there our luggage was
dropped out and the handcarts taken away. We slept
on the ground that night. We were used to it. The next
day we carted what little bedding and luggage we had
into some woman's house and dumped them on the
floor. It was soon after our arrival, I remember that
Mr. Beesley heard a man playing on a tin whistle. He
said to me, 'If that man can play a tune on a tin
whistle, he can play a flute,' so he went and got
acquainted with him. I think he was later the leader of
the military band. . . (Mr. Beesley carried his
violin with him and we used to gather around the fire
at nights and sing and listen to the music.)

"There is one woman who, whenever I meet her
always says, 'Now, lassie, do your share.' She was in
our company and they put her to pull on a handcart
with an old man. Very often he would say to her,
'Lassie, now do your share,' and she has never forgotten
it." [29]

---

[29] In Carter, *Heart Throbs,* VI, p. 380.

The Last of the Handcarts
1860

As another season of emigration approached, the European Saints and their leaders busied themselves with preparations for "going home." Asa Calkin, Mormon head of the British missionary work and emigration, wrote in the *Millennal Star* of January 14, 1860, giving probable costs of transportation and supplies. He concluded: "We wish every one who can raise enough to go by handcart not to remain another season with the view of going out some other time with a wagon, but, trusting in the Lord for strength according to their day, to fortify their souls, gird up their loins, and set their faces Zionward." [1]

In an editorial of the following week, he gave specific prices sent him by George Q. Cannon, in charge of emigration in America. Elder Cannon reported that for 1859 the net cost of the handcart emigration from Florence to Salt Lake City had been $22.30 per head. Railroad fare for adults from New York to Florence was $14.50, with $3.75 per hundred pounds for luggage in excess of the one hundred pounds allowed each passenger. He said the market prices fluctuated somewhat, and that they had risen on account of the great rush to the Pike's Peak gold mines. He had paid for oxen, $80 per yoke; for cows, $25; wagons, $96; tents,

---

[1] *Millennial Star,* XXII (1860), 25.

$12; flour, $4.25 per hundred pounds; bacon, 12½ cents per pound; sugar, 10 cents; rice 8 cents; coffee, 13 cents; and soap, 5 cents per pound.

The first of the emigrants, who planned to go to Utah by handcarts in 1860, sailed from Liverpool on the "Underwriter," March 30. On board were 594 Saints, all from the British Mission except 70 from Switzerland.[2] During the voyage there were four marriages and four deaths. The ship reached New York on May 1; and on May 3 the emigrants entrained for Florence.

The last of the Saints to journey by handcarts, sailed on May 11 in the "William Tapscott." It carried 730 Mormons, including 312 from Scandinavia, and 85 from Switzerland. Some planned to go through to Utah, others would remain a season in the States. Smallpox broke out among the Scandinavians soon after they came aboard. With this sickness, and with stormy weather, the voyage was not pleasant. There were ten deaths at sea, four births, and five marriages. Upon reaching New York Harbor, the passengers were vaccinated on June 16, were landed at Castle Gardens on June 20, and set out westward the next day. They arrived at Florence on July 1.[3]

---

[2] *Ibid.,* 234, 331.

[3] *Ibid.,* 331, 443, 459-60, 538. Asa Calkin, released from his labors in Britain, sailed on this ship as president of the company. The "Latter-Day Saints' Emigration Report," published in the *Millennial Star* of Oct. 6, 1860, gave this information on the 1860 emigration from England:

Ship	President of Company	Date of Sailing	P.E.F.	Teams	Hand-carts	States	Total
Underwriter	James D. Ross	Mar. 30	1	106	140	347	594
Wm. Tapscott	Asa Calkin	May 11	17	246	128	340	731

THE NINTH HANDCART COMPANY

Daniel Robinson, who was to lead the Ninth Handcart Company to Utah, had come to Florence from Pennsylvania. He had joined the Mormon Church in 1854, and in early May, 1860, he left his "cozy little home," "beautiful orchard and garden," and with his wife and children set out for Zion. In Pennsylvania, one of their children died. En route on the train to Florence, a second daughter, eight years old, was taken by death.

"As we were traveling under contract the train in which we were riding was not allowed to stop," Robinson relates, "so our little daughter was carried away by a negro porter and buried we know not where." After reaching Florence, their little Johnny, age three, also died,[4] during the two weeks wait for the handcarts to be readied. So it was indeed a sorrowing Captain who was chosen to lead the Handcart Train. But man must go on; the work of the day must be done.

The emigrants who sailed in the "Underwriter," and were to form the Ninth Handcart Company, had reached Florence on May 12. More than three weeks passed before all was completed for their westward journey. On June 5, writes Henry Harrison in his diary, the baggage was weighed out, allowing each person twenty pounds, including clothing and cooking utensils. Harrison's cart was four feet long, three feet wide, the wheels four feet high, and the bed nine inches deep. This vehicle, he was instructed, must be greased three times a week.[5] This was an improvement

---

[4] Daniel Robinson Account, in Carter, *Treasures of Pioneer History*, v, pp. 287-88.

[5] Diary of Henry J. Harrison, copied into the Journal History of August 27, 1860.

over the ungreased carts of some of the earlier companies.

Captain Robinson elaborates on their procedure and
outfits: "When we were called to team up, six teams
were put to lead, the carts were in the rear. The people
pushed the carts. The boxes and carts were painted
beautifully, and had bows over the top. These bows
were covered with heavy canvas. The tongues of the
carts had a crosspiece 2½ feet long fastened to the end.
Against this crosspiece two persons would lean their
weight, this they called pushing instead of pulling. It
was very common to see young girls between the ages
of 16 and 20 with a harness on their shoulders in the
shape of a halter, a small chain fastened to that, and
then fastened to the cart. There were some four or five
to a cart, some pushing, some pulling all day long
through the hot, dry sand, with hardly enough to eat
to keep life in their bodies." [6]

The company, as organized, comprised 233 persons,
with 43 handcarts, and 10 tents. Six wagons, with 38
oxen, accompanied the train.[7] At one o'clock, on June 1,
the caravan started, and traveled seven miles during
the afternoon. They reached Elkhorn River on the
eighth, Fremont on the ninth, and Columbus on the
fourteenth. They ferried Loup Fork on the sixteenth,
and arrived at the Mormon town of Genoa (102 miles
out from Florence) on the twenty-second. Here they
enjoyed an evening of music and dancing.

Wood River was crossed on June 23, buffalo were
encountered four days later, and a baby was born on

---

[6] Robinson, *op. cit.,* 288.
[7] Journal History, Aug. 27, 1860.

July 6. Here Harrison's diary in the "Journal History" ends.

"When we camped at night," says Captain Robinson, "the carts were placed in a circle leaving an open space of about ten feet. The circle was used as a corral for the oxen. The oxen were unyoked inside the circle and then driven perhaps one-half mile away to feed for the night. Here they were guarded until midnight by two of the men and then they were relieved by others. When morning came the oxen were brought in, each man yoking up his own oxen. As soon as breakfast was over we were lined up for another hot day. The carts were loaded with bedding and cooking utensils, and sometimes little children were put in the carts if their feet had gotten too tired to walk any farther. Most of the mothers were seen trudging along on the scorching ground barefooted, leading their barefooted little tots by the hand, pausing now and then, trying to do something to relieve the pain in their blistered feet. . . When we camped for the night we always had prayer and song. We seemed very happy, we were putting our trust in God and were not deceived, for our journey was a peaceful one. Several bands of Indians passed our camp but we were not molested. At one time our food failed to reach camp. I swam the Platte River and made arrangements for provisions to be sent.

"Arriving at the Sweetwater River we found the bottom of the river covered with fish. Everyone had all they could eat, which was a treat after having to eat salty bacon from the time we started until now. We had no meat of any kind, except the salty bacon, because we could not keep it, and we did not see any animals which we might kill. We had to cross the Green River on ferry boats, all except the oxen, who had to swim. We ran very low of provisions at this point and we became weak from hunger." [8]

Here the twenty-five hundred pounds of flour and five hundred pounds of bacon, sent out from the Valley, came to their timely assistance.[9]

"It was a dreadfully hard journey," said Hannah Lapish, when interviewed by the writer in 1919, "especially for me with a six months old baby and a child of 2½ years. My shoes wore out and I got some moccasins. We suffered from lack of food. When provisions were low I traded some of my jewelry at a trading post for 700 pounds of flour. I gave this to the commissary and it was dealt out to the hungry travelers; the last measure, half a pint per person, being distributed on the day we crossed Green River. Here a Church relief train arrived with provisions for us." (Mrs. Lapish later founded the Society of the Daughters of the Utah Handcart Pioneers.)

With the new supplies, the emigrants moved on in comparative comfort. On reaching the site of Henefer on the Weber River, the travelers eagerly accepted Brother Henefer's offer of free potatoes if they would dig them.[10] They still had some steep climbs to make, but additional help was ahead. A man living on top of Big Mountain sent seven yoke of oxen down to pull the carts to the top of the mountain.[11]

Arrival of the company in Salt Lake City, August 27, was reported by the *Deseret News:* "Captain

---

[8] Robinson, *op. cit.,* 289.

[9] *Millennial Star,* XXII, p. 636.

[10] Robinson, *op. cit.,* 289; and William Hemming's account in *ibid.,* 291.

[11] *Ibid.,* 291 (Hemming's account).

Daniel Robinson brought into the city on Monday afternoon the first of the season's handcart companies, in good order, and apparently in general good health.

"The company was composed chiefly of British Saints, with a few families from the Eastern States; in all, about two hundred and thirty souls. They had six wagons, thirty-nine handcarts, and ten tents." One child had died en route, and one ox had been lost. They had come along, continued the *News,* "as well as any company that ever crossed the Plains. Their appearance on entering the city was indeed, if anything, more favourable than that of any previous handcart company." [12]

On emerging from Emigration Canyon they were greeted in the usual fashion, by a large group of welcoming citizens, who escorted them to the camp ground opposite the Eighth Ward Schoolhouse. Here a feast was provided and Ballo's band played "Home Sweet Home."

It had taken eleven weeks to make the journey. The more leisurely gait, the absence of an extended period of hunger, and the presence of wagons sufficient to relieve the weary or sick, along with satisfactory weather conditions may account for the low mortality in Robinson's Handcart Company.

THE LAST HANDCART COMPANY (10th)

The Tenth, and what was to be the last, Handcart Company was organized at Florence in early July, 1860. Some of the party had sailed in the "Underwriter," and had reached Florence by train on May 12. There they were employed to help construct the handcarts. Others, who crossed the Atlantic in the "William

---

12 *Deseret News* of Aug. 29, 1860.

Tapscott," reached the frontier outfitting point on July 1. These latter had but a short wait, as carts and provisions were available on their arrival.

On July 6, the handcart company of English, Swiss, and Danish Saints set out from Florence. Oscar O. Stoddard, who had been on a mission to Michigan, was appointed – by George Q. Cannon – to serve as Captain of the company. Stoddard wrote:

"We went into camp with the carts on the evening of the 4th of July, 1860, and did not camp two nights on the same ground from that time till we did on the 8th Ward Square of Salt Lake City.

"It was three days before we fairly got all together, wagons, teams, and handcarts. There were 21 handcarts and seven wagons, with three yoke of oxen to each wagon." [13] The 124 persons of the company were organized in the usual fashion, by tents and under sub-captains. Elder Paul was chosen chaplain of the English emigrants, Elder Christian Christiansen of the Scandinavian and Swiss.

"Brother Cannon told them at the start," continues Stoddard, "if they would be humble and faithful, not one of them should die on the road to the Valley, which was literally fulfilled."

At Independence Rock, Stoddard learned that flour awaited them at the Three Crossings of Sweetwater. With the fourteen sacks picked up there, he raised the rations to one and one-half pounds per head per day. This was kept up until they reached their destination.

"We landed," concludes Stoddard, "on the Eighth

---

[13] Stoddard's account in Journal History, Aug. 27, 1860; and in *The Contributor*, XIV, p. 546. The other parts of Stoddard's account are devoted almost entirely to the incidents he reported as examples of healing and other instances of divine intervention.

Ward Square in Salt Lake City on the 24th day of September, 1860, having just dealt out one week's rations, and also meeting, on the square, persons under the direction of the Bishopric, with vegetables, molasses, provisions, etc., which were distributed among them as needed or required, so they were well received, and I must say, according to the best of my understanding and knowledge, that this, the last handcart company, came across the plains in as good condition as any one of them." [14]

Despite the success and comparative comfort of this trip, those who made it never looked upon the trek as a pleasure jaunt. My mother, Mary Ann Stucki Hafen, who as a Swiss child of six years, took the five million little steps that brought her over the one thousand miles of plains, deserts, and mountains, had deep recollections which she carried the remaining eighty-five years of her life:

"The train landed us at the point of outfit. Father was a carpenter, and they asked him to stop for a while and help make handcarts, as most of the people were too poor to buy teams.

"When we came to load up our belongings we found that we had more than we could take. Mother was forced to leave behind her feather bed, the bolt of linen, two large trunks full of clothes, and some other valuable things which we needed so badly later. Father could take only his most necessary tools. . .

"There were six to our cart. Father and mother pulled it; Rosie (two years old) and Christian (six months old) rode; John (nine) and I (six) walked.

---

[14] *Ibid.*

Sometimes, when it was down hill, they let me ride too.

"Father had bought a cow to take along, so we could have milk on the way. At first he tied her to the back of the cart, but she would sometimes hang back, so he thought he would make a harness and have her pull the cart while he led her. By this time mother's feet were so swollen that she could not wear shoes, but had to wrap her feet with cloth. Father thought that by having the cow pull the cart mother might ride. This worked well for some time.

"One day a group of Indians came riding up on horses. Their jingling trinkets, dragging poles and strange appearance frightened the cow and set her chasing off with the cart and children. We were afraid that the children might be killed, but the cow fell into a deep gully and the cart turned upside down. Although the children were under the trunk and bedding, they were unhurt, but after that father did not hitch the cow to the cart again. He let three Danish boys take her to hitch to their cart. Then the Danish boys, each in turn, would help father pull our cart.

"After about three weeks my mother's feet became better so she could wear her shoes again. She would get so discouraged and down-hearted; but father never lost courage. He would always cheer her up by telling her that we were going to Zion, that the Lord would take care of us, and that better times were coming.

"Even when it rained the company did not stop traveling. A cover on the handcart shielded the two younger children. The rest of us found it more comfortable moving than standing still in the drizzle. In fording streams the men often carried the children and weaker women across on their backs. The company stopped over on Sundays for rest, and meetings were held for spiritual comfort and guidance. At night, when the handcarts were drawn up in a circle and the fires were lighted, the camp looked quite happy. Singing, music, and speeches by the leaders cheered everyone. I remember that we stopped one night at an old Indian camp ground. There were many bright-colored beads in the ant hills.

"At times we met or were passed by the overland stage coach with its passengers and mail bags and drawn by four fine horses. When the Pony Express dashed past it seemed almost like the wind racing over the prairie.

"Our provisions began to get low. One day a herd of buffalo ran past and the men of our company shot two of them. Such a feast as we had when they were dressed. Each family was given a piece of meat to take along. My brother John, who pushed at the back of our cart, used to tell how hungry he was all the time and how tired he got from pushing. He said he felt that if he could just sit down for a few minutes he would feel so much better. But instead, father would ask if he couldn't push a little harder. Mother was nursing the baby and could not help much, especially when the food ran short and she grew weak. When rations were reduced father gave mother a part of his share of the food, so he was not so strong either.

"When we got that chunk of buffalo meat father put it in the handcart. My brother John remembered that it was the fore part of the week and that father said we would save it for Sunday dinner. John said, 'I was so very hungry and the meat smelled so good to me while pushing at the handcart that I could not resist. I had a little pocket knife and with it I cut off a piece or two each half day. Although I expected a severe whipping when father found it out, I cut off little pieces each day. I would chew them so long that they got white and perfectly tasteless. When father came to get the meat he asked me if I had been cutting off some of it. I said "Yes. I was so hungry I could not let it alone." Instead of giving me a scolding or whipping, father turned away and wiped tears from his eyes.' " [15]

"At last, when we reached the top of Emigration Canyon, overlooking Salt Lake, the whole company stopped to look down through the Valley. Some yelled and tossed their hats in the air. A shout of joy arose at the thought that our long trip was over, that we had at last reached Zion, the place of rest. We all gave thanks to God for helping us safely over the Plains and mountains to our destination.

"When we arrived in the city we were welcomed by the people who came out carrying baskets of fruit and other kinds of good things to eat. Even though we could not understand their language, they made us feel that we were among friends.

"We were invited home by a good family who kept us two or three days, until my parents were rested. Then we were given a little house near the river Jordan, three miles from town, and father was put to work on the public road. He was paid in produce, mostly flour and potatoes, from the Tithing Office." [16]

---

[15] *Family History Journal of John S. Stucki* (Salt Lake City, privately printed, 1932), 43-44.

[16] Mary Ann Hafen, *Recollections of a Handcart Pioneer of 1860* (Denver, privately printed, 1938), 21-27; and from interviews with her.

HANDCARTS SUPPLANTED

The year 1860 witnessed another experiment in transportation. By this time, livestock and produce had become rather plentiful in Utah. So it was planned and proposed that teams undertake the trip from Salt Lake Valley to the Missouri River and back in one season. If this could be done successfully, Utah outfits could be profitably employed, and the enormous expense involved in purchasing wagons and oxen for emigrants on the Missouri could be avoided.

Joseph W. Young, experienced frontiersman and freighter, was placed in charge of a freight train to test the project. With thirty wagons, each drawn by three or four yoke of oxen, and with six or seven mule-team wagons, the train set out from a camp east of Salt Lake City on April 30.[17] On the eastward journey, some supplies were left at depots en route, to be utilized on the return journey. Young and his freight train reached the Missouri River in good time, and in satisfactory condition; and they also made a successful return.

President Brigham Young observed, October 8: "For four years past we have not had much money pass through our hands. At times it seems as though all hell and earth are combined to keep money out of my hands."

Here now was a good opportunity to put their surplus stock to useful employment, and at the same time to help the emigrants. The feasibility of sending teams to the Missouri River and back in one season was demonstrated, and so it was found convenient and profitable to bring the emigrants along with their freight.

---

[17] *Deseret News,* May 2, 1860.

Also, however true it may be that some handcart companies got along better and made faster time than did the ox trains; and however expedient it was at a certain period, to urge emigration by this method; it is nevertheless true that it was a hard, almost inhuman journey, and when a better and easier way was procurable, it naturally was grasped.

Accordingly, Brigham Young was able to write to George Q. Cannon on May 2, 1861: "The four companies for Florence left on the 20th ult. There were upwards of 200 wagons and 4 yoke of oxen to each. They take some 150,000 pounds of flour to deposit at suitable points east of South Pass. We confidently anticipate that the assistance now forwarded will clear Florence of all Saints who may be there wishing to come through this season."

Thereafter this system was employed for the bringing of passengers and freight to Utah, until the coming of the railroad. Federal legislation for the building of a Pacific Railroad was enacted in 1862, and two years later was amended to encourage the project.

As the rail-head pushed westward from Omaha in the middle sixties, the length of ox-train transportation was shortened, until it was entirely displaced upon completion of the railroad to the Salt Lake Valley. Utah joined the rest of the nation in celebrating the driving of the golden spike at Promontory Point on May 10, 1869.

SUMMARY AND CONCLUSION

With the discontinuance of travel by handcarts, we may summarize the extent of their use and appraise the success of the project. In the accompanying table the principal facts and figures are presented.

HANDCART COMPANIES

Co. no.	Captain	Persons	Hand-carts	Wagons	Year	Left Iowa City	Left Florence	Arrived S.L.C.	Deaths enroute
1	Ellsworth	274	52	5	1856	June 9	July 20	Sep. 26	13
2	McArthur	221	48	4	"	" 11	" 24	"	7
3	Bunker	320	64	5	"	" 23	" 30	Oct. 2	less than 7
4	Willie	500	120	6	"	July 15	Aug. 17	Nov. 9	67
5	Martin	576	146	7	"	" 28	" 27	" 30	135-150
6	Evans	149	31	1	1857	May 22	June 20	Sep. 11, 12	(?)
7	Christiansen	330	68	3	"	June 13	July 7	" 13	6 (?)
8	Rowley	235	60	6	1859	—	June 9	Sep. 4	5 (?)
9	Robinson	233	43	6	1860	—	June 6	Aug. 27	1
10	Stoddard	124	21	7	"	—	July 6	Sep. 24	0
	Totals	2962	653	50					about 250

Thus we see that from 1856 to 1860, nearly 3000 emigrants traveled to Zion by handcarts. They employed 653 carts and 50 wagons. The eight companies that left the Missouri River in June or July came through successfully and without undue casualties. In fact, they out-traveled the usual ox teams and often complained of being slowed down by the accompanying wagons. Only the two late companies, caught in the unfortunate combination of a late start and an early winter, suffered terrible loss of life.

Most people, in looking at the handcart emigration, have seen only the tragic misfortune of those late companies of 1856. This was indeed a pitiful episode, one of the most pathetic chapters in the history of the West. But taken in its normal operation, with adequate preparations and proper scheduling, the handcart plan was an economical, effective, and rather beneficent institution.

It is generally conceded that Brigham Young and the other leaders who put forth and encouraged this method of emigration were actuated by a sincere desire to advance the temporal and spiritual welfare of these people.

The economy of handcart travel is undisputed. It enabled hundreds to emigrate who, in all probability, never could have come to America. Also, by this plan the limited resources of the Perpetual Emigration Fund were so spread as to afford assistance to many more emigrants than could have been helped with wagon trains.

A majority of those who traveled by handcart were factory workers or peasants whose economic opportunities were greatly enhanced by coming to the New World. Hard work and sacrifices were not unknown to them, and they did not hesitate to undertake a type of travel simply because it involved strenuous work and difficulties.

Without doubt, handcart travel was an exacting ordeal, for both the body and the spirit, as the personal records and reactions presented in this volume amply testify. But thought of comfort, with these devoted Saints, was not a primary objective.

Concern for material welfare alone could never have produced the handcart migrations. It took consecrated resolution, the sustaining conviction of a deeply religious faith. Spiritual resources buoyed these humble, faithful souls with a strength to endure summer heat and winter cold, fatigue and hunger, discouragement and despair.

Like Israel of old, these modern "Children of God" responded to a Prophet's voice. From their zeal for a new religion, they drew strength. From an abiding faith in God and his overruling care, and from a firm belief in the divinity of the command for Latter-day Saints to gather to Zion, they were enabled to gird up their loins and walk the long scourging trail.

Appendices

Appendix A

OFFICIAL JOURNAL OF
THE FIRST HANDCART COMPANY [1]

June 9th. At 5 p.m., the carts were in motion proceeding Zionwards. The Saints were in excellent spirits, bound Zionwards. The camp traveled about four miles and pitched their tents. All well.

June 10. We remained in camp all day, owing to three yoke of oxen having strayed from the herd. The brethren went out in search of them. The camp was engaged in various duties.

June 11. Early this morning the strayed cattle were brought back. About 8 a.m., the camp started forward and traveled five miles. Pitched tents. Brothers Robinson and Jones' carts broke down.

June 12th. The camp started this morning at 6 a.m. Traveled twelve miles. The road was very dusty. Pitched tents about 2 p.m. All in good spirits.

June 13th. The camp started about 8 a.m. Traveled seven miles. Good roads. All went off well. Visited by a good (many) strangers.

June 14th. The camp started this morning at 6 a.m. In good spirits. Traveled seven miles. Pitched tents about 9 a.m. The roads good. The camp in good spirits. Towards evening Elder James

---

[1] Printed in the *Utah Genealogical and Historical Magazine,* XVII, pp. 247-49; XVIII, pp. 17-21, 49-56. The company left Iowa City on June 9 and arrived in Salt Lake City, September 26, 1856.

Thirty-three persons dropped out en route — seven men, heads of families, and the remainder, women and children (*ibid.,* XVII, p. 249). Those who died en route, with ages and dates of death, were as follows (data from this Journal and the Archer Walters diary): William Lee (12), June 14; Lora Pratter (3), June 15; Job Welling (1½), June 17; James Bowers (44), June 21; Sidney Shinn, June 24; Emma Shinn (2), June 26; Henry Walker (50), killed by lightning, July 26; Peter Stalley, August 17; Robert Stoddard (51), August 31; Walter Sanders (65), September 2; George Neappris (24), September 7; Mary Mayo (65), September 13; James Birch (28), September 17.

Ferguson came to us from the General Camp. About 6 p.m. William Lee, son of John Lee, died of comsumption, age 12 years.

June 15th.   Today is Sunday. The Saints remained in camp and held two meetings. The morning meeting commenced at half past ten. Singing. A prayer by Elder Heaton. Elder Joseph France addressed the meeting. Afternoon meeting commenced at half past one o'clock. Singing, and prayer by Elder Leonard. Elder Edward Frost addressed the meeting. A great many strangers attended the meetings. Good attention by all present. At nine o'clock this morning Lora Pratter, daughter of Richard Pratter, died of whooping cough, age 3 years. At half past seven the sacrament was administered to the two companies. It was a time of rejoicing to all. Elder Ferguson addressed the Saints. About 9 p.m. the above two children were interred at Little Bear Creek.

June 16th.   At half past six a.m. the camp moved off in good spirits. Traveled thirteen miles and rested from half past eleven a.m. till four p.m. at Big Bear Creek. The camp moved off two miles and camped for the night. About nine we had a storm of rain.

June 17th.   At four a.m. the bugle was blown for all to turn out, and at quarter to seven the camp moved off. Traveled ten miles and rested two hours. At twenty past two we pitched our tents. The journey was performed without any accident. No wood, plenty of water. About twenty minutes past three Job Welling, son of Job Welling, died, age one year and seven months. Died of canker or inflammation of the bowels.

June 18th.   At four a.m. the bugle sounded for all to turn out. At twenty minutes past five the camp rolled out; and traveled ten miles without any accident. Pitched tents at thirty-five past eight a.m., to give the Sisters an opportunity of washing the clothes. Today the body of Job Welling was interred three feet from the Northeast corner of Mr. Watrous' Farm, Township 80, Range 17, Section 25.

June 19th.   The camp rolled out today at quarter to seven a.m. and traveled fifteen miles. The journey was accomplished without any accident. We camped at ten minutes to twelve p.m. Plenty of wood and water. Several were baptized by Elder John Oakley for their health. Three miles from Greenhustle.

June 20th.   The camp moved off at quarter to seven a.m. Traveled sixteen miles. The road was very hilly and rather rough. It was rather a hard day's travel. About a quarter to eight this morning John Lloyd, wife and family, backed out. He was very much given to drinking whiskey along the road. We passed through the city of Newton this morning about 9 a.m. We rested by a stream from ten to twelve. Pitched our tents at 4 p.m. alongside a beautiful stream of water. Plenty of wood. Several were baptized for their health by Elder Oakley.

June 21st. At ten minutes to seven the camp moved off and traveled thirteen miles. Rested thirty minutes by the side of a stream; and an hour on the top of a hill. No accident happened to the camp. All was well. At ten minutes to one p.m. we pitched our tents in a grove. Plenty of wood and water. At a quarter to five p.m. James Bowers died of quick consumption. Age 44, 24th of January, 1856.

June 22nd. Brother James Bowers was buried near to two other graves a quarter of a mile east of the main line of Fort Des Moines, Section 76, Township 29, Range 72. The camp was called together for meeting at twenty minutes past four p.m. Singing. Prayer by Elder Leonard. The meeting was addressed by Elders Heaton, McArthur, and Ellsworth. Much good instruction was given.

June 23rd. The camp moved out at twenty-five past seven a.m. Traveled ten miles. Pitched tents by 10 a.m. The roads were rather rough in some parts and a little hilly and somewhat dusty. We passed two middling good streams of water, a good camping ground, plenty of wood and water, four miles from Fort Des Moines. Passed a small town this morning seven miles from the Fort.

June 24th. The camp rolled out at thirty past six a.m. Traveled eleven miles. The roads were a little rough and somewhat dusty. The day was exceedingly warm, through which it was rather hard for the handcart boys. Pitched tents at thirty past one p.m. Plenty of wood, water, about a half a mile from the camp on the left side of the road. An old mobocrat came and tried to make a fuss with our captain. Sidney Shinn, son of James and Mary Shinn Jr., died this morning. Buried thirty yards south of the bridge on Four Mile Creek, on the east bank, under an elm tree.

June 25th. The camp rolled out this morning at twenty-five past six a.m. Traveled nineteen miles. A gentle breeze blew all the way; it was quite refreshing. The roads good; supplied water at six miles, and at nine. Pitched tents at forty-five past one p.m. alongside of a river bank. Plenty of wood.

June 26th. The camp moved off this morning at thirty past six a.m. Traveled ten miles. Forded the River Racoon about one mile from the camping ground. Passed the town of Balley. At 12 p.m. we again forded the Racoon and camped on the west bank. Plenty of wood and water; the road good with the exception of two or three hills. Emma Shinn, daughter of Robert and Eliza Shinn, died this morning of whooping cough, age two years and eight months.

June 27th. Emma Shinn was buried this morning twelve feet southeast of a walnut tree on the west bank of the Racoon, nearly opposite the sawmill. At seven a.m. the camp rolled out and traveled ten miles. Good roads. Camped at thirty past ten a.m. in a beautiful valley alongside of a good stream. On the right side of the road on the west bank of the stream there is a beautiful spring of water.

June 28th. The camp moved off at forty past five and traveled sixteen miles. The road was good with the exception of some parts of it being rather hilly. The water rather scarce for about thirteen miles. We got supplied with water at Bear Station. Pitched tents at 1 p.m. Pretty good camping ground; plenty of water; wood rather scarce. We had a heavy thunder storm about six p.m. One of the tents was blown down and another rent from top to bottom.

June 29th. We remained in camp all day and rested our bodies. The day was fine. Several strangers were in the camp. At twenty past four p.m. the Saints met together for meeting, singing, and prayer by Elder Crandall. The meeting was addressed by Elders Hargreave, Ellsworth, McArthur, Leonard, and Crandall on a variety of subjects for the benefit of the Saints.

June 30th. The camp moved out at fifty-five past 6 a.m. Traveled sixteen miles. We traveled twelve miles without resting. The roads were but middling; part of the way somewhat hilly. No water for twelve miles. Pitched tents at ten past one p.m. All in good spirits. Plenty of wood and water.

July 1st. The camp moved out at ten past seven a.m. and traveled fifteen miles. The road was rather rough. Passed one creek of water. Camped on the side of the creek. Plenty of water. Wood plentiful; about a half a mile from the camp. About half past ten p.m. we had a severe thunder storm. One tent was blown down and another rent.

July 2nd. We remained in camp untill fifty past three p.m. owing to Brother McArthur's company having lost a boy by the way. At the above hour we started and traveled ten miles. Rested about half an hour on the bank of the river Nishnabotna. Camped two and one half miles west northwest of Indian town on the banks of a river. Plenty of wood. A most delightful camping ground.

July 3rd. The camp moved out at forty-five past nine a.m. and traveled fourteen miles. Rested at the side of a creek six miles from where we started. Very little water as we came along. After traveling twelve miles, we turned down a road to the right two miles and camped by the side of a creek with plenty of water. Little wood. About twenty of the camp lost their road, but returned about midnight.

July 4th. The camp moved out at ten past seven a.m. and (traveled) twenty miles. We passed two creeks the first ten miles, the other ten, no water. The roads good. Camped at fifteen past three p.m. alongside of a good creek of water. Plenty of wood. Fourteen miles from Council Bluffs. All in good spirits.

July 5th. The company remained in camp today to rest and get their clothes washed.

July 6th. Today is Sunday. We remained in camp. Had meeting at twenty past four p.m. Singing, and prayer by Brother Crandall. The meeting was addressed by Elders Galloway, Oakley, Ellsworth, and McArthur. A good many strangers present. Some were attentive, others could not bear the doctrine and walked off grumbling.

July 7th. The camp rolled out at 7 a.m. Traveled fifteen miles. The roads were very hilly. Rested thirty minutes alongside of a good creek. For about eight miles there was little or no water. Passed a few houses about two miles from the camping ground where a good many old Mormons were staying. Pitched tents about five p.m.

July 8th. The camp moved out at 7 a.m. and traveled sixteen miles over a very rough road up and down hills. One handcart broke down by the way. The camp rested at Pigeon Creek for two and a half hours. Cooked dinners and got nicely rested. Crossed the Missouri by the steam ferry-boat a little below Florence. Got to the camping ground at Florence at fifty past four p.m.

July 9th to 12th. We were busy engaged repairing the handcarts. On the 10th, Sister Isabella Stevenson backed out with an old apostate.

July 13th. The saints met in meeting at four p.m. The saints were addressed by Elders McGraw, Ellsworth, and McArthur.

July 14th to 16th. Engaged getting our outfit for the plains.

July 17th. The camp rolled out at eleven a.m. Traveled two and one-half miles to Summer Quarters.

July 18th and 19th. We remained in camp till Saturday, finishing the carts and getting the balance of our outfit.

July 20th. The camp rolled out at 6 p.m. and traveled seven miles. Pitched tents half past nine.

July 21st. The camp rolled out at nine a.m. and traveled eighteen miles. Crossed the Elkhorn by the Ferry Boat and camped about 5 p.m. Before all the tents were pitched, we had quite a thunder storm, and continued more or less all the night.

July 22nd. The (camp) rolled out at twelve p.m. and traveled seventeen miles along a good road. Passed five dead oxen. Camped at half past seven p.m. at Liberty Pole camping ground close to the Platte River.

July 23rd. The (camp) rolled out at half past seven a.m. and traveled fourteen and one half (miles). Camped at Loop Fork at four p.m. An excellent camping place. Good feed for cattle. The roads were rather heavy and the day very warm. Water scarce.

July 24th. The camp rolled out at half past seven a.m. Traveled nine miles. The roads pretty good. Camped at twelve p.m. at Shell Creek.

July 25th. The camp rolled out at seven a.m. and traveled nineteen miles. The (roads) were pretty good with the exception of about five miles. Rather sandy. Camped at six p.m. two miles from Loop Ferry Fork.

July 26th. At nine a.m. the camp rolled towards the ferry, where (we) were detained five hours in crossing. At half past five p.m. the camp again moved on about three miles, where we were overtaken by a most terrific storm of thunder and rain. In the open prairie without tents. Two brothers and two sisters were knocked down by lightning. Brother Henry Walker from Carlisle was killed. Age fifty-eight. He was a faithful man to his duty. We again moved on for one and one quarter miles and camped for the night. Traveled six miles.

July 27th. Brother H. Walker was buried this morning four miles west of Loop Fork Ferry on sandy rise, right hand side of the road. At 12 p.m. the camp rolled out and traveled two and a half miles to a better camping ground, where we remained for the rest of the day. A beef was killed at night for the camp. About eight p.m. a meeting was called. Brothers Oakley, France, and Ellsworth addressed the meeting.

July 28th. At fifteen past seven a.m. the camp rolled out and traveled twenty miles. The roads in many parts were heavy. We rested two hours and had dinner. We turned up to the right about half a mile and camped for the night at half past six p.m.

July 29th. At nine a.m. camp rolled out and ascended a bluff to the right of the camping ground. Traveled fifteen miles. The roads in some parts a little sandy. Camped at quarter to three p.m. about four miles from the upper crossing. Plenty of wood and water. Two good springs on the west side of the camp ground. One of them dug out by Brother Card.

July 30th. The camp rolled out at seven and traveled twenty-five miles. A great part of the road very sandy and heavy for hand-carts and wagons. No wood, no water till we camped, and that not very plentiful. Still plenty for camping purposes. Camped at fifteen past six p.m.

July 31st. The camp rolled out at seven a.m. and traveled eighteen miles. The road leading from the camp is a very heavy sandy road and continues so for about thirteen miles. It is also very hilly. Camped about fifteen minutes past six p.m. alongside of Prairie Creek. No wood, but plenty of buffalo chips. There is a well about seven miles from where we camped last night on the right hand side of the road.

August 1st. The camp rolled out at eight a.m. Traveled sixteen miles. The road (is) in good condition. Crossed Prairie Creek twice. The second crossing, the hand (carts) had to be carried over by the brethren. There was a little difficulty in getting the wagons over, the banks of the creek were so steep. We also crossed Wood River by the means of a good bridge. We came very close to a herd of buffalo. Brother Ellsworth went out with his rifle. Wounded two but not sufficient for him to get them. At thirty past six p.m. we camped alongside of Wood River. Plenty of wood and water. A good camping ground.

August 3rd. We remained in camp all day and attended to such duties as we were necessitated to do. Meeting at seven p.m. Brothers Oakley, Butler, and Ellsworth addressed the Saints.

August 4th. At a quarter to eight a.m. the camp rolled out and (traveled) eighteen miles. Good roads. Camped at quarter to three p.m. near to the Platte.

August 5th. At eight a.m. the camp rolled out and traveled sixteen miles. The road pretty good with the exception of one or two places. Camped about four p.m. Wood a plenty. Water rather scarce, still plenty for camping purposes.

August 6th. At nine a.m. the camp rolled out and traveled twelve (miles). Roads good. Camped about two p.m. on Buffalo Creek four miles from the crossing of B. Creek. We killed four buffaloes today. The camp got quite a good supply of meat.

August 7th. At fifteen to nine a.m. the camp rolled out, and (traveled) twenty-five miles. The roads good, with the exception of about two miles which is rather sandy. There is no water after leaving the crossing. Camped at about thirty past eight p.m. No water but by digging for it. No wood. Plenty of chips.

August 8th. At fifteen to nine a.m. the camp rolled out from this place of desolation and traveled thirteen miles without water. The roads good. Camped about thirty past two alongside the Platte. By turning off to the left about one half mile you will find a good camping ground but no wood. There is another camping ground about two miles ahead. By some means Father Sanders got left behind. The brethren have been out on foot and horse. As yet they have not succeeded in finding him.

August 9th. The camp rolled out at ten past one p.m. and traveled thirteen miles. Brother Thomas Fowler found Father Sanders this morning about five miles ahead of the camp. The road for about seven miles is very heavy sandy road; hard pulling for handcarts and ox teams. Camped beside the Platte about two miles from Skunk Creek about fifteen eight p.m.

August 10th. About 9 a.m. the camp was called together for meeting. Elders Ellsworth, France, and Oakley addressed the Saints. A good meeting. The camp rolled out at ten past eleven a.m. Traveled fourteen miles. For two or three miles the (road) is sandy and bluffy, but they can be greatly avoided by winding them. Camped at Cold Springs camping ground about six p.m. A most excellent place for a camp.

August 11th. The camp rolled out at fifty past seven a.m. and traveled seventeen miles. The roads were pretty good with the exception of some that are rather sandy, but that can be avoided by turning off a little either to the right or left. Plenty of water every three or four miles. One of our milk cows died near the camping ground. We crossed over a small creek and camped close to the Platte opposite to two or three small islands, where there is wood, but rather difficult to get at. We had two buffaloes brought into camp tonight killed by the brethren appointed for that purpose. We camped at four p.m. All well.

August 12th. We remained at rest today to cut up buffalo to dry for the journey; and repair the handcarts.

August 13th. The camp rolled at thirty past nine a.m. and traveled twelve (miles). The roads were rather heavy owing to last night's rain. Camped about five p.m. alongside of Bluff Fork. We forded the river previous to camping.

August 14th. The camp rolled at ten past eight a.m. and traveled eighteen miles. The first twelve miles was nearly all over heavy sandy bluffs. Right from the camp it made heavy pulling. The last six miles the road was pretty good. One of the covered handcarts broke down. Camped about seven a.m. alongside the Platte.

August 15th. The (camp) rolled out at one quarter to eight a.m. traveled fourteen miles. For the first six miles the sand was fully as bad, if not worse, than yesterday. We crossed four creeks, took dinner at Goose Creek. For the next eight miles the road was good. We forded Rattle Snake and camped about a half a mile from the old Rattle Snake camping ground. Camped about one quarter past six p.m.

August 16th. The camp moved off at a quarter to eight a.m. and traveled sixteen and three quarter miles. A good part of it heavy sandy traveling. Other parts of the road was good traveling. We crossed small creeks, had dinner on the banks of Camp Creek. Camp about seven p.m. on the east bank of Wolf Creek. Buffalo chips not so plentiful here. Good feed for the oxen.

August 17th. The camp moved out at a quarter to nine a.m. and traveled twelve miles. We crossed over Wolf Creek and ascended the Sandy Bluff. We crossed the bluff to the left instead of going up the old track. It is easier for handcarts and for ox teams. The road today was very sandy for several miles. Passed over several creeks. Camped at four p.m. on the side of the Platte opposite to

Ash Grove. Brother Peter Stalley died today. He was from Italy.

August 18th. The camp rolled out twenty past seven a.m. and traveled nineteen miles. The road was very good today. Forded Hustle Creek. Passed no other creek during the day. Had dinner alongside of a slough. Passed over a sand ridge. Two dry sloughs on the left hand side of the road about four miles from the Platte. Camped at twenty to seven p.m. on the side of the Platte.

August 19th. The camp rolled out at a quarter to eight a.m. and traveled twenty miles. The road today in parts was very sandy. Especially crossing the cobble hills it was very sandy. We crossed Crab Creek today. Camped about thirty past (?) p.m. on the Platte opposite ancient Bluff ruins.

August 20th. The camp rolled out at thirty past seven a.m. and traveled twenty miles. The road was tolerably good till we came to the last five miles, when it became very sandy in some parts, especially in crossing over sand bluffs. Camped on the side of the Platte forty-five past six p.m.

August 21st. The camp rolled out at thirty past seven a.m. and traveled sixteen and one half miles. The road today was tolerable good. No water for fourteen and one half miles. Camped on the Platte two miles beyond Chimney Rock at four p.m. Buffalo chips rather scarce.

August 22nd. The camp rolled out at twenty past seven a.m. and traveled twenty-one miles. The road today was good. We were detained three hours on the road by a thunder storm. Twelve miles without water. Camped about thirty past seven p.m. on the Platte about half a mile from Spring Creek. Buffalo chips and wood scarce. Poor feed for cattle.

August 23rd. The camp rolled out at five past eight a.m. and traveled fifteen and a half miles before we struck the Platte, where we camped. Wood plentiful on the south side by fording for it. The river from two to three feet deep. About six miles of the road was rather sandy. Camped about two p.m. on the side of the Platte near ————. Killed a buffalo tonight.

August 24th. The camp did not travel any today. We were busy with the hand carts. At six p.m. we had a Sacramental and Saints' meeting. A good time of it.

August 25th. At half past seven a.m. the camp rolled out and traveled nineteen miles. For six or seven miles the road was rather sandy. At a quarter to five p.m. we camped not far from the Platte. Good feed. Plenty of wood.

August 26th. The camp rolled out twenty past seven a.m. and traveled seventeen miles. For about fourteen miles the road was very sandy. Heavy drawing. Forded the Platte opposite to Laramie. Camped at thirty-five past five p.m. on the side of the Platte four miles from Laramie. Good feed, plenty of wood.

August 27th. The camp rolled out at quarter past seven a.m. and traveled twenty-one miles. The roads good with the exception of about four miles, rather rough and rocky. At a quarter to five p.m. we camped at Bitter Cottonwood. Wood and water plenty. Feed scarce.

August 28th. The camp rolled out this morning at thirty past eight a.m. and traveled fifteen miles. Eight miles from Bitter Cottonwood Creek to the Platte, three from that to a good spring, and pretty good feed on the right side of the road. Four from that to the Horseshoe Creek. Good feed and plenty of wood and water. Camped about thirty past four p.m.

August 29th. The camp rolled out at fifteen past seven a.m. and traveled twenty-five miles. The road was pretty good. Sixteen miles to the Platte where we took dinner. Traveled two miles and forded the Platte. Camped about thirty past six p.m. on the Platte. Plenty of wood; feed pretty fair.

August 30th. The camp rolled out at twenty-five past seven a.m. and traveled nineteen miles. The road pretty fair. Forded the Platte again. Traveled about six miles and camped by the side of a creek. Plenty of wood, water, and feed. We passed two emigrants from California. By them we were informed that five wagons were waiting on us at Deer Creek. Camped at about thirty past six p.m.

August 31st. The camp rolled out at quarter to seven a.m. and traveled twenty-four miles. The roads were very good. Camped at Deer Creek about thirty past five p.m. Found the wagons waiting on us. A most excellent camping ground. Plenty of wood, water, and feed for the cattle. Robert Stoddard died of consumption, age 51. Buried about four hundred yards from the left hand side of the road.

September 1st. We remained at Deer Creek today to rest ourselves and the cattle. Busy repairing the hand carts. Killed a cow.

Had a good meeting at night. Addressed by Brother Ellsworth and the brethren from the Valley. We spent a first rate day of it.

September 2nd. The camp rolled out at a quarter to seven a.m. and traveled twenty miles. The road tolerable good, but very dusty owing to a heavy wind. Camped beside the Platte. Plenty of wood. Feed scarce. Crossed a creek eleven miles from where we started. Walter Sanders (died) last night. Buried this morning about three hundred yards from the south side of the road. Age sixty-five.

September 3rd. The camp rolled this morning at thirty past eight a.m. and traveled eleven miles. It was very heavy pulling owing to the dust and a heavy wind. Crossed the Platte a mile and a half below the upper crossings. A good place to ford. Camped beside of the Platte at thirty past four p.m. Plenty of wood. Feed middling.

September 4th. The camp rolled out this morning and traveled twenty-six miles. The roads were very good for traveling. Had dinner by the side of Mineral Spring Creek. Camped at Little Stream Creek at thirty past five p.m. About a half an hour after getting into camp it got very cold and rained for several hours so that we could not light a fire.

September 5th. We remained in camp today owing to the inclement state of the weather. It rained and snowed alternately for the whole of the day (so) that we could not cook hardly anything.

September 6th. About four a.m. this morning the weather became more settled, but we found to our sorrow that twenty-four head of our cattle were missing, owing to the negligence of Robert Shinn and James Shinn Jr., who were on guard. We had to remain in camp again today as the cattle were not found till about three p.m.

September 7th. The camp rolled out this morning at thirty past seven a.m. and traveled twenty-two miles. The road was good for the first fourteen miles. Camped to have dinner beside a most beautiful creek of water. For the next eight miles the road is very sandy and heavy. Camped at thirty past six p.m. by the side of Sweetwater, two miles from the crossing. A good camping ground. Good feed for the cattle. George Neappris died this evening. Age 24. Emigrated from Cardiff in Dan Jones' company.

September 8th. This morning George Neappris was buried on a sand ridge directly east of three rocky mounds. Two and a half miles from the crossing on the bend on the north side of the river. The camp rolled out at forty past nine a.m. and traveled fourteen miles. Crossed Sweetwater by a good bridge. The roads were in many parts rather rough. Had dinner beside an old trading post close by the Devil's Gate. Camped beside Sweetwater at thirty past five p.m. not far from a company of apostates.

September 9th. The camp rolled at thirty past seven a.m. and traveled sixteen miles. The roads continued rather rough with a heavy headwind. Camped at five p.m. beside Sweetwater. An excellent camping ground. Killed a cow.

September 10th. The camp rolled out at forty past seven a.m. and traveled eighteen miles. The roads tolerable good to Sweetwater crossing. After that it was sandy for seven miles. Camped at six p.m. on Sweetwater. A very indifferent camping ground. Poor feed.

September 11th. The camp rolled out at forty past seven a.m. and traveled nineteen miles. The first part of the journey the roads pretty good. No water for twelve miles. You will then come to a good stream of water and good feed. Take the left hand road. Traveled eight miles to a creek. A poor camping ground. Middling feed. Camped at six p.m. About 11 p.m. Brother McArthur's company came up. They had traveled nearly night and day to overtake us.

September 12th. The camp rolled out at forty-five past seven a.m. and traveled twelve miles. The greatest part of the road very hilly and rough. A good spring of water about six miles from where we started this morning. Camped at forty-five past one p.m. Good camping ground. Feed pretty fair. Plenty of good spring water, about two hundred yards from the road, right side.

September 13th. The camp rolled out at forty past seven a.m. and traveled twenty-eight miles. The (road) was very good. We took the cut-off six miles from where we started. There is (a) good creek of water and plenty good feed about two hundred yards from where the road crosses the creek. Nine miles farther on there is another good creek and feed. It is not far from the head of Sweetwater. Camped at nine p.m. at the Pacific Springs. Here we came up with the main body of Captain Bank's company. They had ten days clear start of us from Florence. Mary Mayo died of Diarrhea. Age 65. Buried close to the big mountain left hand side of the road.

September 14th. The camp rolled out at nine a.m. and traveled three miles where there was plenty of feed for the cattle.

September 15th. The camp rolled out at seven a.m. and traveled twenty-six miles. A creek of water twelve miles from where we started. Also feed. Here we rested two hours. Sixten miles we camped at Little Sandy. We got plenty of water by digging for it. Plenty of wood and pretty good feed. Camped at nine p.m. Very good roads.

September 16th. The camp rolled out at thirty past eight a.m. and traveled twenty-three miles. Good roads. Crossed a splendid creek of water five miles from Little Sandy. Camped on the banks of Big Sandy at seven p.m. Plenty of wood on the opposite side of the river. Poor feed for cattle.

September 17th. James Birch, age 28 died this morning of diarrhea. Buried on the top of sand ridge east side of Sandy. The camp rolled at eight and traveled eleven miles. Rested four hours by the side of Green River. Forded the river about four p.m. and camped about six p.m. Good feed and camping ground.

September 18th. At eight a.m. the camp rolled out and traveled twenty-two (miles). Good roads. Camped on Ham's Fork at seven p.m. Good feed for cattle; and wood.

September 19th. The camp rolled at thirty past nine a.m., and traveled twenty-three miles. The roads good. A poor place for feed. Camped at nine p.m.

September 20th. The camp rolled out at forty-five past six a.m. and traveled nine miles to Bridger. The road rather rough and rocky. Camped at Bridger for the day. At fifteen past ten a.m. Killed a first rate fat ox. Shod several of the oxen.

September 21st. At seven a.m. the camp rolled and traveled twenty-two miles. The roads were good. Crossed several creeks. Passed a sulphur and soda spring. Camped at six p.m. Plenty of wood and feed, but no water.

September 22nd. The camp rolled out at thirty past five a.m. and traveled twenty-three miles. Had breakfast six miles from where we started. About three p.m. met with Brigham's and Heber's sons. They were glad to see us. About half past five we were taken in a thunder storm and traveled an hour and a half in it. Camped at six p.m. Plenty of water and feed. Wood rather scarce. The wagons with the tents did not arrive till twelve midnight. We were cold and wet. Still we felt alright.

September 23rd. The camp rolled out at 12 p.m. and traveled eighteen miles. The roads were pretty good. We forded the Weber about one p.m. and had dinner on the Weber banks. Camped about thirty past six p.m. Wood, water, feed plenty. We were visited by a few Indians.

September 24th. The camp rolled out at seven a.m. and traveled twenty miles. The roads were rather rough and rugged. Camped about thirty past six p.m. Wood, water, feed plenty.

September 25th. The camp rolled out at seven a.m. and traveled twenty miles. Crossed canyon eleven times. The roads a little rough. Had dinner at the bottom of the Big Mountain. Crossed the Big Mountain in two hours and fifty-five minutes. Camped at the foot of the Little Mountain at six p.m.

September 26th. The brethren from the city sent us a wagon with provisions as we were rather short. At thirty past ten a.m. the camp rolled and traveled thirteen miles. About eight miles from the city we were met with Governor Young and his counselors. The Nauvoo brass band, the Lancers, and a great many others. We were first rate received in the city. Provisions of all kinds came rolling in to us in camp. The brethren of the city manifested great interest towards us as a company, which caused our hearts to rejoice and be glad.

EDMUND ELLSWORTH, *Captain*
A. GALLOWAY, *Secretary.*

Appendix B

CAPTAIN McARTHUR'S REPORT
ON THE SECOND HANDCART COMPANY [1]

On the 19th of May, 1856, our company, which had crossed the sea with us, were divided, by President Daniel Spencer, into two handcart companies, Brother Edmond Ellsworth to take charge of the first and I, Daniel D. McArthur, to take charge of the second company. Then every move was made to get our carts ready, which job was a tedious one, but by using all our efforts, the first company was enabled to start on the 9th of June, and the second on the 11th, about 11 o'clock. This second company numbered 222 souls, and were bound for Florence, and from thence to the Valley, at which place (Florence) we arrived on the 8th day of July, distance, 300 miles, or there abouts. We had the very best of good luck all the way, although the weather was very hot and sweltering, but let me tell you, the saints were not to be overcome. Our carts, when we started, were in an awful fix. They moaned and growled, screeched and squealed, so that a person could hear them for miles. You may think this is stretching things a little too much, but it is a fact, and we had them to eternally patch, mornings, noons and nights. But by our industry we got them all along to Florence, and being obliged to stop at Florence some two weeks to get our outfit for the plains, I and my council, namely, Truman Leonard and Spencer Crandall, went to work and gave our carts a thorough repair throughout, and on the 24th of July, at 12 o'clock, we struck our tents and started for the plains, all in the best of spirits. Nothing but the very best of luck attended us continually. Our train con-

---

[1] This report was made by Captain McArthur to Wilford Woodruff on January 5, 1857, and is taken from the L.D.S. Journal History, under date of Sept. 26, 1856. In it we note that seven persons died en route, and one disappeared.

sisted of 12 yoke of oxen, 4 wagons, and 48 carts; we also had 5 beef and 12 cows; flour, 55 lbs. per head, 100 lbs. rice, 550 lbs. sugar, 400 lbs. dried apples, 125 lbs. tea, and 200 lbs. salt for the company. On the 28th of August, we arrived at Laramie, and on the 2nd of September we met the first provision wagons from the Valley. On Deer Creek we got 1000 lbs. of flour, which caused the hearts of the saints to be cheered up greatly. On the 14th we camped at Pacific Spring Creek, and there I took in 1000 lbs. of more flour, so as to be sure to have enough to do me until we got into the Valley, for I was told that that would be the last opportunity to get it. On the 20th we reached Fort Bridger, and on the 26th of September, we arrived in this Valley, with only the loss of 8 souls. 7 died, and one, a young man, age 20 years, we never could tell what did become of him. We brought in our 48 carts, 4 wagons, 12 yokes of oxen, save one, which we had left at Fort Bridger, 10 cows, (one cow died and one we left at Fort Bridger,) and the 5 beeves, we ate, of course. We laid still 5 Sundays and three week days all day, besides other short stops while traveling from the Missouri River here.

My company was divided into two divisions and Brother Truman Leonard was appointed captain over the first division and Brother Spencer Crandall over the second. We had six tents in each division and a president over each tent, who were strict in seeing that singing and prayer was attended to every morning and night, and that peace prevailed. I must say that a better set of saints to labor with I never saw. They all did the best they could to forward our journey. When we came to a stream, no matter how large it might be, the men would roll up their trousers and into it they would go, and the sisters would follow, if the men were smart enough to get ahead of them, which the men failed many times to do. If the water was high enough to wet the things on the carts, the men would get one before the cart and one behind it and lift it up slick and clean, and carry it across the stream.

I will state a couple of incidents that happened in one day, and one other circumstance that took place. On the 11th of August a man came to camp pretending to be starved nearly to death, and wished me to give him some provisions, for he had had nothing for many days but what he had hunted for. So I gave him bread and

meat enough to last him some four or five days and he acted as
though he had met with some friends indeed. He said, that he had
been robbed by some Californians somewhere near Fort Bridger,
with whom he was in company on their way to the States, and on
the 16th, while crossing over some sand hills, Sister Mary Bathgate
was badly bitten by a large rattlesnake, just above the ankle, on the
back part of her leg. She was about a half a mile ahead of the camp
at the time it happened, as she was the ring leader of the footmen
or those who did not pull the handcarts. She was generally accompanied by Sister Isabella Park. They were both old women, over 60
years of age, and neither of them had ridden one inch, since they
had left Iowa camp ground. Sister Bathgate sent a little girl back
to me as quickly as possible to have me and Brothers Leonard and
Crandall come with all haste, and bring the oil with us, for she
was bitten badly. As soon as we heard the news, we left all things,
and, with the oil, we went post haste. When we got to her she was
quite sick, but said that there was power in the Priesthood, and she
knew it. So we took a pocket knife and cut the wound larger,
squeezed out all the bad blood we could, and there was considerable,
for she had forethought enough to tie her garter around her leg
above the wound to stop the circulation of the blood. We then took
and anointed her leg and head, and laid our hands on her in the
name of Jesus and felt to rebuke the influence of the poison, and
she felt full of faith. We then told her that she must get into the
wagon, so she called witnesses to prove that she did not get into the
wagon until she was compelled to by the cursed snake. We started
on and traveled about two miles, when we stopped to take some
refreshments. Sister Bathgate continued to be quite sick, but was
full of faith, and after stopping one and a half hours we hitched up
our teams. As the word was given for the teams to start, old Sister
Isabella Park ran in before the wagon to see how her companion
was. The driver, not seeing her, hallooed at his team and they being
quick to mind, Sister Park could not get out of the way, and the
fore wheel struck her and threw her down and passed over both her
hips. Brother Leonard grabbed hold of her to pull her out of the
way, before the hind wheel could catch her. He only got her out part
way and the hind wheels passed over her ankles. We all thought that
she would be all mashed to pieces, but to the joy of us all, there

was not a bone broken, although the wagon had something like two tons burden on it, a load for 4 yoke of oxen. We went right to work and applied the same medicine to her that we did to the sister who was bitten by the rattlesnake, and although quite sore for a few days, Sister Park got better, so that she was on the tramp before we got into this Valley, and Sister Bathgate was right by her side, to cheer her up. Both were as smart as could be long before they got here, and this is what I call good luck, for I know that nothing but the power of God saved the two sisters and they traveled together, they rode together, and suffered together. Sister Bathgate has got married since she arrived in the Valley. While we were leading our handcart companies through the States and on the plains, we were called tyrants and slave drivers, and everything else that could be thought of, both by Gentiles and apostates.

Your humble servant in the Gospel of Christ,

DANIEL D. McARTHUR

Appendix C

REPORT BY
F. D. RICHARDS AND DANIEL SPENCER [1]

President Brigham Young:

Dear Brother:—We left Florence (Winter Quarters) K.T., on the evening of the 3rd Sept., accompanied by Elders C. H. Wheelock, J. Van Cott, G. D. Grant, W. H. Kimball, Joseph A. Young, C. G. Webb, W. C. Dunbar, James McGaw, Dan Jones, J. D. T. McAllister, N. H. Felt, and James Ferguson; G. D. Grant being selected as captain of our company.

The rear of our season's emigration had started on the road, with the exception of Elder Wm. Walker with 10 wagons, laden with a portion of P.E.Fund baggage.

Previous to leaving Florence we sent Elder Jos. A. Young back to ascertain, if possible, the whereabouts of Elder Walker. He rode back 50 miles, and, learning that Walker's train was yet some 25 or 30 miles in the rear, returned to join us for the plains.

Elder E. Snow accompanied us to our camp, 3 miles west of Elk Horn, and on the morning of the 5th, having completed his business with us, returned to the States.

We overtook our rear company of wagons, in charge of Captain L. [J.] A. Hunt, during the forenoon of the 6th, and nooned with them about 10 miles east of the Loup Fork. He has in his company 240 persons, 50 wagons, 297 oxen and cows, 7 horses and mules, and some 4 church wagons. The majority of this company have light loads and good teams, and are generally well provisioned. They would probably ferry the Loup Fork on the 7th.

On the evening of the 7th we overtook Elder Edward Martin,

---

[1] This report by Richards and Spencer regarding the Perpetual Emigration Fund, the emigration of 1856, and the trip West, was made after their arrival at Salt Lake City and is printed in the *Deseret News* of Oct. 22, 1856. They had managed the emigration from Britain, where Richards had served as President of the Mission.

about 40 miles from the Loup Fork, with the rear of our P.E.F. Emigration for this season. He had with him some 576 persons, 146 hand-carts, 7 wagons, 6 mules and horses, and 50 cows and beef cattle; also one wagon mostly loaded with church goods. His company was in most excellent spirits, and, though he had the greater proportion of the feeble emigrants, the health of his camp was very good; and he was able to average about 100 miles a week, without fatiguing his company.

Here, from a company of returning Californians met the previous day, we learned of the increased hostility of the Cheyennes, and that they had already made a successful attack upon A. W. Babbitt's ox train. Of the four teamsters in that train two were killed, and one wounded; and a woman named Wilson (as was presumed from the tracks) was severely wounded and taken prisoner, and her child, about two months old, was murdered. The wagons were plundered, but, as we subsequently learned, most of the property was retaken by Captain Wharton of Fort Kearney.[2]

Refreshed by our short interview with Captain Martin's company, we drove about 10 miles further and found br. Hodgetts' camp. This company is composed of 150 persons, 33 wagons, 84 yoke of oxen, 19 cows and some 250 head of heifers and other loose cattle. This includes br. Thomas Tennant and family, with 4 wagons and 1 carriage. Br. Hodgetts' company, though generally pretty heavily laden, were in good traveling condition, making excellent progress.

On the 9th inst. we met with two brethren, from br. J. G. Willie's company of hand-carts, in search of 30 head of cattle that had strayed from their camp about 50 miles in advance.

Accompanied by br. James Ferguson, we this day visited Captain Wharton at Fort Kearney, and received a confirmation of the news of the attack of the Cheyennes upon Mr. Babbitt's train. The troops had made an attack upon a Cheyenne village and killed 10 warriors. This increased the rage of the Cheyennes, and from that time we were informed that they had divided into war parties for the purpose of attacking small parties of emigrants.

Here we met a returning Californian who had escaped from one of their assaults, with the loss of his wife killed, and his boy, some 3 or 4 years old, taken prisoner.

[2] See Hafen, ed., *Relations with the Plains Indians, 1857-1861* (Glendale, Calif., 1959), *Far West and Rockies Series,* IX, p. 17ff.

Captain Wharton declared himself incompetent to afford any protection to emigrants, and had some doubts of his ability to maintain the post, for want of troops. Mr. Babbitt had left Fort Kearney for Utah a week previous, with Thomas Sutherland and a driver.

As we were leaving the fort for our camp on the north side of the Platte, a discharged soldier came to Capt. Wharton with the news of another massacre by the Cheyennes. This soldier had accompanied Thomas Margetts and James Cowdy, and their families, from Laramie, and on returning from a buffalo hunt, when about 125 miles from Fort Kearney, found the wagon plundered and the murdered remains of his traveling companians.

The soldier's account of the affair, as given to brs. Willie and Atwood, will give you the particulars and is as follows:

STATEMENT [11 paragraphs, omitted from this report]

On the 12th we overtook and camped with br. Willie's company, at North Bluff Creek, consisting of 404 persons, 6 wagons, 87 handcarts, 6 yoke of oxen, 32 cows, and 5 mules. They were considerably weakened by the loss of their oxen, which they had failed to recover, but were in good spirits and averaging from 14 to 16 miles a day. Here we forded the Platte to the south side, and were followed by the handcarts. Never was there a more soul-stirring sight than the happy passage of this company over that river. Several of the carts were drawn entirely by women, and every heart was glad and full of hope.

We spent the afternoon of the 15th inst. with br. A. O. Smoot, about 20 miles west of Ash Hollow. There were in his company 88 souls, 42 wagons, 265 oxen, 6 cows, 15 mules and horses, and 1 carriage. They had provisions for 23 days. Br. Smoot lacked drivers, having only 33 men fit for duty. His oxen were in good condition, but his loads were very heavy. Gilbert and Gerrish's train of 17 wagons was traveling in company with him.

On the 16th inst., 37 miles in advance of br. Smoot, we camped with br. O. P. Rockwell, who had 5 wagons and 11 yoke of oxen in charge, in addition to three families, viz., Grimshaw, Cook, and Barnes, whom he had turned back towards Laramie, deeming them too weak, to pass in safety. Br. Rockwell accompanied us to Fort Laramie, where we arrived on the morning of the 19th. Col. Hoffman received us with much kindness, as also did J. W. Tutt, the sutler. Here we received a small recruit of mules and provisions, and purchased some good buffalo robes for the P.E.Fund passengers in the rear.

On the 23rd inst. we parted, at the Platte Bridge, with Capt. Dan Jones, who met his brother and remained to recover a cached threshing machine. Here also we purchased a few more robes for Capt. J. G. Willie's company.

During the forenoon of the 24th, after leaving our camp at Willow Springs, we met Messrs. Hawley, Lambson, Amy and party on their way to the States, and advised them to wait at Laramie for the company of missionaries reported in their rear.

Same day, and near Independence Rock, we nooned near Patriarch John Smith and two other brethren, who had come out with flour for the companies. Br. Smith returned with us. The same evening, and about 8 miles farther on, we camped with Elder P. P. Pratt and company, all in good health and most excellent spirits, and promising fair for an honorable and successful mission.

On the 27th, 15 miles east of the Pacific Springs, we nooned with br. Wm. Smith and two other brethren from Farmington, with 2 wagons and flour for the companies. We counseled them to cache their flour and go on to meet br. Willie and his company, which they agreed to do.

On the 28th, 3 miles east of Big Sandy, we camped with br. Talcott, who also had flour for the companies. We gave him the same counsel, to go on with his teams to help br. Willie.

On the 29th we camped with br. Croft's company, consisting of 58 persons, 14 wagons, 80 yoke of oxen, 30 horses, and 130 loose cattle; they are principally from Texas and the Cherokee lands. They were healthy and in good spirits, and gave us a most hospitable reception. This was the last company passed by us on the road.

At Bridger, on the 1st of Oct., we were welcomed by Major Burton and a small party of the mountain boys; and on the evening of the 4th were happy to receive your welcome and blessing at home.

Assuring you of our continued exertions to promote the welfare of God's kingdom, and praying that your life may be spared long to God's people, as also the lives of your Council, we remain, sincerely and obediently, yours in Christ,

F. D. RICHARDS,
DANIEL SPENCER,
Agents P.E.Fund

Appendix D

JOURNAL OF THE
FIRST RESCUE PARTY [1]

Tues. Oct. 7. Left G. S. L. City, going east, to meet the emigrating companies. Camped tonight at the foot of the Big Mountain.

Wednesday, Oct. 8. Passed over the Big Mountain and camped in East Kanyon; had a light snowstorm.

Thursday, Oct. 9. Had good roads; camped in Echo Kanyon.

Friday, Oct. 10. Camped near a little grove at the head of Echo.

Saturday, Oct. 11. Traveled down the "Old Pioneer Road;" camped tonight at a big hollow, good feed and water.

Sunday, Oct. 12. Arrived at Fort Bridger. Left some of our flour, feed, etc., at this place. Got some beef, etc. Camped here tonight.

Monday, Oct. 13. Left Fort Bridger; camped tonight at Black's Fork; met Brothers Smoot, Dan Jones and others; some teams returning that had been back on the road and got tired of waiting.

Tuesday, Oct. 14. Brother Smoot returned with us to meet his son, camped tonight on Black's Fork. Again sent on an express to meet the company and report back to us their situation, whereabouts, etc. The express was carried by Cyrus H. Wheelock, Joseph A. Young, Stephen Taylor, Abel Garr.

Wednesday, Oct. 15. Traveled to Green River. Left some flour, feed, etc. Camped tonight on Big Sandy at 8 o'clock.

---

[1] From Journal History, Nov. 30, 1856. This account of Robert T. Burton's relief train is of great importance in checking and dating the tragic events it records so tersely and prosaically.

This rescue party is the one that endured such hardships, persisted with such heroism, and brought the first help to the stalled handcart emigrants. The relief party's activities are elaborated in the chapter at page 119.

Thursday, Oct. 16. At the Big Sandy we met Capt. Smoot; camped here tonight; let him have some flour, beef, and teams and 18 men.

Friday, Oct. 17. Started late; camped on Little Sandy. Feed scarce; looked like a storm.

Saturday, Oct. 18. Clear and fair, storm passed to the right and left us. Camped tonight on the head of Sweet Water. Good feed and wood. Looked like a storm.

Sunday, Oct. 19. Killed one beef. Started in the afternoon; camped below the mouth of Willow Creek. Tonight commenced storming; very cold; good feed.

Monday, Oct. 20. Stayed in the same place today. Brother Willie came to us near night fall.

Tuesday, Oct. 21. Started early in the morning to meet Capt. Willie's company; camped with them tonight; dealt out flour and clothing to them. William Kimball and several others returned with him with teams, etc. Snow deep.

Wednesday, Oct. 22. Traveled 17 miles. Snow growing deeper and deeper all the way. Camped tonight under the Wallahualtah Rock.

Thursday, Oct. 23. Stayed in the same camp. Snow deep; could not travel.

Friday, Oct. 24. Clear and fair, some warmer; started on. Camped tonight below the Three Crossings of Sweet Water. Snow still deep. Saw a large herd of buffalo three miles distant.

Saturday, Oct. 25. Wind blowing hard; camped tonight below the Wallahualtah Rock. Snow going away slowly. Weather some warmer.

Sunday, Oct. 26. Traveled 19 miles; camped near the Devil's Gate; found the express that had been sent on at this place, waiting further orders. Had heard nothing from the company behind.

Monday, Oct. 27. Remained in the same place. Feed tolerably good. From this point sent another express to the bridge on Platte River, Joseph A. Young, Abel Garr, Dan Jones, to find the company if possible, and report back their situation, whereabouts, etc.

Tuesday, Oct. 28. Remained in the same camp. Weather fine; snow going away. At night cloudy; snow began to fall fast. After prayers, ceased snowing.

Wednesday, Oct. 29. In the same camp. Fine warm morning; continued through the day.

Thursday, Oct. 30. Good weather; snow going away slowly; remained in the same camp. Express returned tonight at 7 o'clock and reported that the companies on the Platte River had been camped there several days, not far apart.

Friday, Oct. 31. Fine and clear; started this morning to meet the company of hand carts; met them on Greasewood Creek; camped with them tonight; dealt out to them flour, clothing, etc.

Saturday, Nov. 1. Started back for the Valley. Brothers Grant and Robt. T. Burton went back (further East) to meet Brother Hodgett's [wagon] company, four or five miles; about noon it commenced snowing. Snowed until late at night; camped near Independence Rock.

Sunday, Nov. 2. Camped tonight at Devil's Gate, snow deep, very cold.

Monday, Nov. 3. Remained at same place. So cold that the company could not move. Sent an express to G.S.L. City, Joseph A. Young, and Abel Garr, to report our situation and get counsel and help.

Tuesday, Nov. 4. Cold continued very severe. People could not move; stowed away the goods of the trains in the houses. Capt. Martin's camp moved 3 miles and camped.

Wednesday, Nov. 5. Weather continued cold; neither of the companies moved. Capt. Hunt's company arrived here at 8 p.m.

Thursday, Nov. 6. Colder than ever. Thermometer 11 degrees below zero. Stowed away the goods of Capt. Hunt's train. None of the companies moved; so cold the people could not travel.

Friday, Nov. 7. Remained very cold. Could not travel. Stowing away goods, trying to save the people, stock, etc.

Saturday, Nov. 8. Wind did not blow so hard; some warmer this morning; hunting up the horses and cattle to move on the morrow; camped at the same place.

Sunday, Nov. 9. Fine, warm morning. Hand-cart company and Capt. Hodgett's company moved on at 11 o'clock a.m. Capt. Hunt's company not yet done caching goods.

This evening had a meeting of the officers of the companies to appoint brethren to remain with the goods left here by Captains

Hodgett's and Hunt's companies. Dan Jones left in charge or president, F. M. Alexander and Benjamin Hampton counselors, with 17 other brethren from the two companies. The brethren were instructed in their duties.

During our stay here, we had meetings every evening to counsel together and ask the Lord to turn away the cold and storm, so that the people might live.

Monday, Nov. 10. Very fine morning. Capt. Hunt's company fixing to start, getting up cattle, etc. The last wagon moved on about 2 o'clock. Capt. Grant, Cyrus H. Wheelock, Stephen Taylor and Robt. T. Burton moved on at 3 o'clock; camped tonight with Capt. Hodgett.

Tuesday, Nov. 11. Started early in the morning; overtook the hand cart company at 10 o'clock. Brother Ephraim K. Hanks was with them from the Valley, brought good news; camped tonight on Bitter Cottonwood.

Wednesday, Nov. 12. Fine morning, warm for the season; sent on an express to the South Pass. It returned at 5 o'clock this morning, and four teams with some flour. Camped above Three Crossings.

Thursday, Nov. 13. Very pleasant morning. Companies all moving on finely. Camped again on the Sweet Water, at the lower end of the 16 mile drive.

Friday, Nov. 14. The weather very pleasant; all the companies moving on. Camped on the 16 mile drive, about 4 miles from Sweet Water. Good feed, not much wood. No deaths in camp tonight. Capt. Hunt's company ahead, Capt. Hodgett near.

Saturday, Nov. 15. Weather continued fine and warm; traveled on 8 miles and camped on Sweet Water; not much wood, nor very good feed.

Sunday, Nov. 16. Met 10 teams from the Valley. Brother Call's company, on Rocky Ridge; camped in a little cottonwood grove; good wood and feed.

Monday, Nov. 17. Fine, warm day; camped on the branch of Sweet Water.

Tuesday, Nov. 18. Cloudy, snowing in afternoon; met several teams, Wm. Kimball, James Ferguson, J. Simmons, Hosea Stout and others; camped tonight at our station on Sweet Water.

Wednesday, Nov. 19. Snowing in the morning sent an express

to the city. Company moved on, all in wagons; 3 o'clock. Capt. Grant and Robt. T. Burton, after seeing the ox trains, moved on after the company. Camped tonight on Dry Sandy.

Thursday, Nov. 20. This morning Brothers Grant and Kimball, and others started for the City. Robt. T. Burton was left in charge of the companies; camped at bend of Big Sandy.

Friday, Nov. 21. This morning fair, but cold; met more teams; sent some back to the ox-trains with flour, etc. Camped on Black's Fork.

Sunday, Nov. 23. Fine day, some cloudy; snowed again at night. Camped at Fort Bridger.

Monday, Nov. 24. This morning took in supplies for the company from Brother Lewis Robison's. Started late. Camped on the Muddy, good wood and feed; very cold.

Tuesday, Nov. 25. This morning started another express to the City, Cyrus H. Wheelock, Bullock and others. Sent two other teams to the ox-trains. Camped on Bear River; plenty of wood.

Wednesday, Nov. 26. Cold, but clear. Camped tonight in the head of Echo Kanyon; met Brother Little and others from the City.

Thursday, Nov. 27. This morning snowing a little; camped tonight on the Weber River. Had another express from the president.

Friday, Nov. 28. Today the road was sideling; got all the wagons over safe. Camped in East Kanyon; met several of the brethren here.

Saturday, Nov. 29. Passed over the Big Mountain, snowing fast. Stopped snowing after noon. Passed over Little Mountain; camped in the head of Emigration Kanyon; met supplies.

Sunday, Nov. 30. This morning started early; arrived in S.L. City a little before noon with all the hand cart company and several families from the ox-trains.

Had in the trains 351 horses and mules, 104 wagons, and 32 oxen.

Appendix E

CAPTAIN GRANT'S REPORT
FROM DEVIL'S GATE [1]

Devil's Gate, Nov. 2, 1856

President Brigham Young:

Dear Brother: – Knowing the anxieties you feel for the companies still out, and especially for the Hand-cart Company, I have concluded to send in your son Joseph A. and br. Abel Garr on an express from this place.

We had no snow to contend with, until we got to the Sweet Water. On the 19th and 20th of October we encountered a very severe snow storm. We met br. Willie's company on the 21st; the snow was from six to ten inches deep where we met them. They were truly in a bad situation, but we rendered them all the assistance in our power. Br. William H. Kimball returned with them, also several other brethren. The particulars of the company you have doubtless learned before this time.

(They arrived on the 9th inst, as already noticed.– Ed. [of *Deseret News*])

Previous to this time we had sent on an express to ascertain, if possible, the situation and whereabouts of the company yet back, and report to me. Not thinking it safe for them to go farther than Independence Rock, I advised them to wait there. When we overtook them they had heard nothing from the rear companies, and we had traveled through snow from 8 to 12 inches deep all the way from Willow creek to this place.

Not having much feed for our horses they were running down very fast, and not hearing anything from the companies, I did not know

---

[1] Printed in the *Deseret News,* Nov. 19, 1856. This is the report of Captain George D. Grant of the rescue party. It was sent by messengers Joseph A. Young and Abel Garr, who arrived at Salt Lake City at 4 a.m. on Nov. 13.

but what they had taken up quarters for the winter, consequently we sent on another express to the Platte bridge. When that express returned, to my surprise I learned that the companies were all on the Platte river, near the upper crossing, and had been encamped there nine days, waiting for the snow to go away, or, as they said, to recruit their cattle.

As quick as we learned this, we moved on to meet them. Met br. Martin's company at Greasewood creek, on the last day of October; br. Hodgett's company was a few miles behind. We dealt out to br. Martin's company the clothing, &c, that we had for them; and next morning, after stowing our wagons full of the sick, the children and the infirm, with a good amount of luggage, started homeward about noon. The snow began to fall very fast, and continued until late at night. It is now about 8 inches deep here, and the weather is very cold.

It is not of much use for me to attempt to give a description of the situation of these people, for this you will learn from your son Joseph A. and br. Garr, who are the bearers of this express; but you can imagine between five and six hundred men, women and children, worn down by drawing hand carts through snow and mud; fainting by the wayside; falling, chilled by the cold; children crying, their limbs stiffened by cold, their feet bleeding and some of them bare to snow and frost. The sight is almost too much for the stoutest of us; but we go on doing all we can, not doubting nor despairing.

Our company is too small to help much, it is only a drop to a bucket, as it were, in comparison to what is needed. I think that not over one-third of br. Martin's company is able to walk. This you may think is extravagant, but it is nevertheless true. Some of them have good courage and are in good spirits; but a great many are like children and do not help themselves much more, nor realize what is before them.

I never felt so much interest in any mission that I have been sent on, and all the brethren who came out with me feel the same. We have prayed without ceasing, and the blessing of God has been with us.

Br. Charles Decker has now traveled this road the 49th time, and he says he has never before seen so much snow on the Sweet Water at any season of the year.

I am sorry to inform you of the death of br. Tennant, among those who have fallen by the way side.

Br. Hunt's company are two or three days back of us, yet br. Wheelock will be with them to counsel them, also some of the other brethren who came out.

We will move every day toward the valley, if we shovel snow to do it, the Lord helping us.

I have never seen such energy and faith among the "boys," nor so good a spirit as is among those who came out with me. We realize that we have your prayers for us continually, also those of all the Saints in the Valley. I pray that the blessings of God may be with you and all those who seek to build up the kingdom of God on the earth.

GEORGE D. GRANT

Appendix F

JOSEPH A. YOUNG'S REPORT
NOVEMBER 16, 1856 [1]

Brethren and sisters, as I have the latest news from companies yet on the plains, and as you are all anxious to hear from them, I have been the first one called upon to speak to you this morning.

You are aware that Capt. Geo. D. Grant's relief company left this city on the 7th of Oct., to go and meet the immigration. Capt. Grant kept an express in advance until we reached the Devil's Gate, when he sent three of us on to the Platte river, to see if we could find the companies or hear of them.

We traveled until the 28th, when we met Capt. Edward Martin's company of hand carts and Capt. Hodgett's wagon company, at a place called Red Buttes, 16 miles below [above] the Platte bridge. We met Capt. J. A. Hunt's wagon company 26 miles below the bridge [10 miles below Martin's].

The brethren and sisters appeared to be in good health and spirits. Capt. Martin informed us that about 56 out of 600 had died upon the plains up to that date. Those who had died were mostly old people.

On the 29th I returned from Capt. Hunt's to Capt. Martin's company. Capt. Martin had started early in the morning, and when I overtook them their cry was, "let us go to the Valley; let us go to Zion."

I camped with them that night in the snow, at a place called Rocky Avenue, near the [36 miles east of] Devil's Gate. The next day I journeyed on towards Capt. Grant's company, and on the 31st rode into their camp and found all well.

---

[1] Given in the Tabernacle on Nov. 16 and printed in the *Deseret News,* Nov. 19, 1856.

In the morning [On Nov. 3] Capt. Grant sent me and br. Abel Garr on an express to this city. We found plenty of teams at Fort Bridger, and by this time the hand carts have all the assistance necessary to take them up and bring them in within nine days from tomorrow. There were teams enough, so soon as they could meet them, to bring them right through as fast as horses and mules can travel, and such will be done.

All the companies requested me to inform the Saints in the valleys that they desired your faith and your prayers, and that they would endeavor to merit them in their journey and after their arrival.

That the blessings of God may attend them is my sincere desire. Amen.

Appendix G

HARVEY CLUFF'S ACCOUNT
OF THE RESCUE [1]

. . . I attended the October conference of that year which
opened on the 6th as usual, having walked from Provo to Salt Lake
City. On that day President Brigham Young at the opening of the
first Session made a call upon the people to furnish teams, provisions
and clothing to aid the late handcart companies in as the winter
season was fast hastening on, snow having already fallen upon the
mountains. The response to the call of President Young was most
remarkable. On the following day October 7th 22 teams – two span
of mules or horses to each wagon and each wagon loaded to the bows.
There were about fifty young men in the company. Being in Salt
Lake City and of an ambitious turn of mind, I volunteers to go. One
thing which attracted me, in addition of the interest in the handcart
people, was my brother Moses. He was on the plains returning from
a mission to England.

Of the most prominent men of the company who went out in that
memorable expedition of relief I mention Geo. D. Grant; Robert T.
Burton; Joseph A. Young; William H. Kimball; Daniel W. Jones;
John R. Murdock; Eph H. Hanks; Issac Bullock and Brigham
Young, Jr.

This relief party proceeded eastward as rapidly as possible and in
due time passed over the South Pass, the backbone of the continent,
being the divide point of the waters flowing into the Atlantic Ocean
east and the Pacific Ocean west. Nine miles brought us down to the
Sweetwater river where we camped for the night. On arising in the
following morning snow was several inches deep. During the two
following days, the storm raged with increasing fury until it attained

---

[1] Extract from the Journal of Harvey H. Cluff, 1836-1868, in Brigham
Young University Library – a reminiscent account.

the capacity of a northern blizzard. For protection of ourselves and animals, the company moved down the river to where the willows were dense enough to make a good protection against the raging storm from the north. The express team which had been dispatched ahead as rapidly as possible to reach and give encouragement to the faultering emigrants, by letting them know that help was near at hand. Quietly resting in the seclusion of the willow copse, three miles from the road I volunteered to take a sign board and place it at a conspicious place at the main road. This was designed to direct the express party who were expected to return about this time. So they would not miss us. In facing the northern blast up hill I found it quite difficult to keep from freezing. I had only been back to camp a short time when two men rode up from Willies handcart company. The signboard had done the work of salvation. Had Captain Willie and his fellow traveller, from his company, continued on the road they certainly would have perished as they would have reached the Sweetwater where the storm first struck us. The handcart company was then 25 miles from our camp, and as they had travelled that distance without food for themselves or horses and no bedding, they must have perished. I have always regarded this act of mine as the means of their salvation. And why not? An act of that importance is worthy of record and hence I give a place here.

Preparations were made and early in the morning of the following day we were on the road pushing our way for Captain Willies camp. The depth of snow made travelling extreemly difficult and the whole day was spent before we reached camp. It was about sun set when we came in sight of the camp; which greatly resembled an Esqumeax Village fully one mile away. The snow being a foot deep and paths having been made from tent to tent gave the camp that appearance. As we reached an eminance overlooking the camp, which was located on a sagebrush plain near the river a mile away. When the people of the camp sighted us approaching, they set up such a shout as to echo through the hills. Arriving within the confines of this emigrant camp a most thrilling and touching scene was enacted, melting to tears the stoutest hearts. Young maidens and feable old ladies, threw off all restraint and freely embraced their deliverers expressing in a flow of kisses, the gratitude which their tongues failed to utter. This was certainly the most timely arrival of a relief party recorded in history,

for the salvation of a people. Five hundred people with handcarts a
scanty supply of clothing, bedding and less supply of provision, upon
the plains in snow ten inches deep. The limited supply of food
ordinarily would be very small, and of this limited supply scarsely a
bite of substantial of food was left in camp. Think of it ye mountaineers. Four hundred miles from any possible supply of provisions.
You no longer wonder at the joy manifested by that perishing people
when they saw salvation pull into their camp. Twenty odd wagons
drawn by four animals to each and each wagon loaded to the bows
with vegetables, meat, flour, groceries, clothing for both sexes, and
bedding and footwear. To give an idea of the critacle condition of
those people I will say that our camp was pitched about fifty yards
from the tents of the emigrants and each meal was over in our camp
and the boans and crumbs from our meals were thrown out on the
snow, young men would geather them up knaw and suck them as long
as they geathered any substance. Of course caution was necessary in
dealing out provisions as too liberal a supply of food at first would,
no doubt, prove fatal, after being in a starving condition for days.
Six well loaded wagons teams and teamsters were left with this
company and the rest of us pushed on for as yet we had no information as to where the other two handcart and two independent wagon
companies were. On arriving at Devils Gate we found the express-
men awating our coming up, for as yet they had no word as to where
the companies were. Here we were in a dialema. Four or five hundred
miles from Salt Lake and a thousand emigrants with handcarts on
the dreary plains and the severity of winter already upon us. With
snow ten inches deep in the low altitude, what must it be a month or
two months hence on the Rockey Mountains when we return. Devil's
Gate is formed by the Sweetwater river cut through a mountain of
granite rock 1000 feet in length 130 feet wide with perpendicular
walls of 400 feet in hight. Irregular ranges of low hills or mountains
dot the irregular plains. The hills are covered sparcely with ceaders
and scruby pitch pine timber. The plains formly were pasture for
buffalow, deer and antelope, but those animals except, an occasional
antelope, had gone to other parts. For Devils Gate consisted of a
small stocade and a few log houses, located on a plane near where the
river enters the deep gorge through the mountains.

Our camp was pitched in a lovely cove in the mountain across from the fort where we had plenty of fuel and forage for animals. Deliberations on the uncertanty as to the best course to persue in our dialema resulted in selecting two good horsemen who were to ride as rapidly as horses could endure. Four days was the extent of time they were to be gone. If the emigrants were not found within that length of time the two men were to return and the conclusion would be that the companies had gone into winter quarters. The return of the two horsemen at night of the forth day brought the news that companies were on the uper crossing of the Platt river, sixty-five miles away. Ah! then there was hurrying to and froe! and on the following day, every team but one, and all the men but ten started out on force march for to meet the companies, who as soon as the two men found them, began anew their journey from the place where the first snow storm tied them up until the news of approaching help reached them then new life, as it were, invigerated them, when they could sing as my father did.

Come let us anew
Our journey persue

The one team and ten men immediately began hauling from the hills the ceader and the pine wood to the stockade and clearing the snow off so the emigrants could be comfortable when they arived. For several days we made every effort possible to get things in good shape. It was a Sunday evening when the handcart veterans pulled into the quarters provided for them. Every room nook and corner was taken. Wagons and tents were filled to their utmost capasity, to protect the people from the northern blizzard then raging. Every possible assistance from the boys from Utah was freely given. And these young hardy men from the Rockies were a mighty force and power in the salvation of that people. No more efficient help could have been furnished. They had crossed the dreary plains, new what hunger, thirst, starvation, weary, travelling, with sore feet ment; hence with the subsiquent experience in the vallies gave them the vim to endure and they did endure and they worked valiently for the poor emigrants. But oh! what a sight to see. Aged men, women, children and young maidens plodding along through the snow several inches deep, with icicles dangling to their skirts and pants as they walked along pushing and pulling their handcarts, the wheels of which were burdened with snow. The roaring fires of cedar and pitch pine wood soon cheered the weary souls and the youthful of both sexes were singing the songs of Zion arround the campfires. Herein lies the secret or cause of the success which the Latter day Saints have had in coming out from Babylon, and crossing the plains into a wilderness.

Here at Devils Gate I met my brother Moses returning from a four years mission to Great Brittain. He had been detailed at the frontier to take charge of what was termed the "Church Heard" but in reality it was an individual speculation, except perhapse a few head included for the benifit of the handcart companies for beef when no wild game could be secured. I was also selected to assist my brother in driving and hearding these several hundred head of texan cattle with the promice, as made to my brother, that I should receive pay. Fifty-two years have passed since then and not one dollar has ever come into our hands. What will the principal and interest, at compound amount too in the next world? The Lord will judge the case.

Northern blizzards prevailed, the thermometer showing ten to twenty degrees below zero, making it utterly impossible to proceed homeward; finally a lull in the raging wind from the north enabled the handcart companies to cross the river and go up to the cove where we had camped as previously mentioned. Men of old age and women were carried across the river on the backs of these sturdy mountain boys. In this instance, as in many others, the value of the boys from Zion was of great help to the weary Saints. Camp was made, tents set, supper over and the people retired for the night when a snow storm accompanied by a raging wind from the north, came over the mountain and with a terrific whirl arround the cove, levelled every tent to the ground. Here again the Utah boys found that their services verry much needed. To rescue the people from beneath their tents and re-set the tents in the dark hours of the night was a very trying ordeal for the boys and also the people, but marvilous as it may seem, not a single person was seriously injured. Now again the blizzard set in with increased fury, the snow covering the grass compelling the cattle and horses to forage upon the willows along the river bottoms. Cattle died daily. The situation was, indeed, verry criticle. No power could save the people from death but that of God. To our rescue O Lord God Almighty seemed the fervent prayer constantly offered to our Heavenly Father. The carcases of dead cattle were preserved in a frozen state from wolves, for food for the people in case we should be winter bound; which really seemed ineviatable. Over four hundred miles of mountainous country lay between the emigrants and their destined home in Utah where snow in winter frequently falls to a depth that stopes all travel by teams. The only glimmer of hope that seemed to reconcile our feeling and that was the utmost confidence in President Brigham Young's inspiration that he would keep companies coming out to meet us and thereby keep the road opened. They knew, or at least the boys from Utah knew, that presidents foresight and excellent judgement would be sufficint to grasp the situation of the emigrants and their needs in such an inclement season and therefore teams and supplies would be forwarded train after train until the last Saint should arive safely in Zion. These relief companies following one after another and only but a few days apart would keep the road open, thus insuring the possibility of our companies moving out as soon as they could leave Devil's Gate. Patience finally rewarded our hopes. "The cloudes ye so much dread" finally lifted and we start out homeward bound. Our travel was very slow at first. Five or ten miles a day was all we could make, but that was more satisfactory than remaining in camp. The independent ox trains cached the most of their merchandise at the stockade Devils Gate before leaving which enabled them to travel more successfully than the handcart people. Jessie Haven conducted one of the independent wagon companey's and with him Moses and I lodged and borded. Our company I mean the company of Bro. Haven, started out ahead of the handcarts which improved or benifited their travel. Elder Daniel W. Jones and several other men were chosen to watch the goods until teams could reach them in the spring.

It was near the middle of November when the line of march was resumed, the ox train taking the lead, thus opening the road. Not many days after the departure of the companies from Devils Gate, they were met by a train of wagons with supplies from Zion. Following this train came another and then another and from that time on the road was kept pretty well opened. As the trains came the number of handcarts diminished as the aged were taken into wagons and made quite comfortable. By the time we reached Ft. Bridger the entire handcart people were being carried with their goods in wagons.

At Green river I was selected to take a light team and hasten on to Salt Lake with a son of C. G. Webb who had his feet frozen so badly that amputation would be necessary. I making a night drive of ten miles I got my feet frosted so that both of my big toes blakened. At the end of the ten miles I turned my oxen out, made a fire of small sage brush sufficient to thaw my boots so I could get them off. Soon after getting into bed, in the wagon, my feet warmed and during the following two hours it seemed that my feet were in coals of fire. On reaching upper end of Echo Canyon I met the brother of the young man I had in charge, who naturally wanted to accompany his afflicted brother home. I therefore took his team and went back to Ft. Bridger and he took my team and returned to Salt Lake. Ariving at Bridger where the remnant of the last handcart company, were wating for assistance, I loaded up my wagon with goods and as many people as could conviently get in and began my way homeward. All the teams of the company were loaded likewise, taking in all but a few carts of the remnants. Reaching East creek at the base of the Big mountain the snow about four feet deep, a recent fall of snow having filled up the track. Now came the tug of war so to speak. Every avalable man was lined up in double file as far apart as the wagon wheels and thus they proceeded up the mountain in advance of the train. At regular distances we would make a side track for the lead team to pull out and fall in behind, thus we continued up and up the four miles and near the summit a cut with shovels had to be made through a snow drift twenty feet deep. The whole day was consumed in getting over the mountain and camp was made between the Big and Little mountains. The journey over the Little mountain into "Emigration" was uneventful beyond the usual cheerfulness which beamed upon every face as they looked down upon Salt Lake Valley, which from this summit spread out in grandure amid the mountains surrounding it wrapped in snow. Into Salt Lake City we pulled that day, ariving in the evening. How inadequate is language to depict, or pen to write, the soul stiring pleasure, and gratitude to the Allwise Creator for our safe arival home. It was near the close of December of the year 1856 when I arived at my home in Provo City. . .

Appendix H

BRIGHAM YOUNG AND HEBER C. KIMBALL ADDRESSES OF NOVEMBER 2, 1856

BRIGHAM YOUNG'S FIRST REMARKS [1]

. . . Do you want to know the reason why I speak of our being so comfortably situated this morning, in so comfortable a meeting house? We can return home and sit down and warm our feet before the fire, and can eat our bread and butter, etc., but my mind is yonder in the snow, where those immigrating Saints are, and my mind has been with them ever since I had the report of their start from Winter Quarters (Florence) on the 3rd of September. I cannot talk about anything, I cannot go out or come in, but what in every minute or two minutes my mind reverts to them; and the questions — where-abouts are my brethren and sisters who are on the plains, and what is their condition, force themselves upon me and annoy my feelings all the time. And were I to answer my own feelings, I should do so by undertaking to do what the conference voted I should not do, that is, I should be with them now in the snow, even though it should be up to the knees, up to the waist, or up to the neck. My mind is there; and my faith is there; I have a great many reflections about them.

Have any of you suffered while coming here? Yes. How many of you sisters present buried your husbands, or your fathers, or mothers, or children, on the plains? How many of you brethren buried your wives? Have you suffered, and been in peril and trouble? Yes, you had to endure anguish and pain from the effects of cholera, toil and weariness. Do you live your religion when you get here, after all the trouble, afflictions and pains you have passed through to come to Zion? and to a pretty Zion! Men and women start across the plains

---

[1] Given on Nov. 2, 1856, to those assembled in the Tabernacle, Salt Lake City, and printed in the *Deseret News,* Nov. 12, 1856.

for this place, and are they willing to wade through the snow? Yes. And to travel through snow storms? Yes. To wade rivers? Yes. What for? To get to Zion. And here we are in Zion, and what a Zion! where it is necessary for the cry of reformation to go through the land, both a spiritual and temporal reformation. God is more merciful than man can be, and it is well for us. Again, when I consider the backbiting of the people and their sins, I will not ask God to be more merciful and have more sympathy towards me, than I have for my brethren and sisters.

A good many teams have already gone out to meet the Saints who are struggling to gain this place; I can hardly keep from talking about them all the time, for while I am preaching they are uppermost in my mind. The brethren were liberal last Sunday in turning out to meet them with teams, and if any more feel desirous of going to their assistance, I will give them the privilege and advise them to take feed, not only for their own animals, but also for those of the brethren who have already gone out, for they will very likely be short. But I should be more particularly thankful if the minds of this community could be so impressed and stirred up, so wakened up, that when these poor brethren and sisters who are now on the plains do arrive they may be able to say of a truth and in very deed, "God be thanked, we have got to Zion." But fearfulness and forebodings of disappointment to them are in my feelings. How far they may be disappointed, I do not know.

I do not wish to be personal in this congregation, but let me say to the authorities, to the elders of Israel, the Seventies, High Priests, Bishops, or any other quorum or class of officers, if you will appoint meetings and have only those present whom we wish to be there, I will then tell you how to commence a reformation. . . May the Lord bless us.– Amen.

HEBER C. KIMBALL'S COMMENTS [2]

. . . Were this people living their religion as faithfully as they ought to, when a person rose up to teach you the principles of life and salvation, his mind would be free, his tongue would be loosed, . . . But at times it is almost impossible for a man to

---

[2] Given in the Tabernacle on Nov. 2, 1856, and printed in the *Deseret News,* Nov. 12, 1856.

speak to this people. . . This may be measureably due to a murmuring spirit, which I am rather inclined to believe some of you have, and I will tell you wherein. Some find fault with and blame br. Brigham and his Council, because of the sufferings they have heard that our brethren are enduring on the plains. A few of them have died, and you hear some exclaim, "What an awful thing it is! Why is it that the First Presidency are so unwise in their calculations? but it falls on their shoulders." Well, the late arrival of those on the plains cannot be helped now, but let me tell you, most emphatically, that if all who were entrusted with the care and management of this year's immigration had done as they were counseled and dictated by the First Presidency of the Church, the sufferings and hardships now endured by the companies on their way here would have been avoided. Why? Because they would have left the Missouri river in season, and not have been hindered until late September.

There is a spirit of murmuring among the people, and the fault is laid upon br. Brigham. For this reason the heavens are closed against you, for he holds the keys of life and salvation upon the earth; and you may strive as much as you please, but not one of you will ever go through the straight gate into the kingdom of God, except those who go through by that man and his brethren, for they will be the persons whose inspection you must pass. I tell you this plain truth, and you may do what you think best with it.

Three hand-cart companies have arrived in safety and in good season, and with much less sickness and death than commonly occur in wagon companies. Does it make a man sick to labor and be diligent? Let me sit down and be inactive in mind and body, let me cease building and making improvement, or doing something useful, and I should not live six months, nor would br. Brigham, because we have become so inured to occupation.

If the immigration could have been carried on as dictated by br. Brigham, there would have been no trouble. . . Our brethren and sisters on the plains are in my mind all the time, and br. Brigham has given, to those who wish it, the privilege of going back to help bring them in. If I do not go myself, I will send a team, though I have already sent back nearly all my teams, and so has br. Brigham. Those who have gone back never will be sorry for or regret having done so. . . If they die during the trip, they will die while endeavoring to save their brethren; and who has greater love than he that lays down his life for his friends? Manifest your love by your works. . .

When the brethren who have gone back first met them, they felt as though they were truly saviors to them; and when they came into their midst they would not permit them to go ten rods from them, for while one of them was with them they felt as though they were safe, as tho' they would be preserved from misery, from starvation and death.

As br. Brigham has said, I would rather be helping in those on the plains than to be here, if circumstances and duty would permit. We offered our offering and started to go, but the Lord ordered it otherwise and we came home. . . But scores and hundreds have now gone to meet them, and they have had good weather so far, have they not?

I cannot account for the barrier that is between you and the Lord in any other way, only that there is quite a sympathy at work against br. Brigham and his Council. . . We have to acknowledge the hand of God in all things; and that man or woman that feels to murmur and complain is in the gall of bitterness and the hands of iniquity, and does not know it. May God have mercy on you.–Amen.

PRESIDENT YOUNG'S FURTHER STATEMENT [3]

Br. Kimball, in his remarks, touched upon an idea that had not previously entered my mind, that is, that some of the people were dissatisfied with me and my counselors, on account of the lateness of the season's immigration. I do not know but such may be the case, as I am aware that those persons now on the plains have a great many friends and relatives here; but it never came into my mind that I was in the least degree censurable for any person's being now upon the plains.– Why? Because there is not the least shadow of reason for casting such censure upon me. I am about as free from what is called jealousy, as any man that lives; I am not jealous of anybody, . . .

Aside from entire want of foundation, and aside from my free-dom from jealousy and suspicion, there are other reasons why I could not be expected to have indulged in the suspicions of such a

---

[3] Delivered at the Tabernacle, Nov. 2, 1856, and printed in the *Deseret News,* Nov. 12, 1856.

charge. Our general epistles usually go from here twice a year, and the immigration, the gathering of the people, is dictated in those epistles, with a considerable degree of minute detail; I also advance many ideas on the same subject, from time to time, which are written and published; and I write a great many letters on this subject, and many of these are published.

There is not a person, who knows anything about the counsel of the First Presidency concerning the immigration, but what knows that we have recommended it to start in season.— True, we have not expressly, and with a penalty, forbidden the immigration to start late, but hereafter I am going to lay an injunction and place a penalty, to be suffered by any Elder or Elders who will start the immigration across the plains after a given time; and the penalty shall be that they shall be severed from the church, for I will not have such late starts.

You know my life; there is not a person in this church and kingdom but what must acknowledge that gold and silver, houses and lands, etc., do multiply in my hands. There is not an individual but what must acknowledge that I am as good a financier as they ever knew, in all things that I put my hands to. This is well known by the people, and they consider me a frugal, saving man, therefore there is no ground or room for their suspecting that my mismanagement caused the present sufferings on the plains. I presume that Br. Kimball never could have thought of such an idea, had he not have heard it.

Say that we start a company from the Missouri river as late as the first of June, and allow them three months in which to perform the journey, then they have time to travel moderately and one month of good weather for leeway, in which to finish the journey, provided they do not complete it in three months; then they may be ninety days or more in coming a thousand miles, which a child of four years old could walk in that time. They may stop and feed their teams, and after they arrive they will have the autumn in which to look around and prepare for winter. This is my policy, and then during the first half of the journey the cattle can get what is called prairie grass, while it is at its best, for it is easily killed by frost, and cattle must have the privilege of feeding upon it before it is too dry, or frost bitten. The month of June is the best month for that grass, and this all know who are acquainted with the western prairies. Then they come to the mountain grass in the latter part of their journey, which, though probably dry by the time they get to it, is filled with nutrition, nearly as much so as grain, and will fatten cattle.

They can come along moderately, take their time and arrive here in August. They should be here in that month, what for? To help us harvest our late wheat, corn, potatoes; to help get up wood, put up fences and prepare for winter. This plan also puts into the possession of new comers time and ability to secure to themselves their winter's provision. Do you not see that such is the result? I have known this all the time. I have always said, send the companies across the plains early. Companies have suffered loss upon loss of lives and property, but never by the dictation of the First Presidency. Do you not readily understand that if the immigration had been here a few months ago, or by the first of September, that they would have had opportunity to rest, and then to secure wheat, to lay up a few potatoes, to get up wood and lay in the staple necessaries for winter?

But our Elders abroad say, by their conduct all the time, that we here in the mountains do not understand what is wanted in the East, as well as they do. They do not proclaim it in so many words, but their conduct does, and "by their fruits ye shall know them." Their actions assert that they know more than we do, but I say they do not. If they had sent our immigration in the season that they should have done, you and I could have kept our teams at home; we could have fenced our five and ten acre lots; we could have put in our fall wheat; could have got up wood for ourselves and for the poor that cannot help themselves; and thus we might have been providing for ourselves and making ourselves comfortable; whereas, now your hands and mine are tied.

This people are this day deprived of thousands of acres of wheat that would have been sowed by this time, had it not been for the misconduct of our immigration affairs this year, and we would have had an early harvest, but now we may have to live on roots and weeds again before we get the wheat. I look at this matter as plainly as I do upon your faces. I have a philosophical forecast, and I do know the results of men's work; I know what the conduct of this people will produce in their future life. If I have not this power naturally, God has surely given it to me.

Well, what shall be done? Why, we must bear it. The elders East fancy that they know more about what is wanted here than we do, and we have to bear it. Let me have had the dictation of the emigration from Liverpool, and I could have brought many more persons here, and at a cost of not more than from three to five dollars of what it has now cost, provided I could have dictated matters at every point. That is not boasting; I only want to tell you that I know more than they know. But what have we to do now? We have to be compassionate, we have to be merciful to our brethren.

Here is br. Franklin D. Richards who has but little knowledge of business, except what he has learned in the church; he came into the church when a boy, and all the public business he has been in is the little he had done while in Liverpool, England; and here is br. Daniel Spencer, br. Richards' first counselor and a man of age and experience, and I do not know that I will attach blame to either of them. But if, while at the Missouri river, they had received a hint from any person on this earth, or if even a bird had chirped it in the ears of brs. Richards and Spencer, they would have known better than to rush men, women, and children on to the prairie in the autumn months, on the 3rd of September, to travel over a thousand miles. I repeat that if a bird had chirped the inconsistency of such a course in their ears, they would have thought and considered for one moment, and would have stopped those men, women and children there until another year.

If any man, or woman, complains of me or of my Counselors, in regard to the lateness of some of this season's immigration, let the curse of God be on them and blast their substance with mildew and destruction, until their names are forgotten from the earth. I never thought of my being accused of advising or having anything to do with so late a start. The people must know that I know how to handle money and means, and I never supposed that anybody had a doubt of it. It will cost this people more to bring in those companies from the plains, than it would to have seasonably brought them from the outfitting point on the Missouri river. I do not believe that the biggest fool in the community could entertain the thought that all this loss of life, time and means was through the mismanagement of the First Presidency.

I know how to dictate affairs; and no man need to have walked in darkness touching his duty with regard to the foreign immigration. You can read their duty in our epistles, letters and sermons; and what is the purport of those documents on this point? That we are new settlers in a wild and uninhabited country, and are thrown upon our own resources; that we need all our teams and means to prepare for those persons who are coming, instead of crippling us by taking our bread, men and teams and going out to meet them. And if the present system continues, this people will be found like the kilkenny cats, which eat up each other clear to their tails, and they were left jumping at one another; such operations will financially use us up.

Last year my back and head ached, and I have been about half mad ever since, and that too righteously, because of the reckless squandering of means and leaving me to foot the bills. Last year, without asking me a word of counsel, without a word being spoken to me about the matter, there was over sixty thousand dollars of indebtedness incurred for me to pay. What for? To fetch a few immigrants here, when I could have brought the whole of them with one quarter of the means.

What is the cause of our immigration's being so late this season? The ignorance and mismanagement of some who had to do with it, and still, perhaps, they did the best they knew how.

Are those people in the frost and snow by my doings? No, my skirts are clear of their blood, God knows. If a bird had chirped in br. Franklin's ears in Florence, and the brethren there had held a council, he would have stopped the rear companies there, and we would have been putting in our wheat, etc., instead of going onto the plains and spending weeks and months to succor our brethren. I make these remarks because they are true.

As to the companies now out, we must bring them in; and another year we will send men to the Missouri river who understand the right management of affairs, and will send them in the speediest conveyances, so that they may not get the "big head" before they arrive there, and then they may be able to do as we tell them.

Can people come across the plains with hand carts? Ask brs. Edmund Ellsworth, Daniel D. McArthur and William Bunker, who led the three hand-cart companies that have already arrived; and the brethren and sisters in those companies state that they crossed quicker, and easier than the wagon companies.

Those who counseled the companies to come on have nearly all gone back to their assistance, after staying at home but about two days, after their return from a long mission, thus manifesting their faith by their works.

I cannot help what is out of my reach, but I am on hand to send more teams, and to send and send, until, if it is necessary, we are perfectly stopped in every kind of business. Br. Heber says that he will send another team, and I mean to send as many more as he does; I ought to send more than br. Heber, for I am fourteen days older than he is. I can send more teams, but I do not intend that the fetters shall be on me another season.

I will mention something more. You cannot hear George D. Grant, Daniel Spencer and others of the lately returned missionaries speak without eulogizing Franklin D. Richards. They are full of eulogizing Franklin D. Richards, but they need to be careful or they will have the "big head" and become as dead and devoid of the Spirit as old pumpkins. And with them it is, "What could I have done without br. George?" And, "what could we have done without br. Franklin? – and when you hear me calling you Rabbi, know ye that I want to be called Rabbi;" and so it goes, but I suppose that this is not what they do it for.

Don't you know that I know whether you are good for anything, or not, without my praising you? I know all about you, without telling what great things you have done, and what you have not done. But the very spirit some have in them of pride, arrogance and self esteem, has led men and women to die on the plains by scores, at least their folly has. And if they had not have had any such spirit about them, God would have whispered to them to have held a council, and would have stopped them from rushing their brethren and sisters into such suffering. But we must now rescue those people, and may God help us to do it: Amen.

(The above is all of the remarks made at that time, that I deem proper to print at present. B.Y.)[4]

---

[4] This note, at the end of the article in the *Deseret News,* indicated that Pres. Young saw and edited the report of this speech before it was printed.

Appendix I

PRESIDENT BRIGHAM YOUNG'S ADDRESS OF NOVEMBER 16, 1856 [1]

I rise to make a few remarks, to satisfy the feelings of the people and correct their minds and judgment.

You have heard concerning the sufferings of the people in the hand-cart trains; and, probably, you will hear the Elders, for some time to come, those who have lately returned from their missions and those now on the plains, speak about the scenes they have witnessed, and I would like to forestall the erroneous impressions that many may otherwise imbibe on this subject.

Count the living and the dead, and you will find that not half the number died in br. Willie's hand-cart company, in proportion to the number in that company, as have died, in past seasons by the cholera in single companies traveling with wagons and oxen, with carriages and horses, and that too in the fore part of the season. When you called to mind this fact, the relations of the sufferings of our companies this season will not be so harrowing to your feelings. With regard to those who have died and been laid away by the roadside on the plains, since the cold weather commenced, let me tell you that they have not suffered one hundredth part so much as did our brethren and sisters who have died with the cholera.

Some of those who have died in the hand-cart companies this season, I am told, would be singing and, before the tune was done, would drop over and breathe their last; and others would die while eating, and with a piece of bread in their hands. I should be pleased, when the time comes, if we could all depart from this life as easily as did those our brethren and sisters. I repeat, it will be a happy

---

[1] Printed in the *Deseret News* of Nov. 26, 1856. This address was delivered a week after the arrival of the Fourth Handcart Company and two weeks before the coming in of the Fifth Company.

circumstance, when death overtakes me, if I am privileged to die without a groan or struggle, while yet retaining a good appetite for food. I speak of these things, to forestall indulgence in a misplaced sympathy. . .

Not long since I was talking with one of the brethren, who has crossed the plains this season, in regard to the propriety of companies' starting so late. He argued that it was far better for the Saints to be striving with all their might, doing all they could to serve the Lord and keep his commandments; and traveling the road to Zion with intent to build it up and establish the kingdom of God on earth, even though they should lay down their lives by the way, than to stop among the gentiles and apostates. I told him it was a good argument, though it was not exactly according to the will of the people and the will of the Lord, for he wishes to throw temptation and trial before his people to prove them preparatory to their eternal exaltation; consequently if the people have not an opportunity of proving themselves before they die, by the rules of their faith and religion, they cannot expect to attain to so high a glory and exaltation as they could if they had been tried in all things. Yet I believe it is better for the people to lay down their bones by the way side, than it is for them to stay in the States and apostatize. . .

If we could have it so, I would a little rather the Saints could be privileged to come here and serve the Lord, or apostatize, as they might choose, for we surely expect to gather both the good and the bad. You recollect, what I told you last Sabbath, that we can beat the world at anything. If br. Willie has brought in some of the sharks, the gatfish, the sheepheads, and so on and so forth, it is all right, for we need them to make up the assortment; as yet I do not know how we could get along without them; all these kinds seem to be necessary.

I have seriously reflected upon the gathering of the people. They have all the time urgently plead and importuned to be gathered, especially from the old countries where they are so severely oppressed; and they are willing to come on foot and pull hand-carts, or do any thing, so they can be gathered with the Saints. Well, we do gather them and where do many of them go? To the devil.

In Nauvoo we had obligations, to an amount exceeding $30,000, against Saints that we had brought from England with our private means; and there is not to exceed two, of all the persons thus brought out, who have honorably come forward to pay one cent of that outlay in their behalf; and some of them were in the mob when it killed Joseph.

I knew all the time that it was better for many of these persons to stop in England and starve to death, for then they might have received a salvation; but they plead with the Lord and with his servants for an opportunity to prove themselves, and made use of it to seal their damnation and become angels to the devil. They had the opportunity, do you not see that they had? . . .

If br. Willie's company had not been assisted by the people in these valleys, and he and his company had lived to the best light they had in their possession, had done every thing they could have done to cross the plains and done just as they did, asking no questions and having no doubting; or, in other words, if, after their President or Presidents told them to go on the plains, they had gone in full faith, had pursued their journey according to their ability and done all they could, and we could not have rendered them any assistance, it would have been just as easy for the Lord to send herds of fat buffaloes to lay down within twenty yards of their camp as it was to send flocks of quails or to rain down manna from heaven to Israel of old.

My faith is, when we have done all we can then the Lord is under obligation and will not disappoint the faithful; he will perform the rest. If no other assistance could have been had by the companies this season, I think they would have had hundreds and hundreds of fat buffaloes crowding around their camp, so that they could not help but kill them. But, under the circumstances, it was our duty to assist them, and we were none too early in the operation.

It was not a rash statement for me to make at our last Conference, when I told you that I would dismiss the conference, if the people would not turn out, and that I, with my brethren, would go to the assistance of the companies. We knew that our brethren and sisters were on the plains and in need of assistance, and we had the power and ability to help them, therefore it became our duty to do so. . .

You hear the testimony of the brethren with regard to the feasibility of the hand-cart mode of traveling; that testimony and their experience have fully sustained the correctness of the views and feelings of myself and others upon that subject from the beginning. Is is the very essence of my feelings that the people in this house, if we wanted to cross the plains next season to the States, could start from here with hand-carts and beat any company in traveling that would cross the plains with teams, and be better off and healthier. These are my feelings, and they have been all the time. . .

I am ashamed of our Elders that go out on missions, it is a disgrace to the Elders of Israel, that they do not start from here with hand-carts, or with nap-sacks on their backs, and go to the States and from there preach their way to their respective fields of labor. Br. Kimball moves that we do not send any Elders from this place again, unless they take hand carts and cross the plains on foot. When the time comes I expect that this motion will be put to vote. . .

I can go on foot across the plains. As old as I am I can take a hand cart and draw it across those plains quicker than you can go with animals and with loaded wagons, and be healthier when I get to the Missouri river. . .

As to the expediency of the hand cart mode of traveling, brs. Ellsworth, McArthur, and Bunker, who piloted the three first hand-cart companies over the plains, can testify that they easily beat the wagon companies. Br. Ellsworth performed the journey in 63 days and br. McArthur in 61½, notwithstanding the hindrance by the baggage wagons. If br. Willie's company could have had their provisions deposited at Laramie and at Green River, and had been free from wagons, they would have been in this valley by the time they were in the storms.

We are not in the least discouraged about the hand-cart method of traveling. As to its preaching a sermon to the nations, as has been remarked, they are preached pretty nigh to destruction already. We do not care whether the hand-cart scheme preaches to them, or whether it be by the teachings of the Elders of Israel. . . Amen.

Appendix J

ATWOOD'S ACCOUNT OF HIS MISSION AND THE FOURTH COMPANY [1]

. . . I did not go to England for gold or silver, but to preach the gospel and gather the poor. We started home with a goodly number on board the ship Thornton, and they were of the class that br. Brigham wrote for when stating, "if they have not a sixpence in the world, they are the ones to bring here." The people that came from where I was laboring were perfectly destitute; we had to buy every thing for them, even to their tin cups and spoons. And let me tell you, the fare that they had on the plains was a feast to them.

They never regretted having to leave their homes, and they are not insensible of the liberality which has been extended to them by the people of these valleys. They have prayed and fasted day after day, and night after night, that they might have the privilege of uniting with their brethren and sisters in these mountains. Many bore testimony to the gentiles that the day would come, although their heads were silvered o'er with age, when they should see br. Brigham in the Valleys of the Mountains. They had borne that testimony so long that it had become like "sounding brass and a tinkling cymbal" to the wicked around them, who said that their way never would be opened. But the Lord opened the way in a manner they looked not for, and they were willing to draw a hand cart, or to take a bundle on their shoulders, or to come in any other way that might be counseled in order to enjoy the blessings you enjoy this day.

---

[1] Address of Elder Millen Atwood in the Tabernacle at Salt Lake City on Nov. 16, 1856, and printed in the *Deseret News* of Nov. 26, 1856. Mr. Atwood was a leader in the ill-fated Fourth Handcart Company. His address was given one week after the arrival of his company in Salt Lake City. Its purpose was to allay somewhat the excitement, fears, criticisms, and terrors regarding the belated handcart companies.

If you could hear the prayers, and see the tears for the privilege of enjoying what you do this day, you never would feel that you have done too much in assisting them.

I will here say, to those who have come from England and been in these valleys some time, that it seems to your friends that are still there as though you have forgotten them and the promises you made to them at the last shaking of the hand. But when br. Brigham offered his property so liberally, and the word came that they should gather from England, it ran like fire in dry stubble and the hearts of the poor saints leapt with joy and gladness; they could hardly contain themselves.

Will they be willing to pull a hand cart? Yes. I felt it; and I felt that it was the right way, and that it would gather more people than any other that had been adopted, and I have never, since I have been in this church, seen the Scriptures so forcibly fulfilled, as I have seen them this season.

With all their wagons and animals they have scarcely brought one blind or lame man to these mountains, but we have gathered up the lame, the blind and those who had not walked a step for years, and brought them on litters or hand carts to this place.

I never enjoyed myself better than in crossing the plains in a hand cart company. The Spirit of the Lord did accompany us, and the brethren and sisters enlivened the journey by singing the songs of Zion. They would travel 16, 18, 20, 23, or 24 miles a day and come into camp rejoicing, build their fires, get their suppers, rest, and rise fresh and invigorated in the morning.

I have seen some so tired in England, after traveling only 5 or 6 miles to a conference, that they would have to go to bed and be nursed for a week. We stimulated the hand cart companies with the words of br. Brigham, which went through me like lightning. He said, "If they would rise up in the name of the Lord, nothing doubting, no power should stop them in their progress to reach this place." It was in his words that they trusted to perform the journey, and they were determined to see his words fulfilled.

I have walked day by day by the side of the hand carts as they were rolling, and when the people would get weary I have seen them by dozens on their knees by the road side crying to the Lord for strength, and there are scores now in this city who walked from Iowa

city to Fort Bridger, and some who were weak and feeble at the
start grew stronger every day.

So long as you kept the bundle on the hand cart and stimulated
them to lay hold of it, they were filled with the Holy Spirit and it
seemed as though angels nerved them with strength; we could out-
travel the cattle and might have camped 15 miles ahead of them every
night if we had had the provisions with us. I told br. Brigham that
I believed we could beat ox, horse, or mule teams.

The gentiles prophesied, as we came along, that we should never
see the Valleys of the Mountains, and laughed us to scorn, and
ridiculed the idea of men and women's traversing 1200 miles with
hand carts, and they marveled to see the saints travel on so cheerfully. I said to them, I defy you and your rulers, with all your gold,
to gather up a set of men, women, and children that will travel with
hand carts; you have not the influence to do that, but when br.
Brigham speaks the word, see how they go.

They were astonished, and wanted to know what kind of a doctrine
we preached to them to make them willing to undertake such a task.
I told them that we administered the same kind of medicine to all,
and it united them together.

The Saints found, however, a wide difference between singing
about going to Zion, and actually going. You would almost have
thought that they would take wings and fly like doves to their
windows, but when they really got into the work, the tune was a
little different; but the great majority stuck to it, and those who
were good for nothing left us at Florence.

We have not suffered a thousandth part as much as you think we
have. Since I have arrived I have heard such tales of woe, though I
do not know who could have told them to you. I know that br.
Brigham and the honest in heart here have suffered more in their
spirits than we have in our bodies. We did not suffer much; we had
a little bit of snow, but that was nothing; and we had enough to eat
as long as it lasted, and when that was gone you furnished us more;
we fared first rate.

Some that met us would gaze on us, and tears would run down
their cheeks, while we were smiling, laughing and singing, and
wondered what they were crying for; but after they had been two or
three days with us, they would tell us that they had altered their

notions. I am in for hand carts, any way; and if I had a father or mother in old Babylon I would like to see them roll a hand cart across the plains.   .   .

I was surprised when I saw the relief wagons loaded with garments, stockings, shoes, blankets and quilts that had been liberally contributed and sent out to minister to us. I never saw the like, and I marveled and wondered where it all came from.   .   .

I am sorry that you have been put to so great expense in the mountains, in consequence of the lateness of this year's immigration; but had you sent loads of gold and silver they would not have been received with such gratefulness as were the clothing, etc. I never saw such a sight.

I am thankful to you for what you have done for us, and to br. Brigham; he has borne the heat and burden of the day, with his brethren. To think that he had done so much to get the companies part way, and then did so much more to get them in, I could hardly keep from weeping.

   .   .   .   The poor want to come here; and have the brethren and sisters that come from England, those who promised their friends with all their soul and heart that they would help out the destitute, done as they agreed? Have you forgotten the last look they placed upon you, when you parted with them?

The first thing you promised to do was to pay your own immigration, if you had to live in a tent while you did it, and then remember the poor in your native country. Many of you have forgotten those promises; you have not kept those covenants, and if I had time I could read some of your names. You ought to have been in England when they heard that they could come with nine pounds sterling, then you who have made solemn promises to your fathers and mothers, brothers and sisters, relatives and friends, would not let your horses and cattle run by scores on the range, without appropriating some of that property to gather them; and if you had the Spirit of the Lord you would strive far more earnestly to fulfill those covenants. [Voice in the Stand: "They and their property will wither and die, if they do not do it."].   .   .

I do not feel to find fault with the providences of the Lord; and as for the hand carts, I am in favor of them. But, while I think of it, I do not want everybody to think that the women can beat the men at pulling hand carts, for they cannot do it. While there was a man to each hand cart and a couple of women, the women could work their fingers on it like playing on a piano; and the smallest woman had as much to eat as I had. . .

I have the best of feelings to every person; and if any one has aught against me, or has considered that I wronged them in any way when we were in the storm and snow and under small rations, let that person come to me and I will put the matter right. . . I used to look on the hand cart trains with pleasure and say, surely we are in kingdom come. . . Amen.

Appendix K

SONGS OF "THE GATHERING"

FAREWELL TO THE LAND OF MY BIRTH [1]

By Ann Cash

How long in the world I have sigh'd,
From the days of my earliest youth,
When, sick of its sin and its pride,
I sought and I pray'd for the Truth.

It came, and the Gospel I found,
To me it was life, joy, and peace;
Salvation was beaming around,
With hopes of a happy release.

And then I was longing to be
Where the will of my Father is done,
Where the noble, the pure, and the free
On the earth are united in one.

I go where no tryants dare come,
Where oppressors would tremble to tread,
Where the honest in heart find a home,
Where the blessings of heaven are shed.

I go where fair virtue supplies
Rich fountains of blessings for all,
Where the Kingdom of Heaven will rise,
While the nations will crumble and fall.

'Tis with joy I am bidding farewell
To the proud, boasted land of my birth;
I go with the upright to dwell,
Where the *pure* will find heaven on earth.

It is Faith, 'tis not fancy, that paints
The vision of bliss that I see;
I go to the home of the Saints —
To Zion, the land of the Free.

---

[1] Printed in the *Millennial Star* of April 14, 1855.

CHEER, SAINTS, CHEER![2]
By J. F. Bell

Chorus:

Cheer, Saints, cheer! we're bound for peaceful Zion;
Cheer Saints, cheer! for that free and happy land!
Cheer, Saints, cheer! we'll Israel's God rely on,
    We will be led by the power of His right hand!

Long, long in Bab'lon we have liv'd in sorrow,
But God in His mercy hath open'd up our way;
"Hope points before, and shows the bright tomorrow,
    "Let us forget the darkness of today."
           Chorus

See, see the judgments o'er the earth extending,
Pestilence, earthquake, famine, fire, and sword;
Soon shall the rulers of this world "come bending,"
    Shorn of their glory, for "thus saith the Lord."
           Chorus

Come, come away, unto the "hill of Zion;"
Come, come away, to the "temple of the Lord;"
Come ye and hear the roaring of the Lion,
    Where "Ephraim's children tremble" at the word.
           Chorus

Away, far away to the "everlasting mountains;"
Away, far away to the "valley of the west;"
Away, far away to yonder gushing fountains,
    Where all the faithful in latter days are blest.
           Chorus

Sing, sing aloud the song of adoration;
Yea, sing aloud for the goodness of our King;
Ye who are blest to see this great salvation,
    Lift up your voices, and make the mountains ring
           Chorus

---

[2] *Ibid.,* April 28, 1855.

COME, HASTE TO THE VALLEY! [3]
By William Willes

Come, haste to the Valley far off in the West,
    Ye Saints of the Lord, tarry not;
Old Babylon soon will be sorely distres't,
    For very near full is her cup.
Then gather your children, and neighbours all warn
    That the hour of her judgment is near,
For soon great Jehovah will laugh her to scorn,
    And mock when she's quaking for fear.

You've tarried in Babylon, brethren, too long,
    Not thinking her hour was so near;
O mingle no more in her unhallow'd throng,
    For shortly she'll end her career
Dire Famine and Pestilence, Battle and Strife
    Will rage through her coasts far and near,
And if you don't flee, you will be like Lot's wife,
    O'ertaken by judgments severe.

You've a haven of refuge to flee unto now,
    While the storm o'er the nations shall ride,
When the torrents of judgment shall furiously flow,
    To punish foul Babylon's pride.
Secure you may rest till the judgments are o'er,
    And the wicked are banish'd the world;
Enjoying the blessings our God has in store
    Where the banner of Freedom's unfurl'd.

And when our great Saviour in glory shall come,
    To dwell with his Saints evermore,
O then we'll rejoice in our beauteous home,
    For Jesus "all things" will restore.
With him through the great Thousand Years we shall reign,
    No sighing, nor sorrow, nor pain,
And then we shall see our great Father again,
    And in His bright presence remain.

[3] *Ibid.*, June 9, 1855.

HYMN [4]

By John Jaques

Great is the goodness of our God,
To those who do His will;
He, with a Father's watchful care,
Shields them from every ill.

In gathering to their mountain home,
How is His power display'd!
He stretches forth His arm to save,
When prayer to Him is made.

When wildly toss'd upon the deep,
And dead ahead's the gale,
By faith in Him the turmoil's hush'd,
And fav'ring winds prevail.

As up Missouri's turbid stream,
The Saints their course pursue,
From the Destroyer He preserves
The faithful and the true.

When passing o'er the wide spread Plains,
Or through the dark ravine,
With favour of the Lamanites,
His kindness still is seen.

And thus, from strength to strength, they're
To Zion's sacred shrine;
Then let us praise the Lord our God,
In songs and hymns divine.

REJOICE! YE SCATTERED SAINTS [5]

By John Jaques

Rejoice! Rejoice! ye scattered Saints,
Be glad! Dry every tear;
The Lord has heard your cries for aid,
Deliverance is near.

[4] *Ibid.*, June 30, 1855.
[5] *Ibid.*, Nov. 24, 1855.

Rejoice! all ye who've laboured long
  To make the Gospel known,
Who've toiled and struggled many years
  To roll the "little stone."

Rejoice! ye who have fed, lodged, clothed
  The Elders in their need,
Them money given, though scant your means;
  You shall be blessed indeed.

Rejoice! all ye who've been oppressed
  Full many a gloomy day,
Who've prayed the dark and lowering clouds
  Would break and pass away.

Rejoice! ye who have had to leave,
  For truth and for the Lord,
Friends, wealth, fair prospects; you shall have
  Your hundred-fold reward.

Rejoice! Rejoice! ye weary ones,
  Who patiently have borne
The heat and burden of the day,
  Though weak and faint and worn.

A word of cheer you've waited for,
  And now that word has come –
"Search through the land the faithful poor;
  To Zion bring them home."

Rejoice! that now your open door
  To Zion's courts appears;
Rejoice! and to old Babylon
  Bequeath your griefs and fears.

Rejoice! let Israel all rejoice,
  And praise the Lord once more,
That Brigham sends the word, the power
  To save the humble poor.

SONG OF THE SAINT [6]
By C.W.

Farewell, my native land, farewell,
Thou hast no charms for me –
I go with Zion's sons to dwell –
'Mongst noble men and free.

Chorus:

Across the mighty deep we roll,
With spirits bold and free:
Blow gentle gale, fill every sail,
And speed us o'er the sea.

Adieu to priestcraft, pomp, and pride,
Oppression and distress;
I go the laws of God t'abide,
With those the Lord will bless.

No earthly tie or sympathy
Shall cause my heart to grieve;
I leave them all most joyfully,
With Saints of God to live.

What is the joy the world affords,
What are its happiest hours,
Compared with those consoling words,
"Eternal lives are yours?"

I'll go to Zion's peaceful vale,
And learn celestial love,
And there prepare with Gods to dwell
In realms of bliss above.

Oh God! preserve us on the way,
Our lives and health defend;
Let angels guard us night and day,
Unto our journey's end.

---

[6] *Ibid.,* Dec. 15, 1855.

A PRAYER [7]
By M.C.

Father, to thee our voices rise
In earnest prayer and praise;
Give us each day some fresh supplies
  Of thy abundant grace.

We ask thee, mighty God, to grant
The boon which we require –
O let thy children know not want
  In this, their heart's desire –

That we from Babylon may go
To Zion's peaceful shore,
And join with all thy faithful ones
  In praising evermore.

Thou know'st our trials and sufferings here,
How hard they are to bear;
Lord, hasten soon the blessed time
  For us to gather there.

That when thou comest to thy own,
We may among them stand,
And hear thee say, "Thou has well done;
  Sit down at my right hand."

SALVATION'S COME [8]

Salvation's come ye Saints of Latter-days,
Tune, tune your harps and sing in joyful lays;
Rejoice aloud, ye humble, faithful poor;
Salvation even now is at your door.

Salvation's come, ye hungering, thirsting Saints;
God in His love has heard your just complaints,
And in His mercy has devised a plan
For gathering Israel to the promised land.

[7] *Ibid.*, Jan. 19, 1856.
[8] *Ibid.*, May 17, 1856.

Ye who have toiled in Babylon for years,
And eat the bread of poverty in tears,
Rejoice, rejoice, for your salvation's come,
And with the just you shall be gather'd home.

Your faith and prayers have a memorial been
Before the lord, and He your works has seen;
Comfort your hearts, ye poor and ye oppress'd,
For you shall enter into Israel's rest.

Your time has come, no longer be afraid,
Your circumstances have demanded aid,
The brethren have responded to the call,
And say, "In Zion there is room for all."

Yes, you shall haste to Zion's happy land,
Where loving brethren greet you heart and hand,
And cheerfully a place for you prepare,
For your reception when you gather there.

There dwells eternal truth, that ne'er will die,
And springs of knowledge that will never dry,
There you may feast your hungry, thirsty soul –
Let these glad tidings sound from pole to pole.

See the result of the Perpetual Fund,
What an amount of real good it's done;
Ye poor subscribe your pence, ye rich your pounds,
Till not a Saint in Babylon is found.

FAREWELL TO THEE ENGLAND [9]
By I.E.R.

Farewell to thee England – bright home of my sires,
Thou pride of the freeman and boast of the brave,
I have lov'd thee – and never till being expires
Can I learn to forget thee, thou star of the wave.

---

[9] *Ibid.,* July 12, 1856. Composed on the deck of the "Horizon," May 24, 1856.

Farewell to thee England, a long, long farewell,
To every dear scene of my infancy's hours,
Ne'er more shall I roam through each moss-covered dell,
Nor pluck the sweet gems of thy blossomy bow'rs.

Farewell to thee England, and farewell to all
Whose love hath yet hallow'd my pathway below,
Though sadly I leave thee, I would not recall
One hour of the past for the present to know.

Though sorrow may cast its deep shade o'er my soul,
When mem'ry recalls one dear form to my mind,
And anguish of spirit which passeth control,
May crush the lone heart where that form is enshrined.

I wish not to linger thy beauties among,
I dare not be false to the God I adore,
Henceforward my lyre to His praises is strung,
And to Him I relinquish those memories of yore.

Yes England, I leave thee, all dear though thou art,
A country more precious lies over the wave,
With hope for thee, Albion, I turn to depart,
God guard thee my country – protect thee and save.

The rose of thy beauty may fade from thy brow,
The day of thy glory in darkness decline
But a halo of splendour encircles thee now,
Which in regions immortal more brightly shall shine.

There are hearts on thy bosom shall hallow thee yet,
There are spirits too noble, and feelings too pure,
There are creatures too worthy for God to forget,
Whose love like His goodness will ever endure.

His blessing be on thee – thou land of my sires,
Thou pride of the freeman, and boast of the brave,
I have loved thee – and never though being expires
Can I learn to forget thee – thou star of the wave.

THE LATTER-DAY ZION [10]
By J. B. Price

Arise, O glorious Zion,
    Thou city of the Lord;
For unto thee the light has come,
    According to his word;
Thy towers and bulwarks soon shall rise
    Majestic and divine,
And God his glory shall reveal
    Within thy sacred shrine.

For silver, gold; for iron, brass,
    Shall God on thee bestow,
And cause thy holy mountain's breast
    With milk and wine to flow:
To thee the orphan and oppressed
    From every land shall come,
With the afflicted and distressed,
    The blind, the halt, the dumb.

Thy God thy light and sun shall be,
    And glory of thy days;
Thy wall shall sure salvation be –
    Thy gates continual praise;
Those that oppressed and hated thee
    Shall bow, with reverence awed,
And at thy feet acknowledge thee
    The Zion of our God.

DEAR ZION [11]
By Charles W. Penrose

O, ye mountains high, where the clear blue sky
Arches over the vales of the free,
Where the pure breezes blow, and the clear streamlets flow,
How I long to your bosom to flee.
    O Zion! dear Zion!
    Far o'er the sea,

---

[10] *Ibid.*, May 28, 1856.
[11] *Ibid.*, May 31, 1856.

My own mountain home, soon to thee will I come,
For my fond hopes are centred in thee.

Though the great and the wise all thy beauties despise,
To the humble and pure thou are dear;
Though the haughty may smile, and wicked revile,
Yet we love thy "glad tidings" to hear.
O Zion! dear Zion!
Far o'er the sea,
Though thou are forc'd to fly to thy "chambers" on high,
We will share joy or sorrow with thee.

In thy mountain retreat God shall strengthen thy feet,
On the necks of thy foes thou shalt tread,
And their silver and gold, as the Prophets have told,
Shall be brought to adorn thy fair head.
O Zion! dear Zion!
Far o'er the seas,
Soon thy towers shall shine with a splendour divine,
And eternal thy glory shall be!

THE GATHERING [12]

By Joel H. Johnson

High on the mountain top
A banner is unfurled.
Ye nations now look up,
It waves to all the world;
In Deseret's sweet peaceful land –
On Zion's mount behold it stand!

For God remembers still
His promise made of old,
That He on Zion's hill
Truth's standard would unfold;
Her light should there attract the gaze
Of all the world in latter days.

---

[12] *Ibid.,* Dec. 27, 1856.

His house shall there be reared,
His glory to display,
And people shall be heard
In distant lands to say,
"We'll now go up and serve the Lord,
"Obey His truth, and learn His word;

"For there we shall be taught
"The law that will go forth,
"With truth and wisdom fraught,
"To govern all the earth;
"Forever there His ways we'll tread,
"And save ourselves with all our dead."

Then hail to Deseret,
A refuge for the good
And safety for the great
If they but understood,
That God with plagues will shake the world
'Till all its thrones shall down be hurled.

In Deseret doth truth
Rear up its royal head,
Though nations may oppose
Still wider it shall spread;
Yes, truth and justice, love and grace,
In Deseret find ample place.

ZION [13]

By Rebecca Heaton

Oft while I stand beside the jingling loom,
I think of Zion's peaceful, happy home,
Where men of God with bold ardour fired,
And with the Spirit of their Lord inspired,
Stand ready to receive Jehovah's will,
Which they to us in distant lands reveal;

[13] *Ibid.,* April 4, 1857.

That we may learn the mind and will of God,
  And tread the path the faithful Saints have trod:
'Tis thus the law from Zion's hill goes forth
  To the benighted nations of the earth.
Though canting hypocrites may rage and lie,
  And hell with all her votaries may try
The kingdom of our God to overthrow,
  And nations to their golden idols bow;
The cause of Zion onward still shall roll
  Till truth and light have spread from pole to pole,
And every honest soul shall gather'd be,
  And in the Valley of the West be free.

YE ELDERS OF ISRAEL [14]
By Cyrus H. Wheelock

Ye elders of Israel, come join now with me
And seek out the righteous, where'er they may be:
In desert, on mountain, on land, or on sea,
And bring them to Zion, the pure and the free.

Chorus:
O Babylon, O Babylon, we bid thee farewell;
We're going to the mountains of Ephraim to dwell.

The harvest is great, and the laborers are few;
But if we're united, we all things can do;
We'll gather the wheat from the midst of the tares
And bring them from bondage, from sorrows and snares.

We'll go to the poor, like our Captain of old,
And visit the weary, the hungry, and cold;
We'll cheer up their hearts with the news that he bore
And point them to Zion and life evermore.

---

[14] *Ibid.,* April 11, 1857. Sung by the Saints aboard the "George Washington," as they set sail from England on March 27, 1857.

COME TO ZION [15]

By Richard Smyth

Israel, Israel, God is calling –
Calling thee from lands of woe;
Babylon the Great is falling;
God shall all her towers o'erthrow.
Come to Zion
'Ere His floods of anger flow.

Israel, Israel, God is speaking:
Hear your great Deliverer's voice!
Now a glorious morn is breaking
For the people of His choice.
Come to Zion,
And within her walls rejoice.

Israel, angels are descending
From celestial worlds on high
And towards man their powers extending
That the Saints may homeward fly.
Come to Zion
For your coming Lord is nigh.

Israel, Israel, canst thou linger
Still in error's gloomy ways?
Mark how judgment's pointing finger
Justifies no vain delays.
Come to Zion
Zion's walls shall ring with praise.

[15] *Sacred Hymns and Spiritual Songs.* For the Church of Jesus Christ of Latter-Day Saints. Revised and corrected. 12th Edition. (Liverpool, George Q. Cannon, 1863). The 11th edition, published in 1856, did not contain this song.

A WORD TO THE SAINTS WHO ARE GATHERING [16]

(from Miss Eliza R. Snow's "Poems.")

Think not, when you gather to Zion,
Your troubles and trials are through –
That nothing but comfort and pleasure
    Are waiting in Zion for you.
No, no; 'tis design'd as a furnace,
All substance, all textures to try –
To consume all the "wood, hay, and stubble,"
    And the gold from the dross purify.

Think not, when you gather to Zion,
That all will be holy and pure –
That deception and falsehood are banish'd,
    And confidence wholly secure.
No, no; for the Lord our Redeemer
Has said that the tares with the wheat
Must grow, till the great day of burning
Shall render the harvest complete.

Think not, when you gather to Zion,
The Saints here have nothing to do
But attend to your personal welfare,
    And always be comforting you.
No; the Saints who are faithful are doing
What their hands find to do, with their might;
To accomplish the gath'ring of Israel,
    They are toiling by day and by night.

Think not, when you gather to Zion,
The prize and the victory won –
Think not that the warfare is ended,
    Or the work of salvation is done.
No, no; for the great Prince of Darkness
A tenfold exertion will make,
When he sees you approaching the fountain
    Where Truth you may freely partake.

---

[16] Reprinted in *Millennial Star* of March 22, 1856. A bit of warning for over-enthusiastic converts.

Appendix L

HANDCART SONGS

THE HAND CART SONG [1]

Ye Saints that dwell on Europe's shores,
Prepare yourselves with many more
To leave behind your native land
    For sure God's Judgments are at hand.
Prepare to cross the stormy main
Before you do the valley gain
And with the faithful make a start
    To cross the plains with your hand cart.

Chorus:
Some must push and some must pull
    As we go marching up the hill,
As merrily on the way we go
    Until we reach the valley, oh.

The land that boasts of liberty
You ne'er again may wish to see
While poor men toil to earn their bread
    And rich men are much better fed,
And people boast of their great light.
You see they are as dark as night
And from them you must make a start
    To cross the plains with our handcarts.

---

[1] Words composed by J. D. T. McAllister, who was at the Iowa City out-fitting point helping the first emigrants prepare for their handcart trek. He was at first chosen to lead the second company; but later he was made commissary, and McArthur was appointed captain of the company.–"Diary of John D. T. McAllister," MS., Brigham Young University Library, Provo, Utah. McAllister says he was so busy that he did not journalize from June 1 to Aug. 5, which doubtless explains why no mention of the song is found in his diary.

But some will say it is too bad
The Saints upon their feet to pad
And more than that to push a load
   As they go marching up the road.
We say this is Jehovah's plan
To gather out the best of men,
And women too, for none but they
   Will ever gather in this way.

As on the way the carts are hurled
'Twould very much surprise the world
To see the old and feeble dame
   Lending her hand to push the same.
The young girls they will dance and sing,
The young men happier than a king,
The children they will laugh and play
   Their strength increasing day by day.

But ere before the valley gained
We will be met upon the plains
With music sweet and friends so dear
   And fresh supplies our hearts to cheer.
Then with the music and the song,
How cheerfully we'll march along
So thankfully you make a start
   To cross the plains with our hand carts.

When we get there amongst the rest
Industrious be and we'll be blessed,
And in our chambers be shut in
   While Judgment cleanse the earth from sin.
For well we know it will be so,
God's servants spoke it long ago,
And tell us it's high time to start
   To cross the plains with our hand carts.

A HANDCART SONG
By Lydia D. Alder

Obedient to the Gospel call
We serve our God, the All in All,
  We hie away to Zion.
We do not wait to ride all day
But pull our handcarts all the way
  And Israel's God rely on.

Chorus:

To Zion pull the handcart
  While singing every day
The glorious songs of Zion
  That haste the time away.

Our prayers arise to greet the sun
And when his shining course is run
  We gather round the camp fire,
To talk of God and all his ways,
His wondrous works of Latterdays
  Until the dancing blaze expires.

We climb the hills and far away
Then down where sleeping valleys lay
  While still the miles onward roll.
Till Zion rises on our sight
We pull our handcarts with our might
  Triumphant reach the goal.

And those we left beside the way
To dream where summer breezes play
  Saw in the camp fires' vivid blaze
Fair Zion with her golden skies,
Grand temples there that stately rise
  And satisfied, rest always!

HAND-CART SONG
By Emily H. Woodmansee
(Tune – *"A Little More Cider"*)

Oh, our faith goes with the hand-carts,
    And they have our hearts' best love;
'Tis a novel mode of traveling,
    Devised by the Gods above.

Chorus:

Hurrah for the Camp of Israel!
    Hurrah for the hand-cart scheme!
Hurrah! hurrah! 'tis better far
    Than the wagon and ox-team.

And Brigham's their executive,
    He told us the design;
And the Saints are proudly marching on,
    Along the hand-cart line.

Who cares to go with the wagons?
    Not we who are free and strong;
Our faith and arms, with a right good will,
    Shall pull our carts along.

THE MISSIONARY'S HANDCART SONG
By Elder Philip Margetts [2]
(Tune – *"Oh, Susannah"*)

No purse, no scrip they bear with them
But cheerfully they start
To cross the plains a thousand miles
And draw with them a cart.
Ye nations list, the men of God
From Zion now they come
Clothed with the priesthood and the power
To gather Israel home.

[2] Written for the east-bound missionary handcart company of 1857, by a member of that party, and published in *Millennial Star* of Aug. 15, 1857.

Chorus:
Then cheer up ye Elders,
 You to the world will show
That Israel must be gathered soon
 And oxen are too slow.

Ye pious men whose sympathy
Is touched for fallen man,
A pattern now is set for you,
 Just beat it if you can;
Here's men who're called to go abroad
The Gospel to impart.
They leave their friends and homes so dear
 And start with their handcart.

Now competition is the rage,
Throughout the world 'tis true,
To head the Mormons they must rise
 Far earlier than they do.
For Mormonism it is sound,
Without a crack or flaw,
They know the arts and sciences,
 And we're learning how to *draw*.

Some folks would ask, Why do you start
With carts, come tell I pray?
We answer: When our Prophet speaks,
 The Elders all obey.
Since Brigham has the way laid out
That's best for us, we'll try
Stand off ye sympathetic fools,
 The handcarts now or die.

Then come ye faithful ministers,
With blessings now we'll go,
To gather out the honest hearts
 From darkness and from woe.
Our strength increasing day by day
As from this land we part,
We'll bless the day that we were called
 To go with our handcart.

Appendix M

Roster of Members
of the Handcart Companies[1]

FIRST COMPANY
EDMUND ELLSWORTH, Captain (37)

Argyle, Joseph (37), wife and children
" Jane (33) (wife)
" Joseph (14)
" Benjamin (12)
" Mary (10)
" Frances (5)
" Lorenzo (3)
" Priscilla (1)
Ash, John (36), wife and two children
" Sophia (wife) (26)
" Ellen (1½)
" Elizabeth (2 mos.)
Ash, Sarah (widow) (59)
" Joseph (son) (8)
Bailey, James (53), wife and 5 children
" Mary Ann (52) (wife)
" John (20)
" Thomas (19)
" Alfred (17)
" Mary Ann (15)
" Louisa (12)

Baker, Mary Ann (48), widow and 5 children
" John (19)
" Emma (17)
" Job (15)
" Harriet (11)
" Wilford (4)
Baldwin, Hannah (18)
Bates, Mary Ann (21)
Birch, James (38), wife and 3 children
" Mary Ann (29) (wife)
" Thomas (8)
" Mary Ann (6)
" Edward J. (2)
Birch, William (60) and wife
" Elizabeth (40)
Bond, Samuel (61), wife and 2 children
" Elizabeth (55) (wife)
" Samuel, Jr. (25)
" William (23)
Bourne, Thomas (59), wife and 6 children

[1] The lists are from those in the L.D.S. Church Historian's Office, Salt Lake City, with a few names added from other sources. The ages, where known, are put in parentheses following the names. Some discrepancies result from variations in the time the records were made.

Bourne, Margaret (48) (wife)
"   Mary Ann (22)
"   Margaret (20)
"   James (16)
"   Priscilla (14)
"   Louisa (12)
"   John (7)
Bowen, David (18)
Bowers, James (45), wife and 6 children
"   Mary Ann (51) (wife)
"   Sarah (18)
"   Abraham (17)
"   Isaac (14)
"   Jacob (10)
"   Isaiah (8)
"   Shadrach (6)
Bridges, Charles H. (21)
Brough, Alice (69) (widow)
Brough, William (30)
Bunney, John (28), and wife
"   Ann (25)
Butler, William (28) and wife
"   Emma (25)
Chapman, John (58)
Chester, Ann (20)
Clark, George (55), wife and 3 children
"   Mary A. (51) (wife)
"   Charlotte (18)
"   William (14)
"   Hannah (6)
Commander, James (35) and wife
"   Mary (25)
Devereaux, John (51)
Doney, John (35) and wife
"   Ann (24) (wife)
"   Mary Jane (born on the plains)

Eldredge, Thomas, wife & child
Fowler, Thomas (19)
Franklin, Elizabeth (51) (widow)
Frisby, Absalom (21)
Frost, Edward (33), wife and 2 children
"   Eliza (26) (wife)
"   Isabella (7)
"   John F. (4)
Galloway, Andrew (28), wife and daughter
"   Jane (25) (wife)
"   Annie Eliza (3)
Goode, Maria (25)
Goodworth, Hannah (43) widow and 3 sons
"   Joseph (19)
"   Frederick (8)
"   Richard (5)
Green, William (30)
Ham, Ann (31)
Hanson, George (26), wife and daughter
"   Frances (25) (wife)
"   Clara (11 months)
Harmon, William (52)
Henwood, John (46), wife and 2 children
"   Elizabeth (43) (wife)
"   Richard (19)
"   Elizabeth (16)
Hill, Eleanor (40)
Hunt, Abraham (30) and wife
"   Eliza (30)
Hurst, Abraham and wife
Ivins, Thomas (70)
Jeffries, Eliza (21)
Jones, Daniel (41), wife and 6 children

Jones, Ann (36) (wife)
" Rachel (16)
" Ann (14)
" Daniel (12)
" Marion (7)
" Richard J. (3)
" Sarah (1)
Jones, James (56) and wife
" Sabina (36) (wife)
Jones, Mary Ann
Kettle, John (53), wife and 6
children
" Judith (43) (wife)
" Mary Ann (18)
" Robert (14)
" Eliza (12)
" James (9)
" Samuel (5)
" Hannah (2)
Lee, John (33), wife and 6 children
" Sarah (33) (wife)
" William (12)
" Fanny (11)
" Elizabeth (9)
" Samuel (5)
" Chauncey (3)
" Sarah Ann (9 mos.)
Lewis, Jane (29) Mrs.
Lewis, John (33) and son
" John S. (8)
Lloyd, Benjamin (23)
Lloyd, John (38), wife and 6
children
(dropped out, June 20)
" Elizabeth (38) (wife)
" Mary (11)
" John (10)
" William (8)
" Thomas (5)

Lloyd, Jane (2)
" Martha (4 weeks)
Lloyd, Thomas (24)
" Benjamin
Marshall, Sarah (34) and 6
children
" Lavinia (12)
" Selina (10)
" Tryphena (8)
" Louisa (6)
" George (4)
" Sarah (2)
Mayo (or Mays), Mary (65)
widow
Meadows, Mary Ann (21)
Miller, Sarah T. (or J.)
Morris, William (53) and wife
" Sarah Ann (53)
Moss, Henry (19)
Moyle, John (48), wife and 5
children
" Philippi (40) (wife)
" Elizabeth (19)
" Stephen (15)
" Henry (12)
" Alfred (9)
" John (5)
Murray, James
Nappriss, George (23)
Oakley, John (36)
Passey, Thomas (18)
Phillips, John A. (22)
Powell, John (43), wife and 6
children
" Elizabeth (35) (wife)
" William (15)
" Mary (13)
" Margaret (8)
" Anna (4)
" David (infant)

Pratt, William (31), wife and 4
  children
  " Caroline (31) (wife)
  " Eleanor Saline (12)
  " George (9)
  " Orson (3)
  " Emily (1)
Preater, Richard (29), wife and
  2 children
  " Mary (31) (wife)
  " Salome M. (4)
  " Lora I. (2)
Price, Ann (46), widow and 2
  daughters
  " Emma (19)
  " Eliza (17)
Rasdell, Joseph (or John) (20)
  and wife
  " Elizabeth (22) (wife)
Richins, Thomas (30), wife and
  son
  " Harriet Devereaux (22)
    (wife)
  " Albert Franklin (1 mo.)
Robinson, Eliza (26)
Robinson, John (46), wife and
  4 children
  " Emma (27) (wife)
  " Elizabeth (21)
  " Sarah (19)
  " John (16)
  " Clara (10 mos.)
Sanders, Walter (65) and chil-
  dren
  " Mary (19)
  " James (15)
  " John (13)
  " Thomas (10)
Sheldon, Richard (19)

Shinn, James Sr. (60) & family
Shinn, James Jr. (26), wife and
  child
  " Mary (24) (wife)
  " Sidney (6 weeks)
  " Robert (28) and family
  " Eliza (28) (wife)
  " Mary (7)
  " Louisa Eliza (6)
  " Ann (4)
  " Emma (3)
  " Hannah (22)
  " Ellen (19)
Sprigg, Sarah Ann (18)
Stalley, Peter
Stevenson, Alexander, wife and
  7 children
  " Magdalene (35) (wife)
  " Isabella (27) (dropped
    out July 10)
  " John (13)
  " Magdalene (11)
  " Alexander (7)
  " Orson (5)
  " Joseph B. (3)
  " Marion (1½)
Stoddard, Robert (51), wife and
  3 children
  " Margaret (44) (wife)
  " James (14)
  " Mary (10)
  " Dinah (5)
Stoddard, William (42), wife
  and 7 children
  " Margaret (37) (wife)
  " Caleb (18)
  " Robert (16)
  " Jane (12)
  " Sarah (10)

Stoddard, Hannah (8)
"   Mary (3)
"   Margaret (1)
Taylor, Elizabeth (24)
Vaughan, Eleanor (78)
Walker, Elizabeth (17)
Walker, Elizabeth (24)
Walker, Emma (21)
Walker, Henry (58) and wife
"   Isabella (50)
Walters, Archer (47), wife and
5 children
"   Harriet (47) (wife)
"   Sarah (18)

Walters, Henry (16)
"   Harriet (14)
"   Martha (12)
"   Lydia (6)
Warner, James (60), wife and
daughter
"   Ann (49) (wife)
"   Sarah Ann (14)
Wareing, George (18)
Welling, Job (23), wife and son
"   Frances E. (25) (wife)
"   Job (1½)
Williams, George (18)
Yeo, William

SECOND COMPANY
Daniel D. McArthur, Captain (36)

Aitken, William K. (35) and 2
children
" Cecilia (14)
" Thomas (10)
Anderson, Agnes (52) and 3
children
" Archibald (20)
" John (16)
" James (14)
Arthur, ——, and family (drop-
ped out June 30)
Baranigan, Mary
Bathgate, Mary (59) and daugh-
ter
" Mary (12)
Bell, John (54), wife and 2
children
" Maria (55) (wife)
" James (17)
" Samuel (15)
Bermingham, Patrick Twiss
(26), wife and children
" Elizabeth Kate (24)
(wife)
" Mary Katherine (4)
" Edward J. (3)
" Jane E. (infant)
Bone, Mary Ann (10)
Bowring, Henry E. (33), wife
and child
" Ellen (18) (wife)
" Wallace (4)
Bruner, Susannah (66)
Burdett, Elizabeth (65)

Burdett, Emma M. (19)
Chambers, David (54), wife, son
" Mary (54) (wife)
" David, Jr. (14)
Clotworthy, Hugh (29), wife
and 4 children
" Jean (36) (wife)
" Janet (9)
" Mary (7)
" Thomas (3)
" Jean (2)
" Margaret (2 mos.)
Crandall, Spencer
Crawford, James (23)
Dechman, James
Dorrech, Elizabeth
Downie, Margaret (30)
Dreaney, John (31), wife and 2
children
" Mary Jane (28) (wife)
" Samuel (2½)
" Isabella (4 mos.)
Eardley, Bedson (23) and wife
" Louisa (27)
Elliker, Heinrich (59), wife and
7 children
" Margarethe (54) (wife)
" Heinrich Jr. (26)
" Barbara (24)
" Elizabeth (22)
" Konrad (20)
" Margarethe (18)
" Susanna (14)
" Jonannes (13)

Finlay, William (49), wife and child
" Lindsay (48) (wife)
" Ann (17)
Frew, John (30), wife and 3 children
" Jean (35) (wife)
" James (8)
" Janet (7)
" Mary (1½)
Furrer, Anna
Gale, Mary (47)
Gallop, Thomas (39) and wife
" Agness (36) (wife)
Gardner, Ann (48), and children
" Agnes (20)
" James (18)
" Alex. (16)
" Elizabeth (14)
" Walter (8)
Grainger, Walter (34), wife and 5 children
" Catherine (36) (wife)
" Robert (14)
" Alexander (9)
" Catherine (7)
" Walter (5)
" John (4)
Gray, John (51), wife and 4 children
" Jane (51) (wife)
" Jane (22)
" Franklin (4)
" Mary (2)
" William (5 weeks)
Hall, William (29)
Hardie, Janet (45) and 5 children

Hardie, Phyllis (23)
" Agnes (21)
" John (15)
" Grace (13)
" James (10)
Hargraves, Samuel (39), wife and 6 children
" Agnes (33) (wife)
" Jane (16)
" Mary (13)
" Janet (10)
" John (8)
" Elizabeth (3)
" Margaret (1½)
Hay, Mary (34)
Heaton, William (28), wife and 2 children
" Esther B. (25) (wife)
" Christopher B. (3)
" William McD. (5 mos.)
Hillhouse, William (46), wife and 8 children
" Margaret (52) (wife)
" Janet (24)
" John (22)
" Mary (15)
" Robert (13)
" David (11)
" Elizabeth (6)
" William (2)
" Janet (1 mo.)
Hodgetts, Hannah (18)
Ipson, Niels Peter (22) and wife
" Georgina Keller (27)
Johnstone, George (36), wife and child
" Janet (14) [? 24]
" Isabella (4)

Johnston, William (29), wife
and 3 children
" Elizabeth (21 [?]) (wife)
" David (7)
" Richard (5)
" William (3)
Kennington, Richard (52), wife
and 5 children
" Mary (47) (wife)
" Sarah J. (17)
" William (14)
" Eliza (12)
" Richard (10)
" Mary A. (1½)
Lawrensen, William (55), wife
and 2 children
" Ann (50) (wife)
" Jane (18)
" Margaret (11)
Lawson, William (29)
Leonard, Truman
Lucas, Anthony (58), wife and
3 children
" Mary (57) (wife)
" Eliza (26)
" Ann (21)
" Mary (14)
Lucas, Thomas (25)
Ludert, Josephine (43) & child
" Alphonse (6)
McCleave, John (48), wife and
7 children
" Nancy Jane (40) (wife)
" Margaret (17)
" Mary Jane (15)
" Isabella (13)
" John T. (11)
" Joseph S. (8)
" Eliza (6)
" Alexander (2)

McDonald, Alexander (26)
McDonald, John (24)
McDougall, Joseph (25)
McGowan, Mary (29)
Mathiasen, Mary (21)
Maxwell, Elizabeth (52) and 5
children
" Arthur (30)
" Catherine (25)
" Elizabeth (23)
" Ralph (18)
" Ann (14)
Meikle, Margaret (57) and 3
children
" William (30)
" Isabella (19)
" James (17)
Morehouse, Elizabeth (30)
Muir, George (23), wife and 2
children
" Margaret (26) (wife)
" Mary (2)
" Jean (1)
Park, Isabella (62)
Parker, Robert (35), wife and 4
children
" Ann (36) (wife)
" Maximillian (11)
" Martha A. (9)
" Arthur (6)
" Ada (8 mos.)
Peacock, George (30) and 2
children
" Mary Ann
" George Jr.
Ramsay, Ralph (32), wife and
son
" Elizabeth (33) (wife)
" John S. (15)

Randall, Anna M. (31) and son
"   Oscar J. (1½)
Reed, Elizabeth (20)
Reid, James (39), wife and 4
   children
"   Elizabeth (31) (wife)
"   Elizabeth (11)
"   James (6)
"   Mary (4)
"   John (1)
Richardson, Elizabeth (or Eliza)
   (33)
Richardson, Peter (24)
Russell, Ellen (23)

Sanderson, Rebecca (41) and 2
   children
"   Saran Ann (11)
"   Rhoda (9)
Schies, John (39)
Shields, Elizabeth (26)
Smart, Sarah (26)
Smith, Andrew (28)
Stewart, Agnes with 3 children
Tweedle, Elizabeth (21)
Wandles, Ellen (28) & child
"   Ellen (6)
Wright, Maria (25)
Wright, William (22)

THIRD COMPANY
EDWARD BUNKER, Captain (33)

Axton, Thomas (80), wife and son
" Elizabeth (51) (wife)
" John (11)
Barker, Barbara
Barker, Margaret
Barker, Robert
Bridge, James (49)
Brooks, Samuel (65) and family
" Emma (48) (wife)
" Mary (17)
" George (11)
" Francis F. (6)
Butler, Ann (38) and children
" Elizabeth (13)
" William (8)
Butler, John (26) and wife
" Jane (24) (wife)
Chapel, Joseph (25) and family
" Mary (24) (wife)
" Margaret (1)
Cousins, John (25)
Cousins, Martha (24)
Davies, Ellen
Davies, Elizabeth
Davies, George W. (32) and family
" Hannah (23)
" Joseph (1)
Davies, Mary and family
Edmunds, John (66)
Edmunds, Nathaniel (26) and family
" Jane (23) (wife)
" John (6)

Evans, Abraham (47) and family
" Mary A. (42) (wife)
" Jenkin A. (21)
" Elizabeth (12)
" Mary Ann (7 months)
Evans, David and wife
Evans, Letitia (20)
Evans, Morgan and family
" Ann (19) (wife)
" Gwenllian (7 months)
Evans, Moses
Evans, Thomas and son
Evans, Thomas (37) and family
" Mary (35)
" Thomas (9)
" Emma (8)
" Hyrum (5)
" Elizabeth (3)
" Joseph (1)
" Hannah (74) (widow)
Evans, Thomas David and wife
" Priscilla Merriman (wife)
Giles, Thomas D. (35) and family
" Margaret (34) (wife)
" Joseph (7)
" Hyrum (6)
" Maria (1)
Grant, David (39)
Hughes, Ann (15)
Hughes, Elizabeth (60)
Hughes, William (49) and wife
" Elizabeth (49) (wife)
James, John (27)

James, Sarah (15)
Jarman, Thomas (45) and family
  "   Ann (54)
  "   Richard (11)
  "   John (9)
  "   Margaret (6)
Jenkins, Henry and family
  "   Martha (45) (wife)
  "   Margaret (18)
Jenkins, John (25)
Jenkins, Thomas (36)
Jenkins, William (48) and family
  "   Margaret (47) (wife)
  "   William (14)
  "   Elizabeth (12)
  "   Thomas (8)
Job, Hannah (26) and daughter
  "   Mary (8)
Jones, Margaret
Jones, Owen
Jones, Thomas (58) and family
  "   Ruth (49) (wife)
  "   Eleanor (23)
Jones, William (45) and wife
  "   Mary Ann (50) (wife)
Lane, Elizabeth
Lewis, Daniel (50)
Lewis, David (30) and family
  "   Anne (21) (wife)
  "   Joshua (5)
  "   Mary Ann (2)
  "   John (8 mos.)
Lewis, Elias (21) and wife
  "   Ellenor Roberts (22)
Lewis, Enoch (36) and family
  "   Jane (33) (wife)
  "   John (9)
  "   Martha (7)

Lewis, William (24) and wife
Llewellyn, Rees R. (27) and wife
  "   Anne (20)
Llewellyn, Mary (47) and family
  "   Edmund (21)
  "   John (18)
  "   Ann (17)
  "   Elizabeth (11)
McDonald, John (58)
Mathews, Anne (21)
Mathews, Hopkin (32) and family
  "   Margaret (32) (wife)
  "   Elizabeth (10)
  "   Mary (9)
  "   Margaret (6)
  "   Joan (4)
  "   Alma (3)
Morgan, James (28)
Morgan, Thomas (28) and wife
Morgan, William (25)
Morgan, William (47) and wife
Morris, Morris N. and wife
Orton, Alexander
Orton, Samuel
Owens, Owen (18)
Parry, Ann (21) spinster
Parry, Edward (29)
Parry, Elanor (26)
Parry, John (54) and family
  "   Elizabeth (47)
  "   Winnifred (18)
  "   John (14)
  "   Edward (12)
  "   Elizabeth (6)
Parry, John (38) and wife
  "   Harriet (28)
  "   Brigham B. (infant)

Perkins, Ann (69)
Phillips, Edward (48) and family
" Elizabeth (47)
" Jacob (22)
" Elizabeth (21)
" Sarah (16)
" Margaret (14)
" Mary (9)
Phillips, Louisa (18)
Rees, Isaac (32) and wife
" Hannah (28)
Rees, Margaret (46) and family
" George (15)
" Anne (13)
" Lodwick (10)
Rees, Thomas (39) and family
" Margaret (37) (wife)
" Anne (16)
" Alfred (14)
" Sarah (11)
" Eleanor (9)
" Nephi (8)
" Maria (5)
" Lenorah (2)
Roberts, David (45) and family
" Mary (31) (wife)
" William (12)
" David (11)
" Rosa (6)
" Mary (4)
" Margaret (2)
Roberts, David R. (41) and family
" Catherine (48) (wife)
" Robert (18)
" Thomas (15)
" Daniel (13)

Roberts, Ann (11)
" Elizabeth (9)
" Jane (6)
Roberts, John D. (38) and family
" Anne (33) (wife)
" Jacob (7)
" John Powell (infant)
Roberts, John R. (32) and family
" Mary (34) (wife)
" Elizabeth (8)
" William (5)
" Robert Ed. (2 months)
Thayne, John T. (26) and wife
" Margaret R. (23) (wife)
Thomas, Anne (77)
Thomas, Daniel (37)
Thomas, Edward
Thomas, Eliza
Thomas, Margaret (46)
Walters, Elizabeth (17)
Walters, Hannah (28) & family
" Maria (11)
" Thomas (6)
" Elizabeth (4)
Walters, Sarah (26)
Watkins, William and wife
" Charlotte George (wife)
Williams, Catherine and family
Williams, John (40) and family
" Mary (42) (wife)
" Elizabeth (18)
" Sarah (16)
" Anne (14)
" Jane (12)
Williams, Lititia (20)
Williams, Richard

FOURTH COMPANY
JAMES G. WILLIE, Captain (41)

Ahmanson, John
Anderson, Anne
Anderson, David (17)
Anderson, Marie
Anderson, Nils (or Niels) (41)
" Mette (49) (wife)
" Anna (14) daughter
Atwood, Millen (38)
Bailey, John (51) and family
" Elizabeth (51) (wife)
" Elizabeth (17)
Bird, Mary A. (39) and family
" Ann (20)
" Sabina (17)
" Ezra (14)
" Martha (12)
" Sarah (10)
" Susannah (8)
" William (6)
Bowles, Edward (50) & family
" Ann (52) (wife)
" Thomas (19)
" Enoch (11)
Brazier, George (21)
Brazier, John (19)
Bretton, Mary E.
Browant, Emma (18)
Brown, Castina
Bryant, Ann (69)
Burt, Alexander (19)
Calchwell, Mary A., and family
Campkin, Martha (35) & family
Charles, Sarah

Chetwin, Martha
Chislett, John (24)
Christensen, Anders (21)
Cook, Minea
Cook, Sophia with daughter
Cooper, Ann (36) with family
" Mary Ann (6)
" Adelaide (4)
" Sarah Ann (2)
Cox, Theophilus (25)
Crook, Sophia and daughter
Culley, Benjamin (60)
Culley, Elizabeth (23)
Culley, Jane (22)
Cunningham, James (54) with family
" Elizabeth (48) (wife)
" Catherine (17)
" George (15)
" Elizabeth (12)
" Margaret (9)
Curtis, George (64)
Dorney, Hannah
Dorney, Mary
Douglish (or Daglish), Margaret (29)
Edwick, William (17)
Elder, Joseph
Evans, Amelia (18)
Fannel, Elizabeth
Fannel, Mary
Findlay, Allen M. (26) with family

Findlay, Jessie Ireland (26)
(wife, married on ship)
" Mary McPherson
(mother)
Forbes, Elizabeth (8) with Isabelle Wilkie, widow
Gadd, Sam (40) with family
" Eliza (40) (wife)
" Alfred (18)
" Jane (16)
" William (12)
" Samuel (10)
" Mary Ann (7)
" Sarah (5)
" Isaac (1)
" Daniel (1)
Gardner, James (27) with family
" Hannah (27) (wife)
" Mary A. (6)
" Agnes E. (5)
" Frederick J. (3)
" John W. (7 months)
Gibb, James (67)
" Mary (53) (wife)
Gillman, Chesterton J. (64)
Girdlestone, Thomas (62) with family
" Mary (59) (wife)
" Emma (21) (daughter)
Godfrey, Ann
Godfrey, Richard (21)
Gregerson, Marcan
Griffiths, Catherine M. (32)
Griffiths, Edward (25) (from Wales)
Griffiths, Mary P.

Gurney, Charles (36) & family
" Charlotte (37) (wife)
" Mary A. (15)
" Joseph (13)
Hailey, William, with wife
Hanson, Cassius
Hanson, Nils (or Niels) (43)
" Anna Catherine (42) (wife)
Hanson, Rasmus (40)
" Anna (40) (wife)
Hanson, Rasmus Peter (16)
Hardwick, Richard (50)
Harren, James (29) with family
" Mary (wife)
Herbert, Anna (or Ann) (26)
" Charles (2 yrs., 11 mo.) (son)
Hill, Emily (20) (became E. H. Woodmansee, poetess)
Hill, Julia (22) (became wife of Israel Ivins)
Hodges, Janet (Janetta) (55)
Hodges, Mary (20)
Hooley (or Holley), Thomas (21)
Howard, Ann (30)
Humphries, George (45) with family
" Harriet (47) (wife)
" Edwin (18)
" Ann (16)
" Mary (14)
" Elizabeth (12)
" Hannah (9)
" Selina (6)
" James (1)

Impey, Jesse (31) with family
" Mary A. (29) (wife)
" William (9)
" James (6)
" Ann (4)
" Sarah J. (9 mo.)
Ingra, George (68)
" Elizabeth (75) (wife)
Jacobson, Paul (53)
" Lovisa (53) (wife)
Jacobson, Peter (24) with family
" Anna K. (32) (wife)
" Jens Peter (3)
James, John (53)
James, William (46) with family
" Jane (40) (wife)
" Sarah (19)
" Emma (16)
" Reuben (14)
" Mary Ann (11)
" Martha (9)
" George (6)
" John (5)
" Jane (6 mo.)
Janes, Petrina C.
Jeffry (or Jeffries), William (24)
Jensen, Catherine (24)
Jensen, Johanna Marie (21)
Jenson, Andreas (47) & family
" Anna Christensen (47) (wife)
" Michael (10)
" Anton (8)
Jenson, Carsten
Jones, Ellen (6) (with John Bailey)

Jorgensen, Anders (46) & family
" Elizabeth (42) (wife)
" Hans (12)
" Maren (8)
" Anna (6)
" Jorgen (3)
Jorgensen, Christian
Jorgensen, Maren S. (8)
Kelley, Barbara (29)
Kelly, John (31) with family
" Mary (30) (wife)
" John C. (7)
Key, Rose (50) with family
Kirby, Anna (Hannah) (34)
Kirby, Mary (Maria) (14)
Kirkpatrick, Elizabeth (31)
Laird, James (32) with family
Langman, Rebecca (22)
Larson, Peter (43) with family
" Anna Christine (37) (wife)
" Niels (12)
" Anna Sophie (10)
" Martine (5)
Ledington (Ledingham), William, with family
Linford, John (47) with family
" Maria (42) (wife)
" George J. (17)
" Joseph W. (14)
" Amasa C. (11)
Loutross, Louisa
Madsen, Ole
Madsen, Ole (41) and family
" Anna (46) (wife)
" Johanna M. (16)
" Metta Kirstine (13)
" Anna Marie (10)
" Anders (6)

Madsen, Peter (62)
" Petrea (36) (daughter)
Marsen, Peter, with family
McCullick (McCullock), John (20)
McKey, Joseph (57)
McNeil, Christina (24)
McPhell, (McPhail) Archibald (30) with family
McPhail, Jane (33) (wife)
" Henrietta (15)
" Jane (3)
" Donald
Meadows, Joseph, with wife
Millard, Esther (33)
Miller, Mary A. (30)
Miller, Mercy (26)
" William A. S. (5) (son)
Mortenson, Peter (50) with family
" Lena (47) (wife)
" Anna Kirstine (24) (Peterson)
                      (Peterson)
" Anders Jorgen (22)   "
" Hans Jorgen (18)   "
" Lars (13)   "
" Metta Kirstine (10) "
" Maria (8)   "
" Caroline (5)   "
Moulton, Thomas (45) with family
" Sarah (37) (wife)
" Sarah (19)
" Mary Ann (14)
" William (12)
" Joseph (10)
" James (7)

Moulton, Charlotte (4)
" Sophia (2)
Neilsen, Ella
Newman, Mary Ann (37) and children
" Eliza (17)
" William (14)
" John (12)
" Mary Ann (9)
" Caroline (7)
" Ellen (5)
Nielsen, Bertha
Nielsen, Jens (35) and family
" Else (26) (wife)
" Niels (5) son
Nockolds, John
Norris, Cecelia (26)
Norris, Sarah (Ann) (22)
Oakey, Thomas (42) with family
" Ann (43) (wife)
" Ann (23)
" Charles (18)
" Jane (16)
" Heber S. (14)
" Lorenzo N. (12)
" Rhoda R. (10)
" Reuben H. (8)
" Sarah Ann (4)
Oborn, Joseph with family
" Maria Stradling (wife)
" John
Oliver, Ann (23)
Oliver, James (31)
Olsen, Ann (64)
Ore, Abraham (40)
" Eliza (41) (wife)
Osborn, Ann (24)

Osborne, Daniel (35) with family
" Susannah (33) (wife)
" Susannah (10)
" Daniel (7)
" Sarah A. (3)
" Martha (1)
Page, William (19)
Panting, Elizabeth (28) with family
" Christopher (5)
" Jane (9 mo.)
Peacock, Alfred (18)
Perkins, Mary A. (64)
Peterson, Anders Jorgen (22) (see Mortensen above – 7 children listed under both names)
Peterson, Jens (36) with family
" Anna (33) (wife)
" Johanna (12)
" Metta Maria (10)
" Hans Peter (7)
" Christian (5)
" Peter (4)
" Christian (1)
Peterson, Sophie (Catherine Wilhelmine) (31) & family
" Peter (10)
" Thomas (7)
" Emma Sophie (5)
" Anna Johanne (3)
" Otto August (1)
Phillpot, William (51) with family
" Eliza (36) (wife)
" Julia M. (13) (daughter)
" Martha (11) (daughter)
Pilgrim, Rebecca (30)
Read, James, with family

Reader (Reeder), David (54) with family
" Robert (18)
" Caroline (16)
Reed, William (62) with family
" Sarah (62) (wife)
" Joseph (14)
Richins (Richens), John (22) with family
" Charlotte (21) (wife)
" Hannah L. (1)
Roberts, John (42)
Roberts, Mary (44)
Rogers, Jemima (25 ?)
" Elizabeth (8) (daughter)
Rowley, Ann (46) with family
" Louisa (18)
" Elizabeth (16)
" John (14)
" Samuel (12)
" Richard (11)
" Thomas (10)
" Jane (7)
Rowley, Eliza (30)
Rowley, Jane
Sandberg, Jens (38)
Savage, Levi
Showell, Harriet (30)
" Ellen C.
Smith, Andrew (19)
Smith, Margery (51) with family
" Margery (22)
" Jane (17)
" Mary (15)
" Elizabeth (13)
" Alexander J. (6)
Smith, William (47)
" Eliza (40) (wife)

Stanley, Betsey (Elizabeth) (38)
Steed, Sarah (20)
Stewart, Jane Ann (26) (spinster)
Stewart, Thomas (38) with family
  " Margaret (44) (wife)
  " William (12)
  " Ann B. (10)
  " Thomas
  " John (4)
Stockdale, Mary A. (Marianne) (18)
Stuart, Jane A.
Stuart (Stewart), John (31) with family
  " Ann (30) (wife)
  " John (6)
  " Mary (2 mo.)
Stone, Susannah (Susan)
Summers, Emma (27)
Tassell, Kitty Ann
Teait, Elizabeth
Tesit, Ann
Tite, Elizabeth (25)
Toffield, Ellen (43)
Turner, Richard (66)

Wall, Frederick (34) and wife
Wall, Joseph (17) and sister
Wall, Emily E. (16) (sister of Joseph)
Wandelin, Lars
Ward, Lucy
West, Sarah (23)
Wheeler, Edward (51) with family
  " Ann (54) (wife)
  " Mary (24)
Whitham, Witsom, or Withom, Eliza (42)
  " Joseph (9) (son)
Wickland (Wicklund), Oleo (30) with family
  " Ella (30) (wife)
  " Christine (9)
  " Jonas (5)
  " Sarah Jacobine (3)
  " Ephramine J. (1)
Wilkey (Wilkie), Isabella (48) (had charge of Elizabeth Forbes, 8)
Williams, Sarah A. (22)
Witts, Samuel H. (65)
Woodward, William

FIFTH COMPANY
EDWARD MARTIN, Captain (38)

Acres, Joseph (24) and wife
" Ann (23) (wife)
Allen, Eliza, and daughter
" Eleanora (18)
Allen, Maria (21) daughter of
Mary Allen
Anderson, Ann (47)
Andrews, John J. (44)
Anglesea, Martha (22)
Ashton, William (33) with wife
and 4 daughters
" Sarah Ann (33) (wife)
" Betsy (11)
" Sarah (7)
" Mary (4)
" Elizabeth (2)
Atherton, Ellen (57)
Bailey, John (49) with wife and
4 sons
" Jane (45) (wife)
" Langley (18)
" John (15)
" Thomas (12)
" David (5)
Barlow, Ann (58) with 1 dau.
and 2 sons
" John (17)
" Jane (15)
" Joseph (7)
Barnes, George (41) with wife
and children
" Jane (41) (wife)
" Margaret (15)
" Betsy (12)
" Esther (10)

Barnes, Deborah (8)
" William L. (5)
Bartholme, Bone (26) (from
Italy)
Barton, William (47) with fam-
ily
" Mary Ann (36) (wife)
" Francis (3½)
" Elizabeth (1½)
Beer, Benjamin (44), and wife
" Margaret (44)
Bennett, Harriet (53)
Beswick, Ann (65)
" Joseph (33)
Binder, Eliza (24)
" William (24)
Bird, Thomas (P.) (18)
Bitten, John (26) with family
" Jane (19)
" Sarah S. (17)
Blackham, Martha (47) with
family
" Samuel (21)
" Sarah (16)
" Thomas (13)
Blair, David (43) with family
" Deborah (39) (wife)
" Deborah (8)
" Elizabeth (5)
" David (6 mo.)
Blakey, Richard (36) & family
" Caroline (36) (wife)
" Caroline Jr. (16)
" John M. (6)
" Richard Jr. (2)

Bleak, James Godson (26) with family
" Elizabeth (27) (wife)
" Richard (6)
" Thomas (4)
" James, Jr. (2)
" Mary (infant)
Bowes, Elizabeth (27)
Bradshaw, Elizabeth (48) with family
" Robert (11)
" Isabella (10)
" Richard (6)
Brice, Richard, with family
" Hannah (54) (wife)
" John (12)
" Jane (9)
Bridge, Alfred (21)
Brooks, Alice (21)
Brooks, Nathan (61) with family
" Betty (wife)
Brown (Browne), Elizabeth (35)
Brown, Jane (25)
Burton, Eliza (32) with family
" Joseph F. (6)
" Martha A. (4)
Carter, Ellen (38)
" John (10) (son of Ellen)
Carter, Luke (45) (died on plains)
Clark, Margaret (27)
Clegg, Jonathan, with family
" Ellen (40) (wife)
" William (14)
" Alice (9)
" Henry (3)
" Margaret E. (3 mo.)

Clifton, Robert (50) with family
" Mary M. (45) (wife)
" Rebecca (20)
" Sophia (12)
" Ann (6)
Collins, Richard (37) with family
" Emma (30) (wife)
" Louisa (9)
" Fred James (6)
" David (4)
" George (2)
" Samuel (4 mo.)
Cook, Jemima (28)
Crane, Ann (23)
Crossley, Mary (45) with 3 sons and three daughters
" Mary Ann (23)
" Joseph (19)
" Hannah (15)
" Sarah (12)
" Ephraim (5)
" William (1) (grandson)
Davis (Davies), Edmund (32)
Dobson, Thomas (19) with family
" Alice (49)
" Mary Ann (24)
" Willard (17)
Dodd, Thomas (36) with family
" Elizabeth (36) (wife)
" Alma (10)
" Thomas (8)
" Joseph (6)
" Elizabeth (2)
" Brigham (3 mos.)
Douglas, John (39) with family

Douglas, Mary (36) (wife)
" William (14)
Durham, Thomas (27)
" Mary (27) (wife)
Eccles, Thomas (37) with family
" Alice (34) (wife)
" Mary Ann (11)
" Martha (8)
Edmonds, Charles (56)
Edwards, William (28)
" Harriet (16) (wife)
Elliot, Eliza (18)
Foster, Sarah (25)
Franklin, Thomas (33) with family
" Jane (33) (wife)
" Lydia (14)
Franks, Sarah (23)
Gibbons, Jane (25)
Giles, Aaron (B.) (15)
Gourley, Paul (42) with family
Green, Charles (26) with family
" Ann (22) (wife)
" George (4 months)
Green, Elizabeth (23)
Greening, Mary Ann (27)
Griffith, John, with family
" Elizabeth (30) (wife)
" Margaret A. (16)
" John (11)
" Jane E. (8)
" Robert L. (5)
Grundy, Sarah (41)
Gregory, Ann (63)
Gregory, Mary (59)
Haigh, Samuel (20)
Haigh, Sarah Ann (18)

Halford, John (57)
" Mary (53) (wife)
Harrison, William (40) with family
" Hannah (38) (wife)
" Aaron (18)
" George (14)
" Mary Ann (12)
" Alice (10)
" Olivia (6)
" Hannah Jr. (2)
" Sarah Ellen (1 month)
Hall, Charles (21) with family
" Elizabeth (24) (wife)
Harper, Mary (64)
Hartle, John (70) with family
" Lydia (71) (wife)
" Mary (36) (daughter)
Hartley, Eliza (39) and family
Haslam, Esther (50)
" Joseph (18) (son of Esther)
Hawkey, Hannah (33) with family
" James (14)
" Margaret (4)
" Hannah Jr. (3)
Haydock, Elizabeth (55)
" Mary (21)
Herring, George (16)
" Mary (35)
Heycock (Haycock), Elizabeth (45)
Hicks, Ann (20)
Higgs, Lydia (45)
Hill, Mary (48)
Hill, William (48)
" William Jr. (9) (son)

Hiott, John (33)
Holt, Robert (42) with family
"   Ellen (44) (wife)
"   Margaret (23)
"   James (22)
"   Daniel (16)
"   Alice (13)
"   Joseph (11)
"   Martha (5)
Hooker, Lydia E. (20)
Horrocks, Mary (19)
Housley, George (19) with Harriet
Housley, Harriet (44)
Howard, William (10)
Hulst (Hurst), Sarah (49)
Hunter, George
Hunter, James (23)
Hunter, John
Jackson, Aaron (31) and family
"   Elizabeth (29) (wife)
"   Martha (7)
"   Mary E. (4)
"   Aaron (2)
Jackson, Charles (60) and family
"   Mary (62) (wife)
"   William (21)
Jackson, Samuel, with family
"   June (75)
"   Alice (41)
"   Lydia C. (15)
Jaques, Ann (42)
Jaques, Caroline (16)
Jaques, John (29) and family
"   Zilpah (24) (wife)
"   Flora L. (1)
Jervis, Amelia, and family

Johnson, Ann (18)
Johnson, Elizabeth (50)
Jones, Sarah (55) and family
"   Samuel S. (19)
"   Albert (16)
Jones, William
Jupp, Mary (35)
Kemer, Richard
Kimp (or Kemp), Henry (25)
Kewley, James (54) and family
"   Ann (54) (wife)
"   Margaret 16
"   Robert (11)
"   Thomas (3)
Kirkman, Robert (34) & family
"   Mary L. (33) (wife)
"   Robert (10)
"   John (8)
"   Joseph (6)
"   Hiram 4)
"   James (2)
Leah, James (55)
Leah, Sarah (59)
Ledden, Richard, and family
Lawley, George (55)
Loader, Tamar (22) and family
Lord, Charles (39) and family
Lloyd, James, with family
Maine (or Mayne), John (24)
Marshall, Mariann (34) and daughter
"   Emily (9)
Martin, Eliza (20)
Massey, Daniel (38) and family
"   Rebecca (34) (wife)
"   Silas (6)
"   George (4)
"   Rebecca (1½)

Mattison, Robert (52) and family
" Ann (44) (wife)
" Robert Jr. (20)
" John (15)
" George (12)
" Elizabeth Ann (3)
Mayo, Peter (40) and family
" Ann (40) (wife)
" Mary (9)
" Noah (1)
McBride, Robert (52) and family
" Margaret (41) (wife)
" Jeanetta Ann (16)
" Heber R. (13)
" Ether Enos (8)
" Peter H. (6)
" Margaret A. (2)
Mellor, James (37) and family
" Mary Ann (36) (wife)
" Louise (15)
" Elizabeth (14)
" Mary Ann (10
" James Jr. (8)
" William C. (5)
" Emma N. (3)
" Clara A. (3)
Middleton, William (39) and family
" Amy (43) (wife)
" John (15)
Mitchell, Mary (35) and son
" James (4)
Moore, Elizabeth
Morley, Sarah (29)
Moss, Joseph (49) and family
" Mary (45) (wife)
" Edward (21)

Moss, Peter John (18)
" Joseph Jr. (15)
" James (12)
" Alice (10)
" Hiram (7)
Munn, Edward (22)
Murdock, Mary (72)
Nightingale, Jane (57) and family
" Sarah (31)
" Jemima (21)
" Joseph (16)
Normanton (or Normington), Thomas (38) and family
" Maria (36) (wife)
" Lavinia (10)
" Mary E. (8)
" Hannah (6)
" Robert R. (4)
" Daniel (1)
Oldham, John (33) and family
" Sarah (23) (wife)
" Jane Eliza (4)
" Louis William (6 months)
Ollerton (or Oleston), John (55) and family
" Alice (53) (wife)
" Alice (19)
" Jane Ann (15)
" Sarah (6)
Openshaw, William (60) and family
" Ann (50) (wife)
" Samuel (22)
" Eliza (21)
" Levi (19)
" Mary (15)
" Eleanor (14)
" Mary Ann (10)

Ord, Eleanor (26)
Ord, Thomas (29)
Padley, George (20)
Parker, Caroline (36) (spinster)
Parker, Esther (37) and family
"   Ellen (8)
"   Priscilla (5)
Parkinson, John (37) and family (died on plains)
"   Ellen (37) (died on plains)
"   Samuel (18)
"   Joseph (16) (died on plains)
"   Jane (11)
"   Margaret (8)
"   John (7)
"   Ellen (5)
"   Mary (3) (died on plains)
"   Esther (2) (died on plains)
"   William (infant) (died on plains)
Parks, Elizabeth (26)
Patching, Susannah (47)
Pearce, Robert (31)
Pears, Eliza (19)
Peel, John (41) and family
"   Anna (41) (wife)
"   Naomi (8)
"   Marintha (5)
Peyton, Nathaniel (58) & family
"   Margaret (37) (wife)
"   Eliza (12 weeks)
Platt, Benjamin (23)
Platt, Mary (19)
Porrit (or Parrit), Margaret (40) and family
"   Nathaniel (15)
"   Rebecca (13)
"   Thomas (7)

Pucell, Samuel (50) and family
"   Margaret (53) (wife)
"   Margaret Jr. (14)
"   Ellen (10)
"   William (25)
"   Ann (24)
"   Eliza (25) (wife)
"   Robert (3 months)
Quin, Mary A., and family
"   William R. (24)
"   Mary A. Jr. (22)
"   Harriet (18)
"   Elizabeth (16)
"   George (14)
"   Isabella (7)
"   Joseph H. (5)
Ramsden, Samuel (45) & family
"   Esther (43) (wife)
"   Samuel C. (12)
Rhead (or Reed), Samuel (48) and family
"   Elizabeth (50) (wife)
"   Elitha (15)
"   Samuel (14)
"   Frisbea (9)
"   Walter (6)
Riley, Mary A. (39) and son
"   Thomas (12)
Robinson, Elizabeth (with Solomon Robinson)
Robinson, Elizabeth (with Frederic C. Robinson)
Robinson, Frederic (29)
Robinson, Solomon (23)
Robison, Margaret, and family
Rodwell, John (55) and wife
"   Sarah (59) (wife)
Rogerson, Mary (54) and family
"   James (26)

Rogerson, Bridget (24)
"   William (22)
"   Josiah (15)
"   Sarah Ann (13)
"   John Edward (9)
Ryle (or Royle), Sarah (67)
Severn, William (19) and wife
"   Mary (19) (married on ship)
Shorten, John B. (20)
Shorter (or Shorton), James (14)
Speakman, Hannah (18)
Squires, Henry Agustus (30) and family
"   Sarah Cattlin (28) (wife)
"   Sarah A. (8)
"   Mary E. (6)
"   Catherine H. (5)
"   Clara A. (3)
"   Rosetta A. (11 months)
Steele, James (29) with family
"   Elizabeth (28) (wife)
"   James E. (3)
"   George (1)
Stinson, Samuel, with family
Stone, Jonathan (53)
Stones, James (32) with family
"   Mary (34) (wife)
"   Hannah (7)
"   Sarah E. (7)
"   John O. (5)
"   Erastus J. (3)
Taylor, Elizabeth (53) and family
"   James (39)
"   Sarah (20)
"   Elizabeth (18)
Tasker, Andrew (52)

Thomas, Ann Jane (14)
Thomas, James
Toone, John (43)
Thorn (or Thorne), James (56)
Taylor, Mary (31) with family
"   William (12)
"   Jesse (10)
Thompson, Moses (24)
Thompson, John (30) and family
"   Mary (29) (wife)
"   Mary Jane (9)
Thornton, Hannah (29) and family
"   Wardeman (9)
"   Amanda (5)
"   Sarah Ann (3)
Turner, Robert (30)
Turner, William
Twelves, Charles (37) and family
"   Ann E. H. (36) (wife)
"   Charles S. (13)
"   John (11)
"   Ann E.H. (7)
"   Orson (6)
"   Brigham (3)
Walker, William T. (43)
Walker, James (28)
Walker, Sarah R. (24)
Walworth (or Wallwork), Thomas (27)
"   William (6) (son)
Walsh, William (29) and family
"   Alice (29) (wife)
"   Robert (4)
"   John (3)
"   Sarah (5 months)

Wardell, Hannah (35)
Watkins, John (22) and family
  "   Margaret (23) (wife)
  "   Elizabeth (4)
  "   John T. (1½)
Watts, Charles (18)
Waugh, George P. (68)
Webster, Elizabeth (24)
Webster, Francis (25)
White, Elias
White, Maria (55)
Whittaker, Robert (64)
Wignall, Sarah (48) and family
  "   Sarah J. (25)
  "   Mary Ann (16)
Wignall (or Wignol), William
  (33) and family
  "   Grace (33) (wife)
  "   Joseph (11)
  "   Mary (9)
  "   James (7)
  "   Jane (5)
  "   Grace (3)
  "   William H. (3 mos.)

Wiley, Mary
Wilkinson, Sarah
Williamson, Ann (48) and family
  "   Ellen (23)
  "   Ann (19)
  "   Mary (16)
  "   William (13)
  "   John (11)
  "   Betsy (3)
Wilson, Elizabeth (24)
Wilson, James (26)
Woodcock, Charles (52)
Woodcock, Jane (34)
Woodcock, Joseph (29)
Woodhead, John (20)
Wright, Charles (13)
Wright, Elizabeth (59) and
  daughter
  "   Elizabeth (22)
Wright, Rachel (46)
Wrigley, Ann
Yam, Catherine

SIXTH COMPANY [2]
ISRAEL EVANS, Captain (29)

Ashby, Benjamin (29)
Bentham, Jane
Brighton, William Stewart (28) and family
" 　Catherine (30) (wife)
" 　Janet (6)
" 　Mary (4)
Fishburn, Robert L. (23)
Henshaw, Mary (20)
Jones, Hannah Pendlebury (24)
Miller, —— Sister
Noble, Eliza Priscilla
Reeder, James (27) (died on the plains) and family
" 　Honor Welch
" 　(son) (5)
Thornley, Annie Brighton (16)

---

[2] No roster of the Sixth Company has been found; a few names have been noted.

SEVENTH COMPANY [3]
CHRISTIAN CHRISTIANSEN, Captain (33)

Andersen, Jens Chr. (35) and family
" Margaret Nielson (26) (wife)
" Lauritz Peter (7)
" Andrea Katrine (5)
" Boletta Kristine (3)
" Josephine Brighamina (6 months)
Christensen, Anders C. (49) and family
" Sophia Marie (43) (wife)
" Peter C. (20)
" Annie Margretta (18)
Christensen, Carl C.A. (26)
" Elise Haarby (22) (wife)
Christensen, Mads (32) and family
" Maren Johanne Jensen (wife)
" Rasmus Peter (10 months)
Dorius, Carl Christian N. (27)
" Ellen G. Rolfson (wife)
Dorius, Johan Frederick Ferdinand (25)
Eggertsen, Simon Peter (31)
Folkman, Geo. Christoper (64)
Garff, Nels (46) and wife
" Marie Jacobson (wife) (36) (died on plains)
" Peter N. (10)
Green, William (50)
Handberg, Johanna Christins
Hakanson, Elsa (21)
Hakanson, Anna (17)
Hansen, Embreth (died at Devil's Gate)

Hansen, Anne Margrethe (wife)
Hulberg, —— and wife
Jacobsen, Lars (23)
Jensen, Hans (40) and family
" Sissie Marie (42) (wife)
" Jens (17)
" Karen (13)
" Jacob Hans (11)
" Soren Peter (6)
" Marie Sophie (6 months)
Karlson, Claus Herman (8)
Larson, Andrew (38) & family
" Caroline Andrews (45) (wife)
" Lewis (10)
" Anna Hannah (8)
" Mary Christine (5)
Liljenquist, O.N.
Olsen, Peter (35)
" Ane (33) (wife)
Olsen, Frederick (32) & family
" Maren (Mary) (35) (wife)
" Ole (6)
" Anders (4)
" Levi (six months)
Olsen, Ole Christoffer (31) and family
" Karna Margaret (31) wife
" Caroline (2)
Parks, James P.
Rudd, ——
Salisbury, O.K.
Sorensen, Anna Marie
" Niels (33)
" Julia Marie (born on the plains)

---

[3] This partial list is mainly from the Journal History of Sept. 13, 1857.

EIGHTH COMPANY
GEORGE ROWLEY, Captain (31)

Adams, William (22)
Atkins, Reuben (27)
Atkins, William, and family
Anderson, Heahan
Andrews, Franklin (9)
Andrews, Mary Ann (35)
Arvidson, Mathilde (35)
Barrett, Matilda (16)
Bartlett, Clara (21)
Beesley, Ebenezer (18) and wife
  " Sarah (19) (wife)
Bengtson, Bengta (48)
Bengtson, Tufne (42)
Bertelson, Albertine (22)
Birrel, Agnes (18)
Booth, Emma (32)
Broadbent, Joseph (21)
Broadbent, Sarah (25)
Budd, Louisa (55) and children
  " Caroline (18)
  " George (14)
Cartwright, John (21) and wife
  " Ann (22) (wife)
Chapel, Caroline
Christiansen, Christine S. (24)
Christiansen, Lars C. (36)
Christiansen, Nils Christian
Christiansen, Thomas C. (34)
  " Inger Katrine (34) (wife)
  " Anne Marie (1)
Christoffersen, Rasmine (38)
  and family
  " Chr. Ludvig (8)
  " Carl Johannes (5)

Cook, Emma (20)
Cooper, Richard (or Frederick
  A.) (21)
Coucher, William (26)
Davies, Franklin (or Davis) (8)
Davies, Mary (31)
Davies (or Davis), Elizabeth
  (36)
Davis, Catherine (47)
Davis, James (48)
Dickinson, Mary Ann (32)
Dickinson, Thomas (41)
Dixon, Elizabeth (15)
Duffin, Abraham (46)
Fahy, Catherine (32)
Farrer, Catherine (18)
Farrer, Sarah (16)
Florence, Henry (18)
Foster, Hannah (64)
Fry, Fanny (16)
Gilbert, Joseph (34)
Gledell, Elizabeth (27)
Godfrey, Ann (26)
Hagenson, Christen (30) and
  wife
  " Karen Petra (28) (wife)
Hansen, Martin (32) and fam-
  ily
  " Maren Karina (32)
    (wife)
  " Martine (infant)
Hanson, Aline
Hanson, Maria Jane
Harris, James

Harris, William (43) & family
" Rebecca (43) (wife)
" Jane (19)
" Adelaide or Adeline (14)
Henthorn, Mary (49)
Hibbert, Ann (26)
Hibbert, Benjamin (18)
Hills, Richard
Hobbs, Henry (23) and wife
" Jane (25) (wife)
Hobbs, William (22)
Ince, John (18)
Jarvis, William (41) and family
" Jane (45) (wife)
" Thomas (22)
" Ann (13)
Jones, George (23) and wife
" Harriet (31) (wife)
Jones, Richard (36) and wife
" Sarah (44) (wife)
Jonson, Anders with family
Jonson, Anders (21)
Jonson, Jens or Jons
Jonson, Johannes
Jonson, Ola (34) and family
" Maren (30) (wife)
" Elvina (infant)
Kirkpatrick, Mary (20)
Lamb, Benjamin (46) and wife
" Eliza (45)
Larsen, Peter (49) and family
" Sidse (53) (wife)
" Peter (18)
" Christine (12)
Larson, Mons (35) and family
" Elna (33) (wife)
" Betty (5)
" Karen (3)
" Lehi (2)

Lewis, Ann (20)
Ligget, Joseph (53)
Lindsey, Mark (27) and wife
" Bithiah (26) (wife)
Lorenson, Anders with family
Lyde, Ellen (21)
MacIntyre, Thomas (25)
McKay, Martha (59) and family
" Mary (daughter) (37)
" Ellen " (25)
" Jane " (20)
" Ester " (14)
McKay, Robert (50) & family
" Agnes (51) (wife)
" Mary (20)
" Agnes, jun. (17)
McKenzie, Jane
Magleby, Hans Olsen (24) and wife
" Mary (wife)
Mann (or Munn), William (20) and wife
" Levina (wife)
Martin, Thomas (23)
Mauritzsen, Lars (34) and family
" Maren (35) (wife)
" Johanne M. (13)
" Mauritz (10)
" Maren (9)
" Martina (8)
" Johanna (6)
Maycock, Thomas (26) and wife
" Louisa (26) (wife)
Mitchell, Jane (23)
Moor, Edward (46) with family
" Ellen (wife)
" Hyrum

Morrell, Elise (42)
Morrell, Paul Henry (40)
Munn, William (see Mann)
Nielson, Mathias
Nuns, Mary Ann (19)
Olpin, Henry (54) and family
" Sarah (54) (wife)
" Ellen (21)
" Sarah Ann (15)
" Dorcas (12)
" Julia (9)
Olsen, Niels (30) and wife
" Hanna (29) (wife)
Olson, Joron (Jorgen) (37)
Pearson, Francis E.
Pearson, Sarah A. (20)
Pehrson, Henrich (46) & family
" Bengta (38) (wife)
" Anders (13)
" Oloff (11)
" Kirsti (6)
" Johannes (1)
Peterson, Peter (18)
Petroel, Mary and family
Pitman, Frank (22)
Reid, George (19)
Robison, William (45) and wife
" Jane (45) (wife)
Rowley, George, Captain, and
family
" Anne Brown (30) (wife)
" William (13)
" Joseph Smith (10)
" Alma (6)
Rosburg (or Roseberry), Carl
(33) and family
" Helena Erickson (36)
(wife)

Roseberry, Anna Marie (3)
" Emma C. (infant)
" Niels, Joseph (infant
twins)
Rosenbalt, Ola (35)
Schofield, Joseph (or John)
Schofield, Mary (30)
Schofield, Thomas (19)
Scogings, William (37)
Shanks, Edward (66) and wife
" Mary Jane (53) (wife)
Shaw, Mary (45) and family
" Joseph (14)
" Alice (10)
Smith, John (23) and family
" Frances (23) (wife)
" Alex (2)
" Martha (infant)
Snelgrove, Mary (55)
Simeon, Caroline
Sorensen, Christian (24) and
family
" Christina (24) (wife)
" Petrina (infant)
Sorenson, Karen (53) & family
" Jens Christian (23)
" Sorina Kjerstine (17)
" Anna (15)
" Soren Christian (12)
" Nils Christian (9)
Sorenson, Karen (27)
Stedman, George (28)
Stewart, Fullerton (51)
(spinster)
Strugnell, Henry I. (29) and
wife
" Emma (19) (wife)
Struggnell, Henry Fox (29)

Stungberg, Anne
Thornley, John (25) and wife
"   Margaret (25) (wife)
Thornton, Squire (24)
Titling, C.A.
Tuffley, Sarah (22)
Turnbull, James
Wadd (or Vadd), Soren Madsen (33) and family
"   Anne Marie (24) (wife)
"   Soren Parley (1)
"   Ann Katrine (1)
Ward, Mary with family
Watson, Elizabeth (60)
Whitehead, William (20)
Wilde, Eliza (19)
Wilde, Henry (27) and family
"   Jane (26) (wife)
"   Sarah Elizabeth (8)

Wilde, John Frederick (6)
"   Mary Elizabeth (4)
Wilde, William (53) and family
"   Eliza (19)
"   Thomas (16)
"   Mary (14)
"   Elizabeth S. (8)
Wilson, Charles (33) and family
"   Mary (28) (wife)
"   H.L. (6)
"   J.W. (4)
"   T.W. (1½)
Wolstenholm, Jonathan (48)
Wright, Ann (40) with daughter (14)
Yeats, Esther (16)
Zitting, Carl August (41)

NINTH COMPANY
DANIEL ROBINSON, Captain (29)

Ashdown, Demas (25) and family

Baker, Jane (19)

Bell, Joseph (59) and family
" Edwin (16) (son)

Beverland, James (22) and wife
" Joan (21) (wife)

Birmingham, Sarah (26)

Birmingham, Alfred (21)

Birmingham, Thomas (19)

Booth, Sarah (25)

Brownlow, William (55) and wife
" Mary Ann (57)

Christianson, Christian (21)

Cockin, Hannah (59)

Cook, James (46)

Corbett, William and family
" wife and 5 children

Cousins, Hugh (32)

Curtis, Edwin (20) and wife
" Fanny (18) (wife)

Dalrymple, A.

Facer, George (25) and family
" Mary (20) (wife)
" George H. (infant)

Falconbridge, William (55)

Faux, Jabez (22)

Forscutt, Mark H. (26) and wife
" Elizabeth (25)

Gardner, Christopher (30) and wife
" Augusta E. (32) (wife)

Gibson, John (45) and family
" Mary (40) (wife)
" Wheatley (14)
" Thomas (9)
" Jaques (7)
" Anna (5)

Gorton, Mary Ann (20)

Gough, Richard (31) and family
" Tobiatha (25) (wife)
" Sophia (1½)

Green, Thomas (52) and family
" Margaret (51) (wife)
" Mary Ann (18)
" Thomas Jun. (16)

Harrison, Henry (26)

Hemmings, William (34) with family
" Emma (34) (wife)
" Fanny (8)
" Emma Eliza (11 weeks)

Higgie (or Heggie), Andrew (35)

Hobbs, Annie E. (21)

Holder, Ann (58)

Holder, David (20)

Holder, Edward P.

Holmes, Maria (17)

Hook, Alice (46) and family

Hook, Thomas (23) ?
" Lilace (19)
" Ellen (17)
" Lewis (14)
" Lois (11)

Jackson, Ann (15)
Jackson, Emma (15)
Jacques, Henry, with family
Jones, Thomas (39) and family
" James (17)
" Robert (13)
" George (11)
" Jane (6)
" Sarah (49)
" Gomer (20)
" Ann (13)
" Rebecca (6)
Kipling, Dorothy (38) and family
" Dorothy (8)
Lapish, Joseph (30) and family
" Hannah (26) (wife)
Lavender, Elizabeth (20)
Lavender, Mary (21)
Lavender, Susan (26)
Lewis, John and family
Matthews, Mary (22)
Mawson, Oliver (32)
Meldrum, George (29) and family
" Jane (35) (wife)
" John (11)
" David (8)
" James (6)
" George (3)
" William (1)
McCullock, John (30) and family
" Margaret (26) (wife)
" George (4)
" Charles (2)
McNeill, Charles (53) and family
" Miriam (53) (wife)

McNeill, Alexander (27)
" Miriam jun. (24)
" Archibald (15)
" Isabella (11)
" Ellen (9)
Moffit, David Kay, and family
" Jeanette (42) (wife)
" Jeanette jun. (17)
" Joseph (13)
" William (12)
" Christina (10)
" Alexander (8)
" Mary Ann (5)
Nash, George (39)
Nash, Maria (42)
Nash, Mary (59)
Naylor, Levi (20)
Nichols, Henry (18)
Nichols, Sarah (37)
Ordige, William (40) and wife
" Eliza (41) (wife)
Parkinson, Elizabeth (49) and family
" Thomas (12)
" Samuel (8)
Payne, Ellen (22)
Pierce, Augustus, and family – wife and eight children
Pilling, John (28)
Richards, David (46) and family
" Mary (51) (wife)
" Mariam (13)
" Jane (11)
" William D. (7)
" Rees M. (4)
Richardson, Ann (58)
Robinson, Daniel, wife and two children
Robinson, William (45)

Robison, David
Robison, Franz (19)
Robison, Mary Ann (16)
Rogers, Eliza (21)
Rogers, George and family
Rogers, William (24)
Rogers, Maria (20)
Rothwell, Amelia (33)
Royall, Elizabeth
Shewar, William (35) & family
Sibbett, Hugh G., and family
Siddoway, John (21) and wife
" Mary (22) (wife)
Siddoway, Robert (31) and family
" Isabella (10)
" Richard (8)
" Robert jun. (6)
Slater, Hannah (20)
Slater, Joseph (27)
Smith, Conrad (27) and family
" Eliza (22) (wife)
" daughter (5)
" son (3)
Stevens, Ann (24)
Stoney, Robert (26) and family
" Sarah (23) (wife)
" Sarah Ann (infant)
Stonestrom, John (55) and family
" Christiania (50) (wife)
" Sophia (16)
" Hans P. (10)
Taylor, Harriet (52)
Tempest, Henry (36) & family
" Betty C.
" James
" John

Thacker, Phoebe (45)
Thacker, Pridger (39)
Townsend, John W. (44) and family
" Ann (41) (wife)
" Emma (12)
" Moroni (8)
" Rebecca (5)
" Eliza Ann (3)
" Brigham H. (1)
Wagstaff, John (18)
Walker, William (54) and family
" Elizabeth (54) (wife)
" Elizabeth (21)
" Sarah (18)
Wardle, John (48) and family
" Mary (48) (wife)
" James (19)
Webb, Charles (26)and family
" Jane (23) (wife)
" Emily (3)
" Charles M. (infant)
Webb, Mary Ann (28)
Welch, Joseph (33) and family
" Catherine (33) (wife)
" daughter (8)
" son (6)
" daughter (4)
" son (2)
Whitten, Margaret (29)
Wilgas, Jesse (52) and family
" Sarah (47) (wife)
" Mary Jane (16)
" Joseph (10)
" Aaron (4)
Williams, William
Wright, George (25)

TENTH COMPANY
Oscar O. Stoddard, Captain

Alder, Conrad (35)
" Elizabeth (30) (wife)
Andersen, Carl J.
Andersen, Johan G. (38)
Anderson, Lars (32) and wife
" Ane H. (wife)
Anderson, Niels (24)
Ashton, Samuel (45) and wife
" Mary (40)
Bensen, Bent (35)
Bengtsen, Bengt (36)
Bonderson, Nils (45) and family
" Hanna (49) (wife)
" Anders (15) (son)
Buhler, John (James?) (33)
Chatelain, Louisa (30)
Christensen, Anders (29)
Christensen, Christen (37)
Christensen, Soren (58) and family
" Else (50) (wife)
" Peter (18) (son)
" Lauritz (15) (son)
Fisher, David (32) and family
" Martha (32) (wife)
" Martha Jun. (10)
" David (8)
" Joseph (5)
" Andrew (3)
Fisher, James (or Jacob) (25) and family
Fjeld, Carl Johan (35) and family
" Maren Eline (37) (wife)
" Anne Susanne (13)

Fjeld, Josephine Emiline (9)
" Carl Peter (7)
" Heber Saamund (1)
Frederiksen, Ingeborg (22)
Goosh (or Gvesh), Lorenzo
Halversen, Lars (46) and family
" Agnette (Halvardsdotter) (30) (wife)
" Johanes (6)
Haffam, Zebedee (63)
Hess, Marie (33) and family
" Elizabeth (9)
" Anna (6)
Hirshi, John (27)
Horn, William (38) with family
" Sarah (40) (wife)
" John (13)
" George H. (10)
" Mary Ann (6)
" James (4)
" Moroni (1)
Howard, Margaret (24)
Jackson, Henry (44) and wife
" Maria (43)
Jensen, Gotfredine (27)
Jensen, Jens (30)
Jensen, Soren (22)
Kerby, Francis (36) and family
" Maria (34) (wife)
" Mary (9)
" Alma (7)
" Harriet (5)
" Joseph (3)
" Eliza (1)

Larsen, Gunild (74 or 59)
Larsen, Lars (63 or 59)
Möller, Rasmus (53)
Möller, Matt K. (58)
Nilsen, Gustav (28) and wife
Olsen, Allen (35)
Olsen, Ane C. (3)
Olsen, George (Jorgen) (12)
Olsen, Hokan, and wife
Olsen, Maren (17)
Olsen, Jens Peter (9)
Paul, Elder
Petersen (or Pehrson), Anders (22)
Petersen, Moroni (59) and wife
  " Ane (55) (wife)
Petersen, Nella (20)
Petersen, Dorthea (18)
Petersen, Neils
Rasmussen, Anders (39) and family
  " Karine (40) (wife)
  " Christen (16)
  " Herman (8)
Rasmussen, Rasmus (39) and family
  " Rasmus jr.
  " Maren
  " Anders P.
  " Johan
Roston, Michael (36) and wife
  " Martha (30) (wife)

Sorensen, Bengt (34) and wife
  " Ane (39) (wife)
Sorensen, Ane Chris. (34)
Sorensen, Neils (56) and family
  " Anne H. (50) (wife)
  " Kjersti (25)
  " Johanna (20)
  " Anders (19)
Sorensen, Peter (36) and family
  " Ane M. (34)
  " Christian (7)
  " Kimball (3½)
Stucki, Samuel (37) and family
  " Magdelina (38) (wife)
  " John (9)
  " Anne Maria (Mary Ann) (6)
  " Rosina (3)
  " Christian (6 mos.)
Taylor, Stephen (52) and family
  " Caroline (50) (wife)
  " Elizabeth (18)
  " Sarah (15)
  " Joseph (10)
  " Eliza (28)
  " Dora (6)
  " Car (Caroline?) (4)
Uckerman, Agnette (44) from Norway

Index

Index

Index

Reference should also be made to the alphabetically arranged names in Appendix M, which are not included in this index.

MyMedicare.gov
    greenbough ooo (or all caps)
    ivan m 2 dog

Jenn 988-6149
(720)
prednisone